A New Theory and Practice of Diplomacy

A New Theory and Practice of Diplomacy

New Perspectives on Diplomacy

Edited by
Professor Jack Spence, Dr Claire Yorke and
Dr Alastair Masser

I.B. TAURIS
LONDON • NEW YORK • OXFORD • NEW DELHI • SYDNEY

I.B. TAURIS
Bloomsbury Publishing Plc
50 Bedford Square, London, WC1B 3DP, UK
1385 Broadway, New York, NY 10018, USA
29 Earlsfort Terrace, Dublin 2, Ireland

BLOOMSBURY, I.B. TAURIS and the I.B. Tauris logo are
trademarks of Bloomsbury Publishing Plc

First published in Great Britain 2021
Reprinted 2021

Copyright © Jack Spence, Claire Yorke and Alastair Masser, 2021

Jack Spence, Claire Yorke and Alastair Masser have asserted their right under the
Copyright, Designs and Patents Act, 1988, to be identified as Editors of this work.

For legal purposes the Acknowledgements on p. xviii constitute
an extension of this copyright page.

Cover design: ianrossdesigner.com
Cover image © [top] Khaled Desouki/AFP/Getty Images; [middle] Andrew Caballero-Reynolds/POOL/AFP/Getty Images; [bottom] Valery Sharifulin/TASS/Getty Images

All rights reserved. No part of this publication may be reproduced or transmitted
in any form or by any means, electronic or mechanical, including photocopying,
recording, or any information storage or retrieval system, without prior
permission in writing from the publishers.

Bloomsbury Publishing Plc does not have any control over, or responsibility for,
any third-party websites referred to or in this book. All internet addresses given
in this book were correct at the time of going to press. The author and publisher
regret any inconvenience caused if addresses have changed or sites have
ceased to exist, but can accept no responsibility for any such changes.

A catalogue record for this book is available from the British Library.

A catalog record for this book is available from the Library of Congress.

ISBN: HB: 978-1-8386-0457-8
       PB: 978-1-8386-0456-1
       ePDF: 978-1-8386-0459-2
       eBook: 978-1-8386-0458-5

Typeset by Integra Software Services Pvt. Ltd.
Printed and bound in Great Britain

To find out more about our authors and books visit www.bloomsbury.com
and sign up for our newsletters.

Contents

List of figures	vi
List of tables	vii
List of contributors	viii
Preface *Professor Jack Spence OBE*	xii
Foreword *Professor Sir Lawrence Freedman*	xv
Acknowledgements	xviii
List of abbreviations	xx

	Introduction: The changing theory and practice of diplomacy *Professor Jack Spence, Dr Claire Yorke and Dr Alastair Masser*	1
1	The global diplomatic practice: Constituting an ethical world order *Professor Mervyn Frost*	15
2	Coercive diplomacy and the continued relevance of hard power: The role of competence and context *Dr Jean-Francois Belanger*	37
3	Intelligence and diplomacy: Changing environment, old problems *Dr Daniel W. B. Lomas*	55
4	The power of describing identity in diplomacy: Writing subjects, territory, time and evil at the end of Gaddafi's Libya *Dr Pablo de Orellana*	77
5	The Beijing and Moscow 1972 summits: Strengths and limits of two iconic diplomatic breakthroughs *Dr Barbara Zanchetta*	103
6	Empathy and emotional diplomacy *Dr Claire Yorke*	123
7	Counter-diplomacy: The many ways to say no *Dr Gerrit Kurtz*	141
8	Small state security and diplomacy in the not-so-new Europe: Comparing experiences from the Balkans to the Baltic in the twenty-first century *Professor James Gow*	161
9	South Africa's diplomacy of conflict resolution in the post-apartheid era: The case of the DRC *Dr Flavia Gasbarri*	185
10	Life as a diplomat *Ambassador Nigel Thorpe*	207
	Conclusion *Professor Jack Spence, Dr Claire Yorke and Dr Alastair Masser*	225

Select bibliography	229
Index	237

Figures

1 Diagram summarizing the method. Arrows denote the crossover of representations – signposted by their topoi – from one text to another   83
2 Screenshots of UNSCR 1973, pp. 1–2   85
3 Screenshot of a paragraph reporting on Senators McCain and Lieberman's August 2009 visit to Libya in 19/8/2009 Tripoli to State, 09TRIPOLI677   88

Tables

1 Levels and practices of counter-diplomacy   145

Contributors

Dr Jean-François Bélanger is a Postdoctoral Fellow at Yale's International Security Studies. His latest book project is *Why Competence Matters: Counter-Proliferation and Deterrence*. Using concepts from practice theory and applying them in a strategic setting, the book examines how competence in previous deterrence crises plays an important role in the decision by counter-proliferating states to use force to curb proliferation. His broader research interests focus on questions of competence and coercive diplomacy, asymmetrical deterrence, nuclear restraint and public opinion on international security. He has recently co-authored pieces on the diplomatic strategies of sea powers (*Journal of Global Security Studies*) and the China–India rivalry (Georgetown University Press).

Dr Pablo de Orellana is Lecturer in International Relations at the Department of War Studies, King's College London. His research focuses on how diplomatic communication constitutes the representations upon which policy is made. He has published on diplomacy, North African politics, European affairs, nationalism and identity politics, art history, as well as reviews, essays and features on contemporary art in peer-reviewed as well as less formal publications.

Professor Mervyn Frost is Professor of International Relations in the Department of War Studies at King's College London and is Associate Professor in the Department of Politics and International Relations at the University of Johannesburg, South Africa. In 2019 he spent three months as the Distinguished Visiting Professor of International Ethics at the University of New South Wales in Canberra, Australia, and at the Australian Defence Force Academy. He has written extensively on ethics and international relations. His recent work, with Dr Silviya Lechner, is focused on the 'practice turn' in international relations resulting in three publications.

Dr Flavia Gasbarri is currently Lecturer in War Studies, co-Chair of the Africa Research Group, and member of the Centre for Grand Strategy at the Department of War Studies, KCL. She holds a PhD in War Studies from King's College London, where her research and publications focus on the study of the Cold

War in the Third World, the development of post–Cold War US foreign policy and US-Africa relations. She has also extensively researched and published on US policy in the Rwandan genocide and in the Great Lakes region.

Professor James Gow is Professor of International Peace and Security, Co-Director of the War Crimes Research Group at King's College London, and a Non-Resident Scholar with the Liechtenstein Institute, Princeton University. From 2013 to 2016, Gow held a Leverhulme Trust Major Research Fellowship. He has served as an expert adviser and an expert witness for the Office of the Prosecutor at the UN International Criminal Tribunal for the former Yugoslavia (1994–2004), and as an expert adviser to UK Secretaries of State for Defence. His recent publications include *Impact in International Affairs: the Quest for World Leading Research*.

Dr Gerrit Kurtz is a research fellow for conflict prevention and diplomacy in Africa at the German Council on Foreign Relations based in Berlin. He completed his PhD at the Department of War Studies, King's College London, with a thesis on frontline diplomatic practices in countries with state–society conflicts and their impact on conflict prevention, using South Sudan and Sri Lanka as case studies. Gerrit's research interests include diplomacy, conflict prevention, transition processes, United Nations and peace and security in sub-Sahara Africa. His PhD research benefitted from funding by the UK Economic and Social Research Council and the Heinrich Böll Foundation.

Dr Daniel Lomas is Lecturer in International History at the University of Salford, specializing in British intelligence and security in the twentieth century, and the programme leader of the MA in Intelligence & Security by part-time Distance Learning. His first monograph, *Intelligence, Security and the Attlee Government*, was published by Manchester University Press in 2017, and he has co-authored *Intelligence and Espionage: Secrets and Spies*, published by Routledge in 2019. His work has appeared in *Intelligence & National Security*, *The International History Review*, *Journal of Intelligence History* and *The Historical Journal*.

Dr Alastair Masser is Director of Global Programmes at the Legatum Institute in London. Prior to joining the Institute, he spent almost a decade in politics serving latterly as a Special Adviser in two posts under David Cameron. He holds a PhD in War Studies from King's College London, examining UK-Nigerian development and security cooperation during the coalition government. Alastair is an alumnus of the US State Department's International Visitor Leadership Programme (IVLP) and has taught at the Ministry of Defence's Joint Services Command Staff College (JSCSC) at Shrivenham.

Professor Jack Spence OBE retired from the Department of War Studies in 2020 after more than twenty years. He held a variety of senior posts throughout his distinguished long career, including serving as Pro-Vice Chancellor at the University of Leicester, Director of Studies at Chatham House and Academic Adviser to the Royal College of Defence Studies. He served on the Goldstone Commission which investigated political violence as part of South Africa's transition from Apartheid and has lectured widely throughout his career, including at the UK's Joint Services Command and Staff College, the US Defence Intelligence Agency and State Department, and South Africa's Department of Foreign Affairs. He was awarded an OBE in 2002 for teaching services to the UK Ministry of Defence.

Ambassador Nigel Thorpe is a former British Ambassador and diplomat. He was born in October 1945. After graduating from university (First Class Honours in History) in 1967 he joined Her Majesty's Diplomatic Service in 1969. His career specialized in Central Europe. He served twice in Poland, was a desk officer in the Foreign Office dealing with the Soviet Union and then Head of the newly created Central European Department 1992–6. He concluded his career as HM Ambassador to Hungary 1998–2003. He was appointed Commander of the Royal Victorian Order in 1991. He has spent retirement working in the voluntary sector, especially on homelessness. He also teaches and writes about the communist period.

Dr Claire Yorke is a writer, researcher and academic. Between 2018 and 2020, she was a Henry A. Kissinger Postdoctoral Fellow and Lecturer at International Security Studies and the Jackson Institute for Global Affairs at Yale University. Her writing and research explores the role and limitations of empathy and emotions in international affairs, diplomacy, leadership and policymaking. She completed her PhD in international relations in 2018 at the Department of War Studies, King's College London. In 2014, she was a member of the NATO and Atlantic Council Young Leaders Working Group, reporting to the NATO Secretary General. Prior to academia she worked at the Royal Institute of International Affairs and in the UK Parliament.

Dr Barbara Zanchetta is Lecturer in Diplomacy and Foreign Policy at the Department of War Studies at King's College London. She is the author of *The Transformation of American International Power in the 1970s* (Cambridge University Press, 2014), the co-author of *Transatlantic Relations since 1945* (Routledge, 2012) and co-editor of *New Perspectives on the End of the Cold War: Unexpected Transformations?* (Routledge, 2018). Dr Zanchetta has published articles and book reviews in *International Politics, Studies in Conflict & Terrorism, Diplomacy History, Cold War History, Journal of Transatlantic Studies* and for *H-Diplo*. She is currently working on a monograph tentatively titled *The United States and the 'Arc of Crisis': American Foreign Policy, Radical Islam and the End of the Cold War*.

Preface
Professor Jack Spence OBE

As a key concept in the theory and practice of international relations, diplomacy has a long and impressive history. For Hedley Bull, diplomacy comprised one of the six key institutions essential for the maintenance of what he termed a 'society of states', and an integral part of the international order.[1] The effective conduct of diplomacy has long been based on identifying where the interests of states within that society overlap, and where agreement might be found. It therefore requires a demonstration of certain key values: restraint, civility, patience, empathy and the skilful use of what Sir Ernest Satow characterized as 'tact and intelligence'.[2]

Diplomacy as an institution has always been in a state of near-constant evolution as change occurs in the international system, exemplified by Woodrow Wilson's 'open covenants' which laid the groundwork for a new diplomacy in the aftermath of the First World War. An enduring task of diplomacy has been to provide the 'oil' for maintaining and enhancing the machinery of international cooperation at a variety of levels. Diplomats resident in a country – whether ally or adversary – play a key role in assessing the capabilities and intentions of their hosts. They have a broad range of responsibilities, from providing informed and salient commentary on political issues such as leadership changes and forthcoming elections, to identifying potential opportunities for increased cooperation, to resolving disagreements between nations. This combination of virtues emphasizes the civilized nature of the diplomatic enterprise and the sheer intellectual capacity required to make diplomatic activity meaningful and productive while adding significantly to a country's reputation at home and abroad.

The contemporary theory and practice of diplomacy is no different. Nations, their institutions and representatives continue to interact with each other at different times and in different places to assist in the promotion of what is often only a precarious degree of international order. Painstaking diplomacy is vital to such success as might arise; indeed, it might be described as the 'master' institution insofar as it makes possible that depth and range of a multitude of agreements. Such agreements are achievable only if the interests of the parties, though different, overlap. The art of the diplomat, therefore, is to determine this synergy of interests and 'between reason and persuasion to bring the parties to it'.³

The fruits of diplomatic activity are omnipresent, and too often taken for granted. Painstaking negotiations have played a decisive role in making the world more interconnected, enabling us to communicate and to travel with relative ease. It is easy to forget that every time we post a letter abroad or board an aeroplane, we are taking advantage of international agreements that have been the result of painstaking negotiation.

This question of the value placed on diplomatic activity has taken on a new significance in the face of sustained public criticism of foreign policymakers of a kind that contrasts sharply with the considerable latitude enjoyed by their predecessors for much of the twentieth century. It also reflects the increasing erosion of the traditional distinction between domestic and foreign policy issues. We see this, for example, in the impact of domestic terrorism on national and social media and the necessary pressure on governments to take action to deter and prevent future attacks.

Nevertheless, it is hard to argue that diplomacy remains anything but essential to modern international relations. Most recently – and most dramatically – it has been the COVID-19 pandemic that has illustrated the fundamental need for effective international cooperation and the importance of diplomacy to our shared security and prosperity. As the scholar Jared Diamond has rightly remarked, 'Until the unprecedented danger posed by COVID-19 there has never been a struggle which united all peoples of the world against a widely acknowledged common enemy ... COVID-19 is at last providing world citizens with a shared enemy, an unequivocal quick killer, a threat to the inhabitants of every nation.'⁴

These are some of the many new features of diplomacy that require new perspectives. This collection of papers is the product of many years of reflection with students and colleagues in the Department of War Studies at King's College London. I am profoundly grateful to each of the contributors and especially to my two co-editors, Dr Claire Yorke and Dr Alastair Masser, for their efficiency and commitment to bringing this project to life. The two volumes will, I hope, prove a thought-provoking text for students and practitioners of diplomacy, as well as the general reader with an abiding interest in contemporary international studies. It is my belief that diplomacy will need to continue to evolve to meet current and future challenges of the international order, and to sustain the values that underpin it.

Notes

1. Hedley Bull, *The Anarchical Society – A Study of Order in World Politics*, 4th edition (London: Red Globe Press, 2012).
2. Sir Ernest Satow, *A Guide to Diplomatic Practice* (London: Longmans, 1997), 3.
3. Bull, *The Anarchical Society*, 164.
4. Jared Diamond, 'After the storm', *Financial Times*, 30/31 May 2020, 2.

Foreword
Professor Sir Lawrence Freedman

In 1975 I was working as a research associate at the International Institute of Strategic Studies, my first job since completing my doctorate at Oxford. The Director had asked me to write about the newly formed Nuclear Suppliers Group, which was supposed to control the export of sensitive equipment, materials and technology to prevent further proliferation. As I was completely unfamiliar with the topic I was told that I needed to meet Jack Spence, then a professor at Leicester University. I think we met when Jack was visiting the Institute. He was kind, patient and a source of good advice, pointing me to the underlying politics behind this group, including India's so-called 'peaceful' nuclear explosion of 1974, and what it said about confidence in the nuclear Non-Proliferation Treaty. We stayed in touch thereafter. I did not see much of him when he became Vice-Chancellor at Leicester, but then there were plenty of chances to do so once he became Director of Studies at Chatham House. Jack's contributions in seminars and conferences were always thoughtful and full of good sense, so I was delighted when I heard that he had agreed to teach at King's on his notional retirement in 1997. This might have been expected to last for a few more productive years until his proper retirement. But that never came. Instead for over two decades Jack continued to enchant successive cohorts of students with his wisdom and insight.

During the course of his long career Jack has focused on diplomacy (initially that of the South African government as it faced isolation because of Apartheid) and so it is entirely appropriate that diplomacy provides the focus for these two volumes. It is also important to push it to the fore because of the way that it has been downgraded over this period. Whether or not diplomacy will now start to be appreciated with fresh eyes, there are good reasons why this should be the case. These volumes therefore are timely, providing an opportunity to reflect on the nature and practice of diplomacy.

A starting point might be to distinguish between foreign policy and diplomacy. Strictly speaking you can't have one without the other. Any attempt to implement a foreign policy requires the diplomats going out to explain and negotiate. If diplomats are to do their routine work they need some sense of the broad foreign policy they are supposed to be promoting. But over time the relationship between the two has weakened.

In 1977 not long after my first meeting with Jack a report produced by the No 10 Policy Unit on overseas representation expressed doubts about whether all the expense that went into what we now call 'soft power', including plush and well-staffed embassies as well as the BBC World Service and the British Council, really added a lot of value when the real needs were economic and the most important tasks were trade promotion. The assault was resisted by the Foreign and Commonwealth Office, but even then many could see that the case for the scale of the British diplomatic effort was one that could no longer be taken for granted, especially when funds were scarce.

Moreover it was evident by this time that prime ministers were inclined to keep the big decisions on war and peace for themselves, and wished to be at the fore of any big global initiatives. Attending summits, sorting out big crises and signing treaties could be a welcome escape from the rancour and frustration of domestic politics, with guards of honour and attention by the world's media. Because the spotlight could not be shared foreign ministers (not just the UK's Foreign Secretary) were rarely allowed to strike out on their own. Presidents and prime ministers can often be effective foreign policymakers. They can forge productive relationships with the heads of other governments and international organizations.

But being good at foreign policy is not the same as being a good diplomat. Good diplomats do not find the detail of negotiations tedious. When obliged to attend multilateral conferences and listen to endless speeches, full of platitudes and banality, they don't find it a waste of time or worry about a lack of a decision, but instead get satisfaction when they notice a slight nuance or shift of emphasis which means that a country's position has shifted or some concession is being signalled. More seriously, especially when posted abroad they take it as matter of pride to understand the language and culture of their hosts, as well their politics. This enables them to gauge likely reactions to some new development or identify possibilities for constructive cooperation. They become empathetic, able to appreciate the interests and concerns of other countries.

This is one reason why political leaders can become wary of diplomats. They grumble that they become advocates for these interests and concerns and forget to promote those of their own country. They are forever making the case for concessions that will no doubt delight their foreign interlocutors but could also cause uproar in Parliament or Congress once disclosed. It also used to be the case that foreign ministries were essential in keeping open lines of communication to foreign governments, even in difficult times. Now it is the case that almost all government departments have their own external affairs, and not just those dealing with trade and climate change. A further complication is that governments can be wary about giving their diplomats too much latitude. They do not want to discover that quiet conversations have been had with terrorists, or the political opponents of a friendly government, or any representatives of an unfriendly government. And if they need a back channel at times of crisis political leaders will tend to opt someone they know and trust, and will be recognized by the other side as someone who can speak with authority.

But there is now too much to be managed from the centre. The international agenda is full. There is certainly a lot to do on the trade front as envisaged in the 1977 report (and Brexit will make this even more demanding for the UK). But there are also all the issues thrown up by the digital revolution, from 5G networks to cyber-crime to information campaigns, or states suffering under the weight of debt and political conflict, leading to humanitarian distress, terrorist sanctuaries and outflows of refugees, or the demands of climate change and now pandemics. In the 1990s there were hopes that much of this agenda could be handed over to international organizations who would be able to work out how the necessary cooperation could take place and set norms for individual states to follow. But the effortless days of multilateralism are over. Getting any sort of international agreement is becoming a hard grind. Resolving conflicts can require painstaking talks with disparate, antagonistic and awkward groups. Relations with other major powers are becoming more contentious. The combination of the COVID-19 pandemic and the consequential economic crisis will mean that governments are going to be preoccupied with domestic issues and lack spare capacity for foreign policy at a time when the international system is going to be badly stressed.

Much more is now likely to be done by small groups of like-minded states. New coalitions will need to be formed. Old alliances and agreements may look frayed and dated but with nothing readily at hand to replace them efforts will still need to be maintained. Questions surrounding the trade-offs between economics and security, or the weight to be put on promoting democracy and supporting human rights, will become both more pressing and difficult to answer. The burden of ensuring that governments stay in touch, avoid unnecessary arguments and find new ways to cooperate on their shared problems will fall on those with the skills required to keep conversations going and negotiate agreements where possible. Diplomats! Your time has come!

Acknowledgements

A co-edited series such as this is a collective effort. These volumes have been many years in the making, and over that time we have benefitted from the kind support and generosity of so many.

Firstly, we owe a huge thank you to all of our brilliant contributors. They have shared their expertise and research in these pages to create a vision of diplomacy that is both eclectic and rich. We would like to offer special thanks to Professor Sir Lawrence Freedman and Professor Myles Wickstead who brought their experience and expertise to the Foreword, and have been a wonderful source of encouragement throughout this project.

The Department of War Studies at King's College London has been our shared intellectual home. We owe a genuine thank you to all our colleagues in the department for supporting this project, and for cultivating an environment where academics and practitioners can come together to research and understand the intersection of international relations, diplomacy and conflict. The breadth and quality of expertise within the department makes for a unique interdisciplinary environment that combines academic rigour with policy relevance. As part of this, we want to acknowledge the many students in the department whose curiosity, insights and new perspectives on the world continually shape and inform our own work.

Bloomsbury and I.B. Tauris have offered invaluable support and encouragement throughout this process. Special thanks are due to Lester Crook who started us on this journey, as well as to Jo Godfrey, Olivia Dellow and Tomasz Hoskins for all their advice and support. We also wish to thank the reviewers of both volumes, and all those who have offered comments on the various drafts. Their constructive feedback makes our work stronger, although we acknowledge all errors are our own. Sincere thanks are also due to the many practitioners of diplomacy whose candid insights have improved our understanding of the political context in which diplomacy takes place, and which have helped shape the analysis of this book.

Claire and Alastair would like to thank friends and colleagues at International Security Studies and the Jackson Institute of Global Affairs at Yale University, and at the Legatum Institute respectively who have offered a productive and rewarding environment to complete these books.

They also wish to record a final, and particularly special, acknowledgement. Professor Jack Spence has been a doctoral supervisor, mentor, champion and friend to us throughout our academic careers. Yet, the unwavering support he has offered us is by no means unique. Many of the contributors have their own stories of his generosity and his mentorship, and he is a beloved figure in the Department of War Studies. His desire to help others is not limited to doctoral students and staff. Jack is known to give out his phone number to undergraduates so they can reach him for help and guidance, and he will collect newspaper clippings and articles to send to those who share their research interests with him. His enthusiasm and love for this topic, as well as his extensive expertise and experience, infuse the whole volume. We are so grateful for his help and for championing and leading this project.

Abbreviations

ABMs	Anti-Ballistic Missile systems
AFDL	Alliance des Forces Démocratiques pour la Libération du Congo-Zaïre
AFRICOM	Africa Command (US)
AQ	Al Qaeda
ARCSS	Agreement for the Resolution of Conflict in the Republic of South Sudan
AU	African Union
BALTBAT	Baltic Battalion
BBC	British Broadcasting Company
BRICS	Brazil, Russia, India, China and South Africa
CFE	Conventional Forces in Europe Agreement
CIA	Central Intelligence Agency (USA)
CIGs	Current Intelligence Groups (connected to JIC)
COVID-19	Corona Virus 2019
CSCE	Commission on Security and Cooperation in Europe
DCR	Rassemblement Congolais pour la Democratie
DPRK	Democratic People's Republic of Korea
DRC	Democratic Republic of Congo
EEC	European Economic Community
EU	European Union
EUHOMS	EU Heads of Mission meeting
FBI	Federal Bureau of Investigation (USA)
GATT	General Agreement on Tariffs and Trade
GCHQ	Government Communications Headquarters (UK)
G20	Group of Twenty
G7	Group of Seven
G8	Group of Eight
GDP	Gross Domestic Product
GRU	Russian Main Intelligence Directorate
HUMINT	Human Intelligence
ICBMs	Intercontinental Ballistic Missiles

ICD	Inter-Congolese Dialogue	
IGAD	Intergovernmental Authority on Development	
IMINT	Imagery Intelligence	
ISIL	Islamic State in Iraq and the Levant	
ISIS	Islamic State in Iraq and Syria	
JIC	Joint Intelligence Community	
KGB	Komitet Gosudarstvennoy Bezopasnosti (Russian Committee for State Security)	
LGBTQ+	Lesbian, Gay, Bisexual, Transgender, Queer, +	
LIFG	Libyan Islamic Fighting Group	
MAD	Mutual Assured Destruction	
MENA	Middle East and North Africa	
MDC	Movement for Democratic Change	
MI5	The UK Security Service	
MIP	Military Intelligence Programmes	
MIRVs	Multiple Independently-targeted Re-entry Vehicles	
MONUC	United Nations Organization Mission in the Democratic Republic of the Congo	
MPLA	The Movimento Popular de Libertação de Angola	
NATO	North Atlantic Treaty Organization	
NIP	National Intelligence Programmes	
NSA	National Security Agency	
NTC	National Transitional Council (Libya)	
OAS	Organisation of American States	
OAU	Organization of African Unity	
OSCE	Organization for Security and Cooperation in Europe	
OSINT	Open Source Intelligence	
POTUS	President of the United States	
PRC	People's Republic of China	
R2P	Responsibility to Protect	
RAF	Royal Air Force (UK)	
RPF	Regional Protection Force	
RPF	Rwandan Patriotic Front	
SADC	South African Development Community	
SALT	Strategic Arms Limitation Treaty (I and II)	
SANDF	South African National Defence Force	
SIGINT	Signals Intelligence	
SIS	UK Secret Intelligence Service	

SLBMs	Submarine Launched Ballistic Missiles
SPML/A	Sudan People's Liberation Movement/Army
UK	United Kingdom
UN	United Nations
UNITA	União Nacional para a Independência Total de Angola
UNMISS	UN Mission in South Sudan
UNSC	United Nations Security Council
UNSCR	United Nations Security Council Resolution
US	United States
USIA	United States Information Agency
USSR	Union of Soviet Socialist Republics
WHO	World Health Organization
WMD	Weapons of Mass Destruction

Introduction: The changing theory and practice of diplomacy

Professor Jack Spence, Dr Claire Yorke and Dr Alastair Masser

The theory and practice of diplomacy reflect the ever-changing international order. The challenge for scholars and practitioners alike is to keep pace. Writing in 1961, diplomat and academic Harold Nicolson observed the challenges to diplomacy. In the midst of the Cold War, the world was seen in binary terms: 'we are faced, not with a clash of interests, but with a fight between ideologies, between the desire on the one hand to defend individual liberties and the resolve on the other hand to impose a mass religion.'[1] He offered a pessimistic account of a world where old practices were discredited, trust was diminished and truth unobtainable. Yet, in the same year the Vienna Convention on Diplomatic Relations was concluded, and entered into force on 24 April 1964.[2] The Convention established universal norms and codes of conduct for diplomacy that are still observed today, and institutionalized the practice further.

Others have lamented diplomacy's decline, or questioned its continued role.[3] However, such critiques normally reflect an awareness that a country's power has diminished, or is being challenged, rather than confirming that the function and art of diplomacy themselves have become obsolete. Instead, the nature of power is shifting and the status quo of world order is in flux. Whereas the Cold War offered diplomats and politicians alike a sense of certainty about how the world worked, where power resided and who was a friend or adversary, today's diplomacy operates in a world of multiple actors, diverse threats and competing considerations. Perhaps, in reality, it was always this way. But there is clarity and simplicity in hindsight.

Diplomacy has evolved to be responsive to change, and to adapt and innovate in order to continue the dialogue between states and their people. As Adam Watson observed, diplomacy is about 'the management of change, and the maintenance by continued persuasion of order in the midst of change'.[4] Irrespective of whether, or how dramatically, diplomacy has changed it is more, rather than less, relevant today. It remains 'together with the balance of power, which it both reflects and reinforces, [...] the most important institution of our society of states'.[5] Yet new perspectives are needed to recognize shifts in world order, understand the different forms of power and how actors use it, and to make sense of the impermanence and complexity in international relations. These two volumes aim to address this challenge.

Diplomacy is defined in expansive and inclusive terms across these two books. It recognizes the central tenets – negotiation, communications, dialogue, summitry, intelligence and the fostering and maintenance of relationships – whilst offering new ways of looking at these topics. Central to an understanding of diplomacy are concepts of power and order, and their negotiation. However, power, alone, is 'not sufficient to explain the origins and conduct of diplomacy'.[6] The future of diplomacy therefore has to look beyond narrow conceptions of power, interests and security. These volumes expand how power is understood and achieved not only through military, economic or political might, but through the power of identities and ideas and discourses to shape societies and action.

The call for new perspectives in diplomacy and the questions posed to all contributors include: What do recent shifts in world order mean for how diplomacy is practiced? How does technology and communications change the nature of interactions, and what new challenges and opportunities do they present? How should academics study diplomacy, and how can the dialogue between policy and research be cultivated and fostered to be mutually beneficial? Looking to inspire new generations to study a topic that is important to all of us, what do universities need to teach? And why? What skills and experiences are essential to equip the next generation of diplomats, irrespective of the department or agency or organization in which they serve? Whose voices do we need to hear, and whose perspectives must we seek to realize a better, more inclusive global order and more constructive diplomacy? What does this mean for how we re-evaluate the objectives of diplomacy? What assumptions are outdated and obsolete? Finally, how can we build on the core components and constants of diplomacy that have existed throughout history, and make diplomacy a distinct and invaluable part of the dialogue between states?

Such questions are integral to how we understand the full diversity, breadth and potential of diplomacy in international relations. This can be seen in the wide range of prefixes commonly attached to signify diplomacy's different forms, such as: summit diplomacy, counter-diplomacy, environmental diplomacy and even (albeit not featuring in these volumes) yoga diplomacy.[7] Each points to the different means and manifestations of the central elements of diplomacy and show the many ways by which it is practiced and how power and interests are negotiated and pursued.

Diplomacy is considered to be both distinct to, and inseparable from, foreign policy. Foreign policy refers to the guiding strategies and approaches that states adopt that underpin their engagement with others. Foreign policy approaches might prioritize maintaining a balance of power, containment, isolation, multilateralism or ethics.[8] Although politicians and political leaders may determine foreign policy priorities and lead the decision-making, the process itself is iterative and symbiotic. Foreign policy is not a linear process emanating solely outwards from the heart of government. It responds to a rapidly changing political landscape, and the ability of non-state actors to bring issues to prominence and call for change. It can be influenced by powerful lobby groups or political campaigns, or the voices of individuals who are able to capture a mood or a moment to provoke a new approach.

War and diplomacy are equally not mutually exclusive, nor does war necessarily signify a failure of diplomacy. The two have often gone hand in hand. As Jan Melissen argues, 'All too often the task of diplomacy has not been to prevent armed conflict, but rather to help bring it about at the right moment, and the termination of wars, virtually without exception, involves an important element of diplomatic negotiation.'[9] We see in Samir Puri's analysis how proxy groups in Ukraine have been used by Russia to achieve strategic and diplomatic ends (Volume Two), and in Pablo de Orellana's account how discursive representations of foreign actors can be used to legitimize the use of force, drawing on the case of the US intervention in Libya (Volume One). Moreover, the advent of nuclear weapons has meant diplomacy becomes more pressing as a means by which to avoid war and diffuse conflict, especially between the nuclear powers, and those with nuclear aspirations.

The nature of emerging threats and the means by which to address them call for a need for a re-balance towards diplomacy and dialogue. In the years following the tragic terrorist attacks on American soil on 11 September 2001, foreign policy initiatives in many countries placed greater emphasis on the role of military and security levers of power, sometimes at the expense of funding for diplomatic initiatives and resources. The terrorist threat has been international in reach, uniting allies against a shared adversary, and in response has involved military interventions by the United States, the United Kingdom and their allies in Afghanistan and Iraq. Yet the war against terrorism has proved insufficient at mediating and minimizing the threat.

More recently, the 2020 global coronavirus pandemic raises new challenges for the interconnectedness of states, and their domestic and international stability, as borders were closed, planes grounded and trade and travel restricted. Yet it has simultaneously, and paradoxically, proven the limitations of political boundaries, and the transnational nature of global threats and their ability to disrupt national and international order.

The response to the problem requires multilateral cooperation, both to control the pandemic and to find a solution. Already, there is scientific and medical cooperation with discussion of concerted efforts to pool patents and develop a vaccine. Interestingly, in the longer term, based on the success of countries in handling the health crisis, and talk of the United States withdrawing from the World Health Organization (WHO), the international community may turn towards states like Taiwan, New Zealand and Germany as health leaders instead of the United States.

Similarly, multilateral action on climate change will be critical. Bush fires in Australia from June 2019 until early 2020 spread over ten million hectares of land, killing at least 34 people, and millions of wildlife, underscored the urgency of the matter.[10] A litany of examples of environmental degradation, including polar ice caps melting, threatening those living close to sea level, and the acceleration of deforestation of the Amazon in Brazil have wide-reaching implications for the global ecosystem and illustrate the need for collective action.

The push for global approaches to climate change reveals how different actors use their power. Smaller states and island nations, for example, are at the forefront of initiatives to slow the rising of sea levels and protect indigenous populations. For them it is an existential matter, threatening almost one-third of all citizens living just above sea level in small island nations.[11]

As Harris Kummerle points out (Volume Two), the success of multilateral initiatives will depend, in part, on the ability of diplomatic actors to foster environmental identities and build political will domestically. Yet such efforts are aided by active and vocal non-state actors. Among them is Greta Thunberg, a Swedish student, who gained prominence in 2018 for striking from school to protest global inaction on climate change. She has used her platform to galvanize and empower people, especially the young, to call for action from world leaders.

The ability of non-state actors to wield influence is aided by the evolution in technology and communications. This is especially visible in the rise of online violent extremism and radicalization, and the capacity for actors to stoke hate and incite violence. Although initially designed as a free and global commons, the use of these platforms to undermine societal cohesion and threaten security raises valuable questions about the regulation of the internet and its usage. Given its reach, it is a new domain requiring cooperation and coordinated approaches, as well as a reconsideration of common norms. Already, in the aftermath of the Christchurch terrorist attacks in March 2019, New Zealand, France and Canada have been at the forefront of initiatives to increase online regulations against hate and radicalization.

Another challenge has come from the rising movement of people, and the increase of refugees fleeing conflict and persecution in search of a better life. Managing the flow of people and ensuring both their well-being and the stability of domestic societies where some groups are uncertain or hostile about the influx of people have become a pressing international issue, requiring cooperation and coordination, especially in Europe.

As many states seek new ways to work together, and build international consensus, others have sought to undermine alliances. National and ideological identities have risen to the forefront of political concerns. The rise of nationalism from Hungary, to Brazil, and the United States, in part alongside concerns about immigration, has led to states withdrawing from the international stage and promoting nationalist and populist platforms, such as 'America First'. These bonds both celebrate and transcend national boundaries, with connections between nationalist movements cultivated across states. Similarly, alternative forms of identity, such as those championing a new globalism, the political left or issues such as environmentalism are increasingly powerful in connecting communities behind a view of a country's place in the world, with implications for foreign policy and the conduct of diplomacy.

These contemporary challenges to states and societies have manifold implications and variable impacts on people. Solutions to these challenges require not only cooperation between states, but the involvement of companies, non-governmental organizations and the general public. Alastair Masser examines how cross-border security threats create a pressing need for new forms of security cooperation (Volume Two). A more collaborative form of diplomacy offers opportunities for new ideas and innovations, as well as collective approaches to common problems. However, it brings new challenges. And the growth of new and non-state actors to the diplomatic scene raises questions about representation. Are they representing their own interests? Or those of their home states?

As part of fostering new perspectives, the study and practice of diplomacy need to be more inclusive and reflect the diversity of experiences and actors in the diplomatic space. After all, plurality is 'the essential condition of diplomacy'.[12] It is about negotiating, accommodating or overcoming difference. A lot of diplomatic theorizing and thinking is Western-centric, reflecting the experiences and evolution of the European and American systems. This focus should be expanded. This volume admittedly reflects a similar bias, yet it repeatedly encourages us to look at how different states view the world and engage with how other actors leverage power, create meaning and exert influence. As Ofer Fridman observes, for example, in his chapter on Russian information war (Volume Two), the Western binary of war and peace is not universal. Understanding the meaning Russia gives to warfare and peace can give valuable insights that guide how other states interact with it.

It is for this reason, too, that greater attention should be given to small states, and their distinct contributions and engagement in international diplomacy. Studies and theories of diplomacy often focus on the interactions of great powers, and extrapolate universal rules and principles to determine the actions and motivations of all states. But this denies the nuance and differences embedded in the system. James Gow (Volume One) articulates how small states make diverse choices about their diplomacy based on context, timing and the nature of the alliances available and the purpose they serve. And Flavia Gasbarri points to how South Africa used its new-found power post-apartheid to attempt to mediate regional conflicts, and alter its international image (Volume One). As Hillary Briffa shows, whilst small states might have a limited range of grand strategies available to them, they use their size and distinct capabilities to leverage power in different and unique ways.[13] Smaller states can use diplomacy to manipulate more powerful states, or to encourage them to intervene in conflicts in their own interests, such as how a weakened France encouraged America to intervene in Vietnam.[14]

A recurring theme throughout both volumes is the centrality of people to diplomacy, and of the power of individuals, relationships and emotions to affect change. Diplomacy is not an abstract instrument, or a tool of the state; its power and value are in its art and its craft. It is a conscious process of understanding others and building relations. That is not to say it is always done well, but at its essence it is about people and finding ways to negotiate how different people live in, and experience, the world.

Diplomats are at the forefront of these efforts, cultivating the local knowledge and pursuing national interests as official representatives of the state. Yet whilst the role of ambassadors and diplomats remains integral to diplomacy, the nature of the role is changing. Technology brings diplomats closer to the public, and, as Daniel Lomas reveals, their work is under greater scrutiny since the release of WikiLeaks (Volume One). A lot has changed, but a lot remains the same, as evidenced in Nigel Thorpe's personal account of the foreign service (Volume One). Today's diplomats will find his recollections both familiar in many ways, and also emblematic of a different time given the constant and rapid pace of change. The new realities of diplomacy pose additional questions about what it means to practice ethics within this space, and the codes and norms that shape how diplomats engage with others, as Mervyn Frost examines (Volume One). This is connected to the rise of public engagement in diplomacy, prioritizing ethical considerations.

At a political level, leaders are often powerful figures in the success or failure of diplomatic initiatives. Leaders can set the tone and direction for a country's policy, and build or destroy relations with allies and adversaries that can have a bearing on the effectiveness of their country's diplomatic efforts. US President Trump, for example, has become a symbol of the limitations of American power, undermining relations with allies, withdrawing from the international space and hastening the growing influence of other actors. Whereas leaders can also operate above the restrictions placed on diplomats to bring change. Barbara Zanchetta details the power of leaders to realize strategic objectives through their interactions at high-level summits, a central and symbolic feature of modern diplomacy (Volume One).

For all actors, the process of engaging with others should encourage people to reflect not only on the plurality of voices in the international space, but also how different people and communities view the world, how they feel and how the behaviours and discourses of states can have an influence on others. Constance Duncombe, for example, illustrates how US-Iranian relations are guided by emotional legacies on both sides, including the US trauma of the Iranian hostage crisis of 1979, to the humiliation experienced by Iranians at the overthrow of Mohammed Mossadegh in 1953, that current diplomatic initiatives do not always acknowledge.[15] Empathy is therefore key, as Claire Yorke discusses (in Volume One). This means looking inwards, and understanding diplomatic blind spots and local sensitivities. As Cold War political psychologist Ralph K. White has argued, dangerous illusions and images of others can hinder effective decision-making, blinding diplomats to the world beyond their world view.[16] Practitioners and scholars need to reflect on the shortcomings of their own country in the international space, and understand how emotions shape our world view and those of others.

Emotions serve multiple functions and are integral to diplomacy.[17] This includes providing a means by which leaders connect with their publics, or encourage allies to rally behind them in their diplomatic initiatives, as Philippe Beauregard observes (Volume Two). Similarly, as Francesca Granelli notes (Volume Two), bonds of public and social trust and connection help to explain why certain non-state actors and social movements are able to exert influence in the diplomatic space and raise issues to prominence on the international agenda.

The public are a critical component of diplomacy. Although technology and social media have increased connectivity and democratized discourse, the public dimension is actually not a recent development. There has been a conscious process by political figures to open up diplomacy and reduce the secrecy that traditionally surrounded it. In Woodrow Wilson's 1919 vision for a different world order, he wanted to reduce secret diplomacy and make it more transparent. Years later, Strobe Talbott spoke of efforts to make foreign policy less foreign, and more relevant to domestic populations, through town hall events and public engagement.[18] Given the ability of non-state actors to fill the spaces left by official governments, navigating public engagement is a critical function of the government. Interestingly, such practices can reveal disparities between the official view of diplomacy and the more localized and public view. As Thomas Colley (Volume Two) demonstrates, domestic populations often tell different stories of foreign policy and diplomacy to the official and intended narrative. Moreover, as Negah Angah and Inga Trauthig detail (Volume Two), social movements that harness the amplifying capacity of social media and shine a light on calls for change can have a significant impact on how governments think about public diplomacy and outreach in a more comprehensive fashion.

With a vast array of issues with which to contend, the portfolios of diplomats and practitioners have become ever wider. Diplomats today need to speak to world leaders, the media and the wider public both in their host country and back home.[19] In addition, they should be versed in topics that include trade policy, security, economics, health and technology. They should see the bigger picture, whilst simultaneously able to handle the everyday minutiae of the role. Crucially, diplomacy is not confined to foreign ministries, but expands across many government departments as international relations is a part of trade, development, economic and national security policy. Although governments are evolving to respond to the growth of their briefs, it is here that academics and specialists can play a role, offering insights, analysis and new ideas to aid the process.

Yet a tension often exists between academics and policymakers. Some academics are reluctant for their work to be politicized or misused. The questions they want to ask transcend the specific priorities of the government and relate to broader investigations of humankind, the sources of conflict, the nature of society or dynamics of relations between states. Similarly, for some policymakers, the abstractions of academia, and the theoretical constructs or scope of the questions asked, make it hard to apply academic research to the everyday challenges and realities of life in a government department, or in an embassy or consulate overseas. These books are designed to bridge this divide. Many of the contributors have spent time in politics or policy, or engage regularly with government departments, non-state actors and international organizations.

Now, more than ever, there is a need for dialogue between academics, policymakers and politicians. All are united in the business of ideas and of understanding the world around them. Academics can benefit from understanding the constraints, priorities and complexities of the practitioner's world, whilst the freedom of academics to ask big questions and think outside these constraints offers the potential for innovative, creative and new ways of looking at contemporary problems. Andrew Ehrhardt speaks to this in his chapter (Volume Two) on applied history. He reflects on how a deeper appreciation of history and lessons learned might reveal novel and valuable insights that can inform how we engage with alliances today, especially in light of the United Kingdom's departure from the European Union and strained relations between the United States and organizations such as NATO or the World Health Organization.

History has long been extolled as a tool for policy.[20] Former academic-turned-practitioner Henry Kissinger regularly emphasized the centrality of history and philosophy to understand the challenges within government. Many of the chapters across both volumes engage with historical case studies, drawing on archival materials to reveal different sides to familiar stories and paint a richer picture of the character and intricacies of diplomacy past and present. However, additional sources of insight can be found across disciplines, including in the study of politics and international relations, political psychology, sociology, communications and philosophy. Cross-disciplinary and interdisciplinary work reveals new insights and different perspectives, and these volumes reflect and value this diversity.

The purpose of these volumes is to bridge the divide between theory and practice. It aims to speak simultaneously to scholars, practitioners and experts. Both volumes adhere to the central themes of diplomacy, but are intentionally eclectic. Each chapter is united by a commitment to share new ideas and different ways of looking at the world. The volumes follow a loose thematic categorization, navigating the reader through an array of ideas and original scholarship. The two should be understood in dialogue with one another, with connective themes throughout.

The chapters contain a range of methodologies and analytical approaches. However, they lean heavily towards the qualitative and the discursive, reflecting the European and British epistemological tradition. Given the emphasis on how diplomacy is practiced, practice theory features frequently, highlighting attempts to capture and theorize the everyday habits, practices and 'socially meaningful patterns of action'[21] that make diplomacy distinct.

This first volume examines central and traditional themes of diplomacy in new light. Recurrent in many of these chapters is a call to look at states on their own merit as each reflecting their own unique identities, context, history, populations and sources of power. Rather than viewing the state as a homogenous or abstract entity of international relations, it encourages a more nuanced approach to understanding the evolution of diplomatic initiatives and the measures needed on a case-by-case basis to deliver effective policy.

The volume begins with a philosophical approach, with Mervyn Frost offering a much-needed appraisal of the role of ethics in diplomatic practice. He proposes a different conception of practice theory that recognizes how ethics are not for individual diplomats to determine, but are constituted in the global system and practice of diplomacy, and determine the bar for entry.

Security and hard power are interwoven into diplomacy. Jean-François Bélanger next addresses the continued role of coercion within diplomacy. Using the cases of Iraq, Syria and North Korea, he examines the varying role of coercion, and argues that hard power is a necessary, but not sufficient, cause for coercion to work. Furthermore, he points to some of the potential unintended consequences of the misuse of coercion in today's highly volatile and multipolar international order.

Daniel Lomas then offers an analysis of the enduring centrality of intelligence to the conduct and practice of diplomacy. Intelligence is too often considered a distinct area of study and practice, yet in his chapter he emphasizes how intelligence has evolved as an asset to diplomacy and provided a source of diplomatic power. He acknowledges the challenges presented by rapid changes in communications and technology, the shifting boundaries between private and public spaces, as visible in WikiLeaks, and the security challenges facing diplomats and intelligence officials.

Pablo de Orellana speaks to the significance of identity and how identities are constructed, constituted and represented by diplomats within diplomatic discourses. Taking a poststructuralist approach, he details how meanings are given to different forms of identity – 'evil', 'threat', 'friend' – and how this has implications for what is legitimized and rendered possible in the formation of foreign policy action. It reflects, too, the limitations and dangerous blind spots that can be embedded within diplomatic and policy practices that do not consider diverse perspectives and uncomfortable information, pointing out the potential for improvement in how diplomacy is conducted.

Revisiting the importance of summitry in international diplomacy, Barbara Zanchetta positions them as potential sites of diplomatic transformation, capable of altering adversarial relations. She looks back at the diplomacy of President Richard Nixon and Henry Kissinger and compares the successes and challenges of summits for the US opening to China in 1972, and the Détente with the Soviet Union during the SALT negotiations.

Connecting with themes of identity and the value of understanding others in diplomacy, Claire Yorke explores the power of interpersonal relations and the role of empathy. The connection that exists between diplomats and leaders can be an effective means, and valuable asset, to achieve policy objectives. She examines how empathy aids diplomatic relations, and shapes communications and practices in diplomacy, pointing to its role in strategic initiatives.

Although empathy can be about encouraging people to say yes to diplomatic overtures, Gerrit Kurtz looks at the power of 'no'. His chapter shines a light on counter-diplomacy, an underappreciated and understudied element of diplomacy. Operating at bilateral, multilateral and system levels, counter-diplomacy is used by actors seeking to resist or undermine international norms, or manipulate others. It involves disruptive processes and practices that can harm trust and unity, as well as efforts for collective action on global concerns. Such an approach helps policymakers to better understand how diplomacy can be more effective, as well as reiterating the need to look beyond great power politics to the techniques used by smaller states to wield influence in the international space.

Following the theme of how smaller states leverage their power in different ways, James Gow interrogates the ideas of 'smallness' and examines how small states seek security. With a focus on Central and Eastern Europe, and the NATO and EU relations, he argues that alliances are often dependent on the nature and quality of the relationship between small states and their friends and organizational partners as well as the context.

Looking at how smaller states capitalize on new-found power, Flavia Gasbarri turns to South Africa and how its rehabilitation within the international community after the election of President Nelson Mandela led to it playing a greater role within regional mediation initiatives, albeit with varied levels of success. In the process she reiterates the importance of personality in politics.

Finally, former Ambassador Nigel Thorpe offers a personal reflection of life in the British diplomatic service. As an Eastern European expert, who saw the UK's entry into the European Union and the fall of the Cold War, his account reveals how much changes in a short space of time, as well as detailing the everyday realities and practicalities of being a diplomat. His recollections underscore the thrills and challenges of diplomacy, the importance of interpersonal relations and trust to gain valuable insights and access into a host country, as well as the challenges of balancing the personal with the political, given the unique demands placed on officials representing their state.

These chapters all offer new ways of looking at the central tenets of diplomacy, and pose bigger questions for how it is studied and practiced. The future is always unknown, but the chapters in these two volumes are a call to widen the aperture of focus.

Notes

1. Harold Nicolson, 'Diplomacy Then and Now', *Foreign Affairs* 40 (1961): 39.
2. United Nations, Vienna Convention on Diplomatic Relations 1961, Done at Vienna on 18 April 1961. Entered into force on 24 April 1964. United Nations, Treaty Series, Vol. 500, 95, https://legal.un.org/ilc/texts/instruments/english/conventions/9_1_1961.pdf
3. Ronan Farrow, *War on Peace: The End of Diplomacy and the Decline of American Influence* (New York: W. W. Norton, 2018).
4. Adam Watson, *Diplomacy: The Dialogue between States* (London: Eyre Methuen, 1982), 223.
5. Geoff R. Berridge, *Diplomacy: Theory and Practice* (Springer, 2015), 1.
6. James Der Derian, 'Mediating Estrangement: A Theory for Diplomacy', *Review of International Studies* 13, no. 2 (1987): 91–110, 92.
7. Peter Martin, 'Yoga Diplomacy: Narendra Modi's Soft Power Strategy', *Foreign Affairs* 25 (2015).
8. Mervyn Frost, 'Putting the World to Rights: Britain's Ethical Foreign Policy', *Cambridge Review of International Affairs* 12, no. 2 (1999): 80–9.
9. Jan Melissen, ed., *Innovation in Diplomatic Practice* (Springer, 2016), xvi.
10. 'Australia Fires: A Visual Guide to the Bushfire Crisis', *BBC News*, 31 January 2020, https://www.bbc.com/news/world-australia-50951043 (accessed 29 May 2020).

11 Hussain Rasheed Hassan and Valerie Cliff, 'For Small Island Nations, Climate Change Is Not a Threat. It's Already Here', *World Economic Forum*, 24 September 2019, https://www.weforum.org/agenda/2019/09/island-nations-maldives-climate-change/ (accessed 20 May 2020).
12 Adam Watson, *Diplomacy: The Dialogue between States*, 15.
13 Hillary Briffa, 'Can Small States Have a Grand Strategy?' (Unpublished Thesis, King's College London, 2019).
14 See, for example, Pablo de Orellana, *The Road to Vietnam* (I.B. Tauris, 2020).
15 Constance Duncombe, *Representation, Recognition and Respect in World Politics: The Case of Iran–US Relations* (Manchester University Press, 2019).
16 Ralph K. White, 'Misperception and the Vietnam War', *Journal of Social Issues* 22, no. 3 (1966): 1–164.
17 See, for example, Barbara Keys, 'Emotional Diplomacy: Official Emotion on the International Stage', *Journal of American History* 103, no. 2 (2016): 532; Todd H. Hall, *Emotional Diplomacy: Official Emotion on the International Stage* (Cornell University Press, 2015); Robin Markwica, *Emotional Choices: How the Logic of Affect Shapes Coercive Diplomacy* (Oxford University Press, 2018). Barbara Keys and Claire Yorke, 'Personal and Political Emotions in the Mind of the Diplomat', *Political Psychology* 40, no. 6 (2019): 1235–49.
18 Strobe Talbott, 'Globalization and Diplomacy: A Practitioner's Perspective', *Foreign Policy* 108 (1997): 69–83.
19 Tom Fletcher, *The Naked Diplomat: Understanding Power and Politics in the Digital Age* (HarperCollins UK, 2016).
20 See, for example, Richard E. Neustadt and Ernest R. May, *Thinking in Time: The Uses of History for Decision Makers* (Free Press, 1988).
21 Emanuel Adler and Vincent Pouliot, 'International Practices: Introduction and Framework', in *International Practices*, ed. Emmanuel Adler and Vincent Pouliot (Cambridge: Cambridge University Press, 2011), 3–35.

1

The global diplomatic practice: Constituting an ethical world order

Professor Mervyn Frost

We all have an interest in how our state, the one within which we are constituted as citizens, relates to other states. Relations between states are fundamental to so many aspects of our lives. They determine whether we live in peace or go to war; whether our state forms an association with other states to promote trade, tourism, education, scientific cooperation and to protect the environment. The ever-changing pattern of conflict and corporation between states is in part guided by an elaborate practice of global diplomacy. This chapter sets out to explore this practice and in particular its ethical features. What are the fundamental values constituted and pursued by diplomats who participate in this practice?

Ethics matters. Men and women everywhere and the states in which they live profess to be committed to the realization of certain ethical values. They seek to promote justice and to prevent injustice both on the individual level and on the inter-state level. They do not understand themselves or their states to be involved in naked power struggles in which the 'winner takes all'. The ethical commitments are made manifest in the constitutions of international organizations like the UN, the OAU and OAS, in international law generally and in many international treatises. Yet, at first glance, it is far from clear what ethical values underpin our international system and the diplomatic practice that seeks to guide it. Indeed, it might seem as if there is no ethical basis to our international order. This short chapter challenges such a sceptical conclusion by considering an important component of our contemporary international order, the global diplomatic practice. It asks: What if any are the ethical dimensions involved in the contemporary global diplomatic practice? The phrase 'diplomatic practice' refers not to international relations in general, but to the specific practice operated between sovereign states with its well-known components that include: embassies, ambassadors, consulates, consuls, secretaries, diplomatic bags, diplomatic immunities, the ceremony of the presentation of credentials by incoming ambassadors to host governments, the execution of *demarches* under certain circumstances and, occasionally, the expulsion of diplomats from sovereign states.[1]

How might a researcher go about seeking an answer to this question? A first possibility might be to question serving or retired diplomats about their ethical principles and the ethical problems that they might have confronted during their careers. This line of questioning might uncover cases in which individual diplomats experienced a tension between their ethical commitments and the duties they were asked to perform as diplomats. One example is the case of Craig Murray, the British ambassador to Uzbekistan, who complained publicly in 2004 about the Uzbek security forces' use of torture against opponents of the regime. As a consequence of following his conscience he was recalled to London.[2] He subsequently published a book, *Dirty Diplomacy*, about this incident.[3]

Such research would involve an historical investigation seeking out diplomats who had encountered ethical dilemmas. A researcher might move on from an initial search for such cases, to a subsequent listing of the range of ethical justifications the diplomats had used to justify their actions. There is no doubt that this mode of enquiry would uncover a variety of different ethical positions espoused by diplomats from different states. Deon Geldenhuys, in *The Diplomacy of Isolation*, provides insight into the ethics that guided South African diplomats during the years of *apartheid*.[4] These were different from those which guided Elizabeth Wilmshurst, Deputy Legal Advisor to the Foreign Office in the UK, who resigned her position because she believed that the war against Iraq was unethical and illegal.[5]

In examining the specific ethical positions taken up by individual diplomats, the initial description of these might then be supplemented with an in-depth comparison of the diverse ethical theories informing their justifications. These might include arguments referring to natural law, theories of human rights, utilitarian ethical theory or the ethics embedded in specific religious traditions (Islamic, Christian, Judaic, Buddhist, Hindu etc.). Even a cursory knowledge about contemporary international relations would suggest that it is highly unlikely that such a survey would find a common ethical position informing the ethical judgements of all cases in which diplomats confronted ethical tensions in the performance of their duties.

A second approach to exploring the ethical dimensions of diplomacy might involve, not the questioning of individual diplomats encountering ethical problems, but investigating the actions of individual states and the ethical arguments states gave in support of their actions. This might involve an historical investigation of the actions of states and comparing the value-based positions they adopted in response to specific international events. Such an approach informs the contributions to a recent edited book entitled *Values in Foreign Policy*.[6] This mode of enquiry is descriptive, historical and comparative. Here again a researcher might list the different kinds of ethical reasons for action given by states and classify these in terms of the ethical theories on which they were based (rights based, utilitarian etc.). Such a line of inquiry would produce a diversity of ethical positions among the 195 sovereign states active in international affairs.

A third way of researching the role of ethics in international diplomacy might be to move beyond a focus on individual diplomats, individual states, but to focus instead on the diplomats active in an international organizations such as the United Nations or the African Union. The enquiry might proceed by questioning the diplomats at the UN who make policy across all the many issue areas within which it is active with a view to eliciting whether there is a UN-wide ethical position informing its policies and actions. Here again the enquiry would be historical, empirical and descriptive. Here, once more, a moment's reflection reveals that within the UN there is not a single, coherent, ethical position that remains constant over time. There have been (and still are) ongoing disputes within the UN and other international organizations such as the African Union, about the ethics of humanitarian intervention; about the ethical underpinnings of the International Criminal Court; about the ethics of development, environmental protection, the treatment of refugees; and so on. Historical, descriptive and broadly empirical enquiries into the role of ethics in the diplomacy of international organizations will reveal a wide plurality of ethical positions.

A fourth way of investigating this topic might move beyond listing and classifying the ethical arguments used by diplomats and states, to a thoroughgoing philosophical evaluation of the different approaches to international ethics. This could be done with a view to finding the one that best stands up to intellectual scrutiny (and rejecting the rest). A rather specialized component of such an enquiry might involve, for example, evaluating different theories of international justice.[7] This would be a philosophical exercise rather than an empirical or historical one. Here again, even amongst philosophers, there is unlikely to be agreement on a single 'best' ethical theory. An example of a diplomat with a specific recommendation about the ethical approach diplomats ought to take is provided by Harold Nicolson who argued, 'My own practical experience, and the years of study which I have devoted to the subject, have left me with the profound conviction that "moral" diplomacy is ultimately the most effective, and that "immoral" diplomacy defeats its own purposes.'[8] He stressed that moral integrity must be taken as central to what is required of a diplomat. He then simply listed the virtues required of diplomats as truthfulness, precision, calm, good temper, patience, modesty and loyalty.[9] Although diplomats from different states might agree with his general statement, they are still likely to have widely different views on ethical matters relating to human rights, the limits of state sovereignty, the rights of women, theories of international justice in general and so on.

In the light of the diverse approaches to the study of ethics in the contemporary global diplomatic practice outlined above, one thing stands out. This practice exists in a world in which there are many different ethical codes and systems. Given this diversity, a chapter discussing the role of ethics in diplomacy must confront a fundamental question head-on: is there, somewhere, beyond this diversity of value positions, a common set of ethical commitments, common to diplomats from all states? It might be suggested that reason might reveal a common international ethic. A sceptical response to this suggestion seems warranted. 'Reason' is unlikely to reveal one universally accepted ethical/moral code, because, as we know, different people (diplomats, philosophers, ordinary men and women) have different conceptions of what 'right reason' (as Grotius called it) dictates. Natural lawyers do not agree with those advocating a deontological approach, and neither of these agrees with utilitarian theories or rights-based ones and so on.[10]

The conclusion that follows from the discussion above must be to accept that we live in a plural world – a world of ethical diversity, and any search for a definitive 'ethic of diplomacy' is doomed to fail. It is easy to conclude from this that diplomatic activity between sovereign states is not (and never will be) constrained by a common international ethic of diplomacy. Instead, it will be guided by the architecture of power that exists in international affairs at any given time. On this account, all that scholars can do, at the end of their empirical and philosophical enquiries outlined above, is note the diversity of ethical points of view between diplomats, between sovereign states, within international organizations and between philosophers from diverse traditions, and leave it there. The consequences of this conclusion are not happy ones. For they lead us to understand diplomacy as necessarily guided by considerations of *realpolitik* rather than ethics. The role of ethics in the diplomatic practice, on this view, is both negligible and peripheral.

Practice theory: An alternative approach to the study of ethics and diplomacy

There is, though, an alternative way of investigating the relationship between ethics and the contemporary global diplomatic practice. This is provided by practice theory as elaborated by Silviya Lechner and Mervyn Frost in *Practice Theory and International Relations*.[11] It does not set out to investigate, in the empirical and descriptive ways described above, what ethical positions have been chosen, espoused or followed by diplomats, states or international organizations. Instead, it starts from the fundamental insight of interpretive social science that actors and their actions can only be understood from within the social practices in which they are constituted as actors and actions of a certain kind.[12] At every point where researchers attempt to understand actors, actions and the social practices in which they are constituted, the internal point of view is crucial. The point being made here is not about the importance of *context* for understanding actions in such cases, but is a fundamental logical point that the very meaning of an action cannot be grasped without knowing what might be termed 'the rules of the game' pertinent to a given practice. Straightforward external observation will not reveal the meaning of actions within social practices. For example, simply observing some seemingly ritualized behaviour of a group of people will not result in an observer, ignorant of an internal understanding of the practice of states, understanding that these are heads of state and diplomats engaged in a summit meeting.

When we come to applying practice theory to the study of diplomacy, we come to understand that diplomats are constituted as actors of a certain kind within the practice of diplomacy and their constitution as such provides them with a menu of appropriate actions pertinent to this practice and which can only be understood within it. Diplomats are constituted through an elaborate system of mutual recognition within diplomatic practice. Crucially, embedded in this practice itself, as in all social practices, is a complex set of ethical values. An actor only becomes a diplomat by learning how to follow the rules internal to the diplomatic practice and by committing to the ethical value system constituted within it. Diplomats are not properly understood as actors who may choose between ethical codes (be they Christian, rights-based, Islamic, Judaic, Buddhist, etc.). Such a misguided understanding would lead to the kinds of research programmes outlined above, which set out to investigate empirically whether a given set of diplomats had decided to be guided by ethical considerations (or not) and to list the kinds of ethical principles they had followed.

Before proceeding with an elaboration of practice theory as applied to the practice of diplomacy it is important to note that the Lechner and Frost version of practice theory is distinct from that which has been presented recently by several scholars in the discipline of International Relations.[13] These authors see practices as actions. For them a practice is what actors do. Research into this domain would require close observation of diplomatic behaviour in specific contexts such as their actions and interactions within a given embassy or within a given location at a specific historical moment.[14] It would focus on empirically determining what decisions they made and what ethical constraints they observed? In sharp contrast, Lechner and Frost make a crucial distinction between actions and the social practices within which they are meaningful. Many illustrations of the point they make are to be found in sport. For example, what is to count as a goal can be understood only in the context of the specific sport (practice) in which it was scored (netball, soccer, hockey, water-polo etc.). No sense can be made of the notion 'scoring a goal' apart from knowledge of the rules of the game being played.

The fundamental point for the purposes of this chapter is that the ethical values embedded in the contemporary global diplomatic practice are not values, which diplomats may choose to accept or not, as they deem fit. Accepting them is a precondition for participation; it is a precondition for becoming and being a diplomat. This point can be illustrated with reference to university academics, who, by virtue of being participants in the broad practice of university life, are required to uphold the ethical values embedded in it – these include values such as truth, knowledge, academic freedom and so on. Academics who are found to have undermined these values are expelled from university life in disgrace. Similarly, diplomats who undermine the ethics of the diplomatic practice will be excluded from it.

The turn in the argument made in the previous paragraph merits further elaboration. The ways of exploring the ethics of diplomacy briefly set out in the opening sections of this chapter all focused on researching the ethical choices made by individual actors (diplomats, states, international organizations). The starting point of such enquiries, the 'ontology' if you like, is a field of enquiry populated by individual actors who face ethical predicaments and who make individual choices about ethical codes to guide their actions in the face of these predicaments. Actors understood in this way are free to choose their ethical positions and the task for researchers then is to track, catalogue and evaluate their choices. Practice theory challenges this starting point, by focusing on the way in which to be an actor, is to be constituted as such within a specific social practice with its internal rules and ethical components. The point is easy to make across the vast range of human practices: legal, religious, sporting, cultural, political, scientific and the diplomatic. In order to become a participant in any of these, a person has to understand and follow the ethical components that are internal to the practice. The argument now turns to an analysis of our contemporary global practices which are served by the practice of diplomacy.

Global practices

Let us now turn to an examination of the complexities of our global practices. First, participants in global practices – be they individuals, states, international organizations or diplomats – will find themselves simultaneously participating in any number of other social practices. At any moment an individual might be a participant in practices that include a family (as mother, father, child), a church (as parishioner), a corporation (as shareholder, director, sales person or client), a state (as ambassador, politician, civil servant, citizen), a sporting club (as player, owner or supporter) and many others.

Second, we who are simultaneous participants in multiple practices often encounter circumstances in which the ethical requirements for participation in the one pull us in a different direction to those required in others. For example, as citizens we are to pay attention to the ethical value of sovereignty and protect it from threats of one kind or another, including large-scale influxes of migrants. This might pull us in a different direction to what is required of us by our religious practice which demands that we should love our neighbours (including migrants) as ourselves. Diplomats in their daily routines will regularly encounter tensions that arise from the simultaneous multi-practice nature of international life. There are a number of these that are of great significance and will be discussed later in this chapter.

Third, it is important to note that the global diplomatic practice is embedded in and is a key component of a mega practice – the global society of sovereign states. In other words, the diplomatic practice is not a free-standing practice, but is embedded in (is a component of) a larger one. It is only in relation to this higher-order practice that what diplomats do, worldwide, has any meaning.

Fourth, the society of sovereign states is a macro practice; it is a practice of practices. Within the global macro practice of sovereign states, each sovereign state has within itself thousands of other practices, including micro practices (families), meso practices (local sports and cultural clubs) and mega practices (multinational corporations and universal religions). One of the features of sovereign states is that they manage the multiple practices within them so that they might coexist with one another in an orderly fashion.[15] Some do this in an autocratic way, while others are democratic. Similarly, the practice of sovereign states, as a whole, provides an environment in which the multiple transnational practices embedded within it can prosper and flourish (churches, sporting institutions, university networks, corporations, banks etc.).

Fifth, it is crucial to note that the macro practice we know as the society of sovereign states is an anarchy. An anarchy is a practice within which the participant units recognize one another as having a certain set of freedoms in a wider social whole but are not subject to a central government. The society of sovereign states is an anarchical order in which the participant states recognize one another's sovereignty in a global order that exists without a global government. The global diplomatic practice must be understood as a crucial component of this anarchical practice.

Sixth, the participants in the society of sovereign states (everyone, everywhere) including all those in the global diplomatic practice are simultaneously participants in another global macro practice. This is the global rights practice (sometimes referred to as global civil society). The defining feature of this is that it is constituted of individuals who recognize one another as equal holders of fundamental rights – whose rights include equal sets of negative liberties. These include the right to safety of the person; the right not to be tortured, killed, assaulted; the right to freedom of speech, freedom of movement, religious freedom, academic freedom; and the right to own property. A distinguishing feature of the global rights practice is that it has no geographical boundaries. Rights holders consider themselves to have their fundamental rights wherever they happen to be. These rights are not tied to a location or to a specific state. It may well be that in certain places the sovereign state they find themselves in may not be able to protect their rights, but this in no way suggests that they would not continue to claim their rights. Another feature of this rights practice is that the participants do not consider that the rights they have are a gift/grant from some government. This global rights practice being a macro practice contains within it many other practices. A conspicuous component of the global rights practice is the global market within which property holders buy and sell products and services. In this market are thousands of companies, corporations, banks, building societies and partnerships. The global market is a mega force in contemporary international affairs. It is one in which everyone, everywhere participates. The global diplomatic practice and the diplomats within it spend much of their time interpreting the actions and interactions that take place in the macro practice of global civil society. For what happens in it is of crucial importance to the well-being of the sovereign state they serve.

Seventh, both the global practice of sovereign states and the global rights practice are constitutive practices as opposed to instrumental (purposive) practices. Instrumental practices are deliberately constructed by people in order to realize certain objectives which existed prior to the establishment of the practice. An example would be Oxfam which was set up to raise money to help people overcome the dire effects of famine and poverty. In contrast, by participating in constitutive practices people come to hold identities and realize values that can be achieved only within that practice. Participation in a constitutive practice is an end (an ethical value) in itself. Simple examples of constitutive practices are provided by games. To realize the valued identity of being a cricket player and to realize the ethical values to be had in it (fair competition in the beautiful game) one must participate in it whether as player or participant. Such practices are not a means to an end that exists external to the practice; participation in the practices creates the identities and values that are important to those who participate in them.[16,17] The two global macro practices within which the modern diplomatic practice operates are both constitutive practices. In the first, we are constituted as citizens in states that constitute one another as sovereign equals (as opposed to empires with colonies). In the second, the global rights practice, we come to enjoy the freedoms that come with being recognized as a rights holder by other rights holders, whom one in turn recognizes as having the same set of freedoms as they have granted to oneself. This status is highly valued when contrasted with other possibilities such as being recognized as a slave, in a slave-owning society or as less than fully free in some form of racist society.

Finally, eighth, participants in the global macro practices and the global diplomatic practice confront, as do we all, the problems of change and the ethical tensions precipitated by change within the macro practice. Practices everywhere regularly confront pressures to change from a range of sources including demographic developments (ageing, increasing or shrinking populations), pandemics, technological developments (the digital revolution), scientific discoveries (genetic engineering), natural disasters (tsunamis, volcanic eruptions, droughts, floods) and man-made environmental disasters (climate change, deforestation). Confronting such changes compels participants to consider and deal with a multifaceted range of ethical tensions and contradictions that emerge as different practices cope with change.

The ethics embedded in the practice of sovereign states

Since the global diplomatic practice is a functional component of the society of sovereign states it follows that the ethical dimensions of the diplomatic practice will be closely related to the ethics embedded in the practice of states. We need to give an outline of the latter before we can turn to the former. What, then, are the ethical values embedded in the practice of sovereign states? The primary values are freedom and diversity. States constitute one another through an elaborate system within which they recognize one another as free, that is, as sovereign. Both domestically and internationally each participant state is recognized by the others as being entitled (ethically entitled) to decide on (and to pursue) policies that it considers to be in its interests and to promote what it considers to be the most appropriate ethical form of life for its citizens. The interests they are free to pursue include wealth and power. The ethical forms of life they are free to consider might, amongst others, include the pursuit of liberal, social democratic, socialist, Zionist or communist forms of society.

The mutual recognition of one another's freedom points to another ethical value realized in this practice. This is the value of diversity. The freedom enjoyed by the 195 sovereign states ensures that they enjoy the value of diversity in the global practice. The constitution of the global practice rules out the imposition by one state of its preferred form of life on all the others.

The ethical dimensions of the global rights practice

In the global rights practice, as in the practice of sovereign states, the primary values constituted within it are freedom and diversity. In global civil society the participants constitute one another as rights holders with at least an equal set of negative liberties such as the rights to freedom of movement, freedom of speech, freedom of association, the right to own property, the right to safety of the person and so on. The enjoyment of these rights enables participants to realize the second value which is diversity. Rights holders value that other rights holders might use these to pursue life plans and goals that are different from one's own. Some will choose the life of an aesthete, others a life of consumption and indulgence, yet others might choose to devote their lives to following religious forms of one kind or another. In civil society individuals are free to pursue their chosen ways of life subject only to the constraint that they allow other rights holders the freedom to pursue their preferred life plans.

The ethical component of global diplomatic practice

A large component of the everyday activity of diplomats in the global diplomatic practice involves either administration or politics. The former is the routine maintenance and oversight of standardized mechanisms that are useful to states and their citizens globally. These include the issuing of passports, visas and other kinds of travel documents; the oversight of how these are used at borders and the management of cases where disputes arise about the use of such documents. Similarly, diplomats might liaise with their counterparts in foreign countries about facilitating trade between their states. There are also elaborate systems for the management of student exchanges across international borders to both schools and universities.

Quite distinct from everyday administration are the political activities of diplomats. International politics involves disputes between states about the rules of association within the global practice of states. These might be about borders, claims to territory, claims about reparations after wars have ended and disputes about constitutional issues within international organizations. Important among these are disputes about trade relations, international banking, the control of refugees, the treatment of asylum seekers and so on. In an anarchical practice like the society of sovereign states, in which the defining feature of the participants is that they constitute one another as free states, it is to be expected that there will be political disputes about what one might call 'the rules of the game'. Diplomats are regularly involved in negotiations between states which in some cases result in the establishment of international treaties. Where disputes become increasingly intense and the prospect of war emerges, diplomats may be involved in secret diplomacy, away from the glare of publicity, in which they can explore ways of resolving intractable problems. The international political processes have become more complex in recent years with the development of ever more sophisticated forms of international communication that are open to the general public worldwide. It is now possible for governments and leaders to participate directly in international politics through the media and by extensive use of strategic communications. This kind of activity is sometimes misleadingly referred to as 'public diplomacy'. It would be more accurate to call it international politics. These activities are about the push and pull between states – the struggle for power in order to change the rules of international society. What is crucial to note about international politics is that the participating states are all quite rightly considered to be preoccupied with the pursuit of their national interests usually defined as the pursuit of power and material advantage.

The most important ethical dimension of the global diplomatic practice is not to be found in its everyday concerns with administration and politics. Properly to elucidate the fundamental ethical dimension of the global diplomatic practice it is necessary to focus on the practice as a whole and its relationship to the two global macro practices within which it is embedded. Let us now turn to this task.

The global diplomatic practice is, as we have seen, a component of the constitutive practice of sovereign states. Diplomacy, with all its conventions, hierarchies, protocols, formalities, legal immunities, ancient traditions and so on, is not merely instrumental to the practice of sovereign states (although it is that). Beyond serving the instrumental functions of facilitating quick and confidential channels of communication between participant states and its facilitating role in international politics, it also has an ethically constitutive role within the practice of states. It is this constitutive role that is central for any proper understanding of ethics and diplomacy. By participating in the global practice of diplomacy, states confirm and guarantee their commitment to the international anarchy of sovereign free states. In doing this they indicate their commitment to the web of mutual recognition through which the practice of states is constituted. They do this by protecting the embassies and consulates of foreign powers located in their territories and by conferring on their diplomatic personnel all the immunities to which they are entitled.[18] The ethical import of the global diplomatic practice is achieved through diplomats everywhere conducting themselves in terms of the rules internal to the practice and by having the participants in the macro practices recognize and respect them for doing this. To flout the rules of the global diplomatic practice would undermine a state's standing within the global practice. In recent times an extreme example of such a violation is provided by the abuse by Saudi Arabia of diplomatic protections when it allowed (or did not prevent) the murder in its consulate in Istanbul, Turkey, of Jamal Khashoggi, a journalist on 2 October 2018. The Saudi government was condemned internationally for this flagrant abuse of the protections afforded to diplomatic premises.[19]

This way of understanding the practice of diplomacy enables us to understand that while diplomats in their day-to-day tasks might be focussed on securing and promoting the narrow interests of the states they represent, conveying information back and forth between states, managing the system of passports and visas and so on, these activities must always be understood as subordinate to their primary ethical role which is to uphold and protect the rules and ethical values of the two global macro practices which form the architecture within which they operate. The core values constituted within these global practices are, as we have seen, freedom and diversity. For the global anarchical order to persist the constituent states and rights holders need a way of guarding against the major ethical threats to this global constitutional order which are war, empire and/or the dissolution of the global whole. By maintaining the portion of the global diplomatic practice that falls within its sovereign borders, each state plays its role in maintaining the anarchical order. Respecting the rules of diplomacy in its territory, each state displays to all the others that it is prepared to have the actions of its government observed and interpreted by experts from the sending states. These experts are the diplomats. It is the commitment to having one's government and its actions actively watched and interpreted by foreign diplomats that is the ethical glue which guarantees the security of the whole – the society of sovereign states.

It is interesting to note that the channels of communication that are guaranteed within the diplomatic practice are the polar opposite of channels created by states for the purposes of strategic communication. Strategic communication, by definition, is directed towards broadcasting messages outwards from a state with a view to manipulating international public opinion and the opinion of governments and international organizations in a way that will advance the interests of the communicator.[20] A good example of this kind of activity is provided by a whole slew of policies that were pursued by the government of the *apartheid* state in South Africa which spent a fortune on paying journalists abroad to write articles sympathetic to *apartheid* policies. It bought newspaper companies in New York and London and imposed editorial policies on them that would support South Africa's policies of separate development; it established supposedly objective journals in the United States and Britain with the same instrumental aims; and beyond these it engaged in a range of clandestine manoeuvres to manipulate information in support of *apartheid*.[21]

The global diplomatic practice is quite different. By maintaining it, the participant states in the system of sovereign states are not engaged in strategic communication, but in ethically constituting one another as free in a world of diverse free states. In a sense one might say that by playing its role in the global diplomatic practice a state demonstrates that it is a sovereign state in the practice within which sovereign states are constituted as such, constituted as enjoying that ethical standing.

Not only do diplomats posted abroad observe and confirm that their host states are indeed sovereign free states and not subversive actors, intent on the creation of an empire or the destruction of the anarchy. They also play a crucial role in keeping track of the ways in which their host states are supporting or undermining the ethical values embedded in the other great global macro practice, the global rights practice (global civil society). As we have seen the global rights practice has as an integral component, the global market. This is a domain within which individual rights holders either individually or collectively through companies, firms, multinational corporations recognize one another as having the rights which allow them to trade goods and services internationally. Part of the task of diplomats may be understood as providing reciprocal recognition between the participating sovereign states that they all support and uphold the system of individual rights that constitute the global free market.

In conclusion, then, the specific ethical commitments of diplomats must be understood as being directed towards upholding the values of freedom and diversity (both between states and between individuals) made possible by the global anarchical macro practices which form the fundamental constitution of international relations in the world as we know it. They must be understood as playing a crucial part in the constitution of the values encapsulated in these two global macro practices. This understanding of diplomacy is far removed from all those who would portray diplomacy in simple functional terms relating to the provision of secure channels of communication. The global diplomatic practice is not a postal service but plays a fundamental ethical role in the constitution of contemporary international relations.

The ethical challenges within global diplomatic practice

As indicated above, the global practices in which contemporary diplomats participate are not static. They are not like games in which players play match after match while the rules remain constant. Instead, the two global practices have interesting (and often dramatic) histories which exhibit extensive ethical change over time. The macro practice of states has developed from its mediaeval beginnings in which sovereignty was interpreted as being primarily about the absolute authority of kings over their subjects (an ethical claim), through several periods in which countervailing secular forms of government emerged (all based on ethical claims about the proper relationship between government and governed) to balance the power of sovereigns, to the position, today, where states are taken to derive their power from the people (this, too, an ethical position). Of these about 166 are democratic. In interstate relations there has been a shift from pre-imperial political forms, to imperial international relations and most recently to post-imperial forms. Global civil society, too, has been through many changes. The economic component of civil society has changed from mercantilist forms, to imperial ones, and then to its current global capitalist form.

This brief sketch of the history of global institutions is presented merely to illustrate the extent and scope of ethically significant changes that have taken place over the centuries. As indicated earlier the international practices change over time to accommodate new circumstances such as those presented by technological advances, the emergence of new actors and ideologies, and those caused by natural disasters such as epidemics, droughts, earthquakes and unanticipated demographic changes. In the face of change participants in existing practices must, perforce, interpret the meaning of the new circumstances in terms of the ethics internal to the current practices in which they are constituted as who they value themselves to be. In light of such interpretations they then choose how to act. They must move from analysis to policymaking, followed by policy implementation. These interpretive demands are a constant feature of the day-to-day life of diplomats in their global practice.

States' rights versus human rights: The dominant ethical tension of our time

As we have seen, the core ethical values embedded in the system of sovereign states are those associated with freedom and diversity. Similarly, the core values embedded in the global rights practice are the value of individual freedom and the value accorded to the diversity made possible in a society of free individuals. Given that most people in most places are simultaneously participants in both practices, it is important that any tensions between these ethical positions be harmonized or ironed out. A failure to do this would lead to incoherence in the ethical status of the actors and their actions in the global macro practices. Diplomats have a key role in confronting such ethical conundrums.

There is a tension between these two global practices that, on the face of the matter, seems to be unresolvable. This is a tension between states' rights constituted in the global macro practice of sovereign states and individual rights constituted in the global rights practice. If we consider ourselves as individual *civilians*, that is as rights holders in a global practice of rights holders without borders, then it is clear we ought to be able to exercise our freedoms unconstrained by physical borders. For example, if we were to find ourselves in North Africa struggling to make a living under drought conditions, as rights holders we would consider ourselves free to move elsewhere to improve our lot.

Similarly, if we wished to make contracts with others to form new associations across borders, as right holders, we would consider ourselves free to do this. If, for example, as Muslims we wished to form a global Islamic movement to promote Islamic values, we might justify our action by referring to our right to freedom of religion. Similarly, if the state in which we enjoy citizenship is a failed state and cannot provide the services and protections we expect, then as civilians we would consider ourselves free to seek another state willing to protect our rights. There are many other examples that could be given.

However, if we alter the frame and consider ourselves as *citizens* of a sovereign state, then within this practice, we consider that we are within our rights to exclude others, whom for one reason or another, we do not wish to accept as fellow citizens or even as visitors to our state. For, within this practice, the rules of the practice specify that states are entitled to pursue their interests and are not required to open their doors to all who would enter. There is a clear and easily discernible tension between the rights that states may ethically claim for themselves and the ethical rights that individuals are entitled to claim. It is this tension between individual rights and states' rights that has emerged in the internal politics of the European Union, the United States, Myanmar, South Africa and many other states, worldwide. The problem is not confined to asylum seekers, refugees and economic migrants. The same tension between states' rights and individual rights emerges when considering weak and failed states. From the perspective of civil society, those in successful states ought to be concerned about the rights abuses that take place against civilians in such states. When these are egregious abuses then some might believe that there is an imperative to intervene and engage in state building activities to protect the rights of the civilians in those territories. For it does not matter where a failed state happens to be, the people in it are still participants in the global rights practice and can claim support from the other participant rights holders elsewhere. Yet, here again, from the point of view of the society of sovereign states we are justified in putting the interests of our own state first and for not considering ourselves responsible for what happens in other states.

How should those convinced by the insights of practice theory proceed when seeking solutions to such tensions? In the contemporary world diplomats (who are participants in both) have made considerable progress in reconciling and harmonizing the practice of sovereign states and that of global civil society. The key manoeuvre by which this reconciliation has been achieved is by adopting the stance that all sovereign states are required to protect and uphold the rights of all civilians within their territories. The most cogent formulation of this position is to be found in the principle of the Responsibility to Protect (usually referred to as R2P). The emergence of this principle was the result of a massive effort within the global diplomatic practice which started with a Canadian initiative, but was taken up by the United Nations, who then arranged a World Summit in 2005 where the principle was adopted *nem con*.[22] What was accepted as a result of this global exercise in diplomacy was that, first, sovereign states and their governments have a duty to uphold the individual rights of the people in their territories and to protect them from gross human rights abuses such as genocide, ethnic cleansing, war crimes and crimes against humanity. Second, included in R2P is the specification that states have a duty to help those states that are struggling to do this. Third and finally, it stipulates that in extreme cases states may have a duty to intervene militarily where gross human rights abuses are taking place.

In R2P global diplomacy moved towards a harmonization of the ethical commitments of the two dominant practices. The full implications of this principle have not yet been fully articulated or realized in practice. The fact that this principle was accepted unanimously by the General Assembly of the United Nations indicates widespread recognition of this as a solution to the ethical tensions outlined. A central task for diplomats in the coming years will be to promote this interpretation of how things should stand in the global practices and to avoid backsliding towards a previous era in which the ethical commitments between the practices had not yet been harmonized. Indeed, in the not too distant past it was common to think that state sovereignty trumped all other considerations including those associated with human rights. The crucial point for the purposes of this chapter is to see in this example how the global diplomatic practice wrestled and continues to wrestle with an ethical tension that has arisen within the two global macro practices.

Unfortunately, in many parts of the world, including Africa, the United States, and several Asian countries, contemporary diplomacy has retrogressed and this central tension between states' rights and individual rights is re-emerging. A clear example is provided by the foreign policy pursued by the Trump administration in the United States. Such policies include support for Saudi Arabia, North Korea and Russia, all of which have dismal records in bringing their states into harmony with the ethical features of the global human rights practice. Similar retrogression may be seen in the foreign policies advocated by various right-wing, anti-refugee, political parties in some European states, in many African states, and most dramatically in recent events in Myanmar. All these policies are based on a fundamental misunderstanding of the ethical dimensions embedded in contemporary global practices and the harmonization achieved through the adoption of the R2P.

In many ways the adoption of the R2P principle by the international community was an aspirational manoeuvre. It indicated a desirable direction of ethical travel to relieve the existing ethical contradictions and tensions rather than a fully worked out blueprint for the global constitution.

A far more successful resolution of this tension between states' rights and individual rights has been achieved in the European Union. One might say that the most successful realization of R2P has been achieved within the EU. Within it, the twenty-seven member states retain their sovereignty and can enjoy the freedoms associated with it. At the same time the civilians within the EU are entitled and able to enjoy their fundamental human rights across the whole area. Thus, for example, civilians may choose to use their right to freedom of movement to move around the whole area of the EU seeking love, friendship, work, study opportunities, sporting relationships and cultural connections of many kinds. They can do this because all the member states are committed to upholding and respecting their fundamental human rights. The arrangement also makes it easy for companies to divide the various production facilities that go into the creation of a product, situating each in a different place. The most dramatic example of this is to be found in the production processes of Airbus aircraft which involves the manufacture of wings, tail sections, fuselages and engines, all in different locations. The parts and the workers can move freely between them. Within the European Union, while there are still anomalies, an extraordinary harmonization between states' rights and individual rights has been made a reality. This must be regarded as an extraordinary feat of diplomacy between all the countries involved. Unfortunately, as we saw with R2P, there are distressing signs of ethical backsliding taking place. In several member states there are political movements seeking to re-establish the primacy of state sovereignty and to undermine the borderless enjoyment of individual human rights that currently exists within the EU. Such developments are to be found in Poland, Hungary, Germany and most dramatically in Britain which has left the EU. This retrograde move has been led by anti-immigrant movements in these countries and in others. What this shows is that progress towards harmonization of the values embedded in the global practices is not guaranteed or inevitable. Although further progress is possible, and although we have clear indications of what it would look like, ethical backsliding is always a permanent possibility.

Conclusion

In this chapter it has been argued that the moral and ethical principles available to guide diplomats are not principles that individual diplomats are free to choose. Quite the contrary, the argument offered here is one, informed by practice theory, which shows that in order to be constituted as a diplomat, a person has to learn how to follow the constitutive rules within the global practice of diplomacy. In coming to participate in this global practice the diplomats play their part in upholding the ethical values that are constituted within that practice. The argument was presented that the global practice can only be understood as an internal component of the two contemporary global macro practices which are the society of sovereign states and the global rights practice, both of which, as constitutive practices, produce within them certain fundamental ethical values: freedom and diversity. In the society of sovereign states the values achieved are the freedom of the participant states and the diversity between them, and in global civil society the freedoms achieved are the rights of individual men and women and the diversity made possible between them. It was argued that the global diplomatic practice is fundamental to the establishment and maintenance of the ethical values achieved in the two macro practices. Finally, brief mention was made of the ongoing task currently facing the diplomatic practice which is resolving ongoing tensions between states' rights and human rights. The COVID-19 pandemic of 2020 may well bring the salience of individual rights and state sovereignty into clear focus and promote ethical action on a global scale.

Notes

1 For an outline of its main elements see Ernest M. Satow, *Satow's Guide to Diplomatic Practice* (London: Longman, 1979).
2 Andrew F. Cooper, Jorge Heine, and Ramesh Thakur, *Oxford Handbook of Modern Diplomacy* (Oxford: Oxford University Press, 2013), Introduction.
3 Craig Murray, *Dirty Diplomacy* (New York: Scribner, 2007).
4 Deon Geldenhuys, *The Diplomacy of Isolation: South African Foreign Policy Making* (Johannesburg: Macmillan, 1984).
5 See the webpage at http://news.bbc.co.uk/1/hi/uk_politics/4377605.stm (accessed on 22 April 2020).
6 Krishnan Srinivasan, James Mayall, and Sanjay Pulipaka, *Values in Foreign Policy* (London: Rowman and Littlefield, 2019).

7   This might involve comparing, for example, the theories of international justice produced respectively by John Rawls, Michael Sandel and Simon Caney. John Rawls, *The Law of Peoples* (Cambridge, MA: Harvard University Press, 2001); M. Sandel, *Liberalism and the Limits of Justice* (Cambridge: Cambridge University Press, 1982); Simon Caney, 'Cosmopolitan Justice and Cultural Diversity', *Global Society* 14, no. 4 (2000).
8   Harold Nicolson, *Diplomacy* (London; Oxford; New York: Oxford University Press, 1969), 23.
9   Nicolson, *Diplomacy*, 55.
10 For an introduction to some of these topics, see Bernard Williams, *Morality: An Introduction to Ethics* (Cambridge and New York: Cambridge University Press, 1993).
11 Silviya Lechner and Mervyn Frost, *Practice Theory and International Relations*, Cambridge Studies in International Relations (Cambridge: Cambridge University Press, 2018).
12 This approach stems from the later work of Ludwig Wittgenstein as subsequently elaborated by, amongst others, Peter Winch and Richard Rorty. See Ludwig Wittgenstein, *Philosophical Investigations*, trans. T. E. M. Anscombe (Oxford: Blackwell, 1963); Peter Winch, *The Idea of a Social Science* (London: Routledge and Kegan Paul, 1958); Richard Rorty, *Philosophy and the Mirror of Nature* (Oxford: Basil Blackwell, 1980).
13 See, for example, the publications of Emanuel Adler and Vincent Pouliot, eds., *International Practices*, Cambridge Studies in International Relations (Cambridge and New York: Cambridge University Press, 2011); Christian Bueger and Frank Gadinger, *International Practice Theory: New Perspectives* (Basingstoke: Palgrave, 2014).
14 Iver Neumann, *Diplomatic Sites: A Critical Inquiry* (New York: Oxford University Press, 2013).
15 Terry Nardin, *Law Morality and the Relations of States* (Princeton, NJ: Princeton University Press, 1983), Introduction.
16 Note that the fact that some people play a game for the purposes of making money, that is, by becoming professional players, does not detract from the point being made. The professionalization of a game depends on (is parasitic upon) the constitutive nature of the game.
17 One can find fair competition and beauty in many other games, but not that embodiment of fairness and that version of beauty that is found in cricket. Other games embody values internal to them such that they are only realized by those who play or watch them. This requires that they learn the rules of the game and that they understand them from the participant perspective – the internal point of view.

18 Recognizing the global diplomatic practice achieves something not dissimilar to the way in which players of a game (rugby or netball for example) by recognizing the authority of the referee indicate to the other players and to the spectators their commitment to the rules of the game as a whole. This recognition of the referee is a performative, establishing the *bona fides* of the players in the game.
19 To avoid this international criticism, the Saudi government sought to deny guilt and to blame 'rogue elements' in its security services. This had all the markings of a *post hoc* cover-up.
20 Mervyn Frost and Nicholas Michelsen, 'Strategic Communication in International Relations: Practical Traps and Ethical Puzzles', *Defence Strategic Communications* 2 (Spring 2017): 9–34.
21 Eschel Rhoodie, *The Real Information Scandal* (Atlanta: Orbis, 1983).
22 Alex Bellamy, 'R2P@10: Reflections on the Responsibility to Protect at 10', *R2P Ideas in Brief* 5, no. 2 (2015).

2

Coercive diplomacy and the continued relevance of hard power: The role of competence and context

Dr Jean-Francois Belanger

The supreme art of war is to subdue the enemy without fighting.
— Sun Tzu, *The Art of War*

Speak softly but carry a big stick; you will go far.
— Theodore Roosevelt

Coercive diplomacy has never been about the use of hard power. In fact, the practice of coercive diplomacy by decision makers is designed to avoid military interventions or, if used during conflict, to force a halt and get all parties involved back to the negotiating table, or at least de-escalate. It is precisely because both sides would prefer to avoid conflict that coercive diplomacy works. It is perhaps the most salient insight of mixed motives game theory made popular by Thomas Schelling, and the bargaining theory of war developed by James Fearon. Coercive bargaining can yield results only if the actors involved agree they would prefer some form of negotiated settlement instead of war.[1] Coercive diplomacy cannot succeed if one of the parties sees war as the least costly option. However, it is the possession and willingness to use military power behind a coercive threat that give it its credibility.

Yet, there has been important variation in the effectiveness of coercive diplomacy, especially in settings where we should not have witnessed variation. Three recent examples come to mind. In 1994, after two years of back and forth threats between the United States and North Korea, the Clinton administration put together a preventive attack plan to take out Pyongyang's nuclear facilities. The expected cost would eventually dissuade Washington from attacking.

In 2003, after two years of coercive diplomacy against Iraq, the United States believed Saddam Hussein to be lying about his possession of weapons of mass destruction and invaded Iraq in March 2003. Recently, in 2014, President Barack Obama issued a warning to the Syrian regime of Bashar Al-Asad after years of civil war. The United States would not tolerate the use of chemical weapons against insurgents, and doing so would prompt Washington to action. Yet, the red line was crossed, and the United States blinked.

Three cases with three different outcomes. The United States was deterred in 1994, undeterred in 2003, and Syria brushed aside US deterrent threat in 2014 which led to no action. While it is a cursory description of three important cases, it conveys a simple but strong point: hard power is a necessary, but not sufficient, cause for coercive diplomacy to succeed. It was perhaps the quantitative literature in the Cold War that made such a strong link between relative capability ratios and deterrent outcomes.[2] It has since been demonstrated that coercive successes or failures are not strictly explained by relative capabilities but also credibility and preferences,[3] the means available to states[4] and the strategies they employ.[5]

The question put forth by this volume for this chapter asks: *How can such 'hard power' be used to best effect in modern diplomatic practice?* The argument presented here is as follows: like all diplomatic endeavours, the successes or failures of coercive diplomacy were never about raw hard power. It was always about how the spectre of hard power was used in a given context. As most of practice theory, the success or failure of coercive diplomacy was always about how competently it was wielded and used by diplomats and officers of the state.

This chapter focuses on two important facets of coercive diplomacy: (1) the willingness, or not, to use force and its implications, and (2) the contexts in which coercive diplomacy is used and how it affects outcomes. Through these two focuses this chapter reminds the reader that the need for coercive diplomacy is not going away. In fact, it may be more important than ever given how war is slowly being delegitimized as a tool of foreign policy. We can think of the NATO–Russia relationship in the Baltics,[6] the rivalry between India and China that, as of May 2020, has escalated to China moving troops in contested territory,[7] the continued efforts to denuclearize North Korea or the ongoing nuclear diplomacy with Iran. Coercive diplomacy is not going away. However, as this chapter demonstrates, to be effectively used coercive diplomacy has to be supported by a willingness to use force. If it is wielded to fully avoid the use of force, it will lead to more problems than it solves.

The rest of this chapter will be divided as follows. First, I briefly define the terms used throughout this chapter. Second, I discuss the ambivalence in the use of force in the post–Cold War world. Third, I engage with the consequences of this ambivalence, but also examine what competent coercive diplomacy entails. I conclude with a discussion on the modern use of coercive diplomacy and how it will translate with the arrival of new technologies and different conflict domains.

Definitions and caveats

Competence here is understood as *possessing the relevant knowledge, skills and expertise embedded within a specific setting to perform a particular activity in a capable and proficient way.*[8] This definition rests on a postulate from practice theory which recognize practices, that is, how particular groups or individual perform their crafts in and on the world, have to be competent to be of relevance.[9] Additionally, competence is not a marginal concept. Diplomacy done competently can elevate the status of small and medium powers in the international arena such as the United Nations.[10] Coercive diplomacy done competently is one where context is taken into consideration, and where the objective is tailored in such a way as to be acceptable by the party being coerced. It is also a coercive diplomacy where the use of force is implied and ready to be used, not implied but bluffed.

Broadly, coercive diplomacy is a threat employed to modify the behaviour of an adversary. This statement can be broken down into two types of coercive diplomacy: deterrence and compellence.[11] Deterrence is defined as a threat to stop an actor from engaging in an action it desired taking. The difficulty with deterrence is that it is essentially based on events that are not observable. If a deterrent threat is successful, all you can observe is the threat and not the action of the state being threatened. North Korea threatening retaliation if the United States attacked its nuclear installation in 1994 is an example of a deterrent threat.

Compellence is generally understood to be more difficult, but at the same time more visible. Compellence is defined as threatening an adversary so that it modifies its current behaviour. While deterrence is about stopping an action from happening, compellence is about modifying an action currently taking place. An example of a failed compellent threat would be the 1991 Desert Storm operation. The United States threatened to use force against Iraq if it did not leave Kuwait, an action Saddam Hussein had already taken and was not willing to undo. Iraq did not comply. The United States initiated Desert Storm in January 1991.

All threats made by coercive diplomacy inherently imply the threat of the use of force. Schelling makes an important distinction between coercive diplomacy and the actual use of force that we should keep in mind. Coercive diplomacy is about using a state capacity to hurt another as bargaining leverage. It is the psychological possibility of force being used that provides the leverage, not the actual act of using force. Additionally, this does not mean that coercive diplomacy is all about military power. There is a range of possible actions that are deemed coercive but are not at first a threat of using military force. Sanctions are often the first step in coercive diplomacy.[12] For example, sanctions were imposed on North Korea and Iran by the United States and the international community to stifle their nuclear ambitions.[13]

Other coercive means can include negative and positive inducements, which generally take the form of a threat of abandonment coupled with some form of help. One example would be Washington threatening to abandon Seoul as an ally in the 1970s as it was developing nuclear weapons. The positive inducement came in the extension of the US nuclear umbrella to South Korean once it abandoned its nuclear ambitions.[14]

There are two ways through which coercive diplomacy can be used. The first is coercive punishment, and the other is coercive denial. A coercive threat of punishment is based on hurt and retaliation: if you do X, I will deliver Y amount of hurt. A coercive threat of denial is based on denying victory: If you do X, I will deny you objective Y. While both can be used simultaneously, they are generally separated for analytical purposes.[15]

Finally, this chapter is about interstate coercive diplomacy. There has been great work done in recent years on how coercive diplomacy can be used in other domains such as against non-state actors.[16] However, since this present volume focuses on state-to-state diplomacy in the twenty-first century, I have restricted the scope of this chapter accordingly.

Coercive diplomacy and the political will to violence

There is an important tension in the use of modern coercive diplomacy. On the one hand, we have seen episodes where states were fully intent on using force if their threats were not complied with. On the other hand, there have been systemic trends indicating that the use of violence to achieve politics aims is slowly being delegitimized. But without willingness to use force, there is no credible threat. This section highlights this tension.

A diminished appetite for war

On the one hand, there are certainly factors that have made war less palatable as a means of foreign policy, which in turn may have reduced the effectiveness of coercive diplomacy. We can think of the current integration of the world economies,[17] a real or imagined aversion to casualties in war,[18] the rise of international law and its delegitimization of conquest as a tool of statecraft,[19] the growing anti-war sentiment in the United States,[20] nuclear weapons and the potential disaster the use of force between nuclear countries could be,[21] all come together to delegitimize war as means of foreign policy and reduce how palatable it is for decision makers to use.[22]

We can see this logic in action in two specific examples. In 2012, in a now-infamous speech, President Obama warned the Assad regime about the use of chemical weapons in the Syrian theatre. The United States was not directly involved militarily in the conflict, but the president stated:

> We have been very clear to the Assad regime, but also to other players on the ground, that a red line for us is we start seeing a whole bunch of chemical weapons moving around or being utilized. That would change my calculus. That would change my equation.[23]

The Assad regime would use sarin gas at least six times between this declaration and the summer of 2013. On 6 September 2013, the 'Authorization for the Use of Military Force against the Government of Syria to Respond to Use of Chemical Weapons' bill was introduced by Senator Robert Menendez (D-NJ). The bill provided a period of sixty days, with a thirty-day extension, where the US president could authorize the use of force against the Syrian regime. The bill was never voted on.[24] While Assad eventually gave up his chemical weapons supply, US coercive diplomacy alone would not have achieved the objective: it took the intervention of Vladimir Putin to broker an agreement.[25] The fact that the approval of the use of force was never sent to the floor for a vote is indicative of a desire to avoid sending troops in theatre.

We can also think of the emergence of drone warfare as part of the broader US grand strategy as an indicator of reduced willingness by Washington to use conventional military power abroad. In fact, the link between drones and casualty aversion is linear. As James Rogers demonstrates, it was the Obama administration who truly embraced drone warfare. He argues:

> Improvised Explosive Devices (IEDs) had become the terrorist's weapon of choice between 2008 and 2010, causing 60 per cent of US military fatalities on the ground. [...] the mounting death toll affected public opinion and Obama

promised to bring US ground wars to an end. Drones were part of this promise. [...] An astonishing 542 strikes took place during the president's eight-year tenure. For Obama, armed drones were perceived to be a panacea, a technical fix for the risks of war.[26]

In sum, there are systemic and domestic factors pushing for a reduced reliance on the use of force.

Coercive diplomacy and the actual use of force

On the other hand, coercive diplomacy backed up by a strong military commitment can be found in most official defence and foreign policy documents of the modern state. In the United States, almost all official documents touching on the topic of national security and defence will highlight the importance of coercive diplomacy for American grand strategy.[27] The Trump administration's National Security Strategy of the United States white paper makes salient the importance of deterrence to ensure stability both internationally and regionally in an era of multipolarity.[28]

The embeddedness of coercive diplomacy within the grand strategy of the state is not limited to the United States. The French Livre Blanc de la Défense places deterrence as the second pillar of its three-legged defence policy.[29] The UK's Strategic Defence and Security Review places deterrence at the front and centre of its defence policy by stating:

> Defence and protection start with deterrence, which has long been, and remains, at the heart of the UK's national security policy [...]. We will use the full spectrum of our capabilities – armed force including, ultimately, our nuclear deterrent, diplomacy, law enforcement, economic policy, offensive cyber, and covert means – to deter adversaries and to deny them opportunities to attack us.[30]

The same language can be found in China's 2019 defence white paper. It states, 'China's armed forces strengthen the safety management of nuclear weapons and facilities, maintain the appropriate level of readiness and enhance strategic deterrence capability to protect national strategic security and maintain international strategic stability.'[31] As such, coercive diplomacy in the guise of deterrence remains a pillar of national security.

Additionally, states have not fully shied away from the use of force to achieve their objectives. Perhaps the most salient example is the 2003 invasion of Iraq by the United States. On the heels of the Afghanistan campaign, Washington turned its attention to the possible proliferation of nuclear and chemical weapons by Saddam Hussein; Hussein had used chemical weapons in the past in its conflict with Iran.[32] Additionally, nuclear infrastructures were bombed in 1998 in a joint US-UK strikes when Hussein was found in non-compliance of Security Council resolutions.[33] The Bush administration argued their case at the UN and obtained Resolution 1441 which enjoined Iraq to provide proofs it did not possess weapons of mass destruction. Once Hussein failed to deliver to the US satisfaction, Washington invaded the country in March 2003.

Whether the United States actively misled the international community on Saddam Hussein's possession of chemical or nuclear weapons is not debated here.[34] The case is brought to light because the United States followed through on its coercive threat. The United States went to the Security Council specifically to make its threat of retaliation more credible.[35] In addition, the United States never wavered from its commitment to disarm Saddam Hussein despite truly negative views of the war domestically.[36]

In addition, the United States was equally undeterred in 1991. Hussein had famously said that the United States was not a society that could tolerate the cost of war.[37] In turned out to be false in this instance, given the casualty predictions prior to the war were high. Most analysts who were heard on the Senate and House floors cited casualties and wounded in the 50,000 range.[38] The support for this course of action, then, is not easily reconcilable with the casualty aversion literature which supports a lot of the discussions on the hesitancy by states to use military power.[39]

Synthesis: Coercive diplomacy and the use of force

The two arguments presented above point to a simple but fundamental underpinning of coercive diplomacy: political will to violence. While coercive threats can be made, and sometimes be efficient, without the necessary resolve to use military power behind them, they are generally held to be incredible. The United States can probably bluff a lot more than others, but doing so has a cumulative effect that cannot be ignored. These pathologies are discussed below.

Competence, coercive diplomacy and the interconnectedness of threats and promises

There is no doubt that the United States makes good on its coercive threats. The same can generally be said about Russia and China in their respective regions if there is no involvement by outside parties such as Washington. The discussion in the previous section, however, made salient how states have had a tendency to treat coercive diplomacy as if it was a means to obtain objectives without the use of military power, when it is in fact a more cost-effective way of using military power. But the operating word here is 'using'. If coercive diplomacy is employed in situations where the state has no willingness to use its hard power whenever a threat is dismissed, we enter the realm of bluffing and unintended consequences. As Richard Betts argued, the continued reliance on deterrence in the relationship between Moscow and Washington is most likely what led to the continued adversarial relationship between the two.[40] In sum, what we have witnessed in the post–Cold War is mainly an incompetent use of coercive diplomacy that has a tendency to forgo context for cheap gains.

The importance of making good on all coercive threats, known as having a reputation for resolve, has been a staple of the deterrence literature. Systematically demonstrating resolve in crises is important as it provides cheaper credibility in other crises.[41] The cost reduction benefits of strong reputations have been linked to finding more suitable allies,[42] settling disputes diplomatically,[43] enhancing existing coercive threats[44] and reducing the amount of dispute a state will find itself a part of.[45] Alternatively, not making good on threats has the inverse effect and can increase the number of crises a state find itself in.[46] The higher the certainty an adversary has that a coercive threat will not be carried out, the more it will push the boundaries for concessions and gains in the future, which in turn increases the cost of coercive diplomacy for the challenger.[47] Eventually, this logic leads to unintended escalation and conflicts.

The discussion on the accumulation of reputation is generally focused on the question of committing to, and executing, threats. We speak less about interconnectedness when it comes to reassurances and promises. Coercive diplomacy is not strictly about threats supported by military power. It is also the effective use of reassurances and promises (rewards) in tandem with threats to reach the desired outcome.[48] Reassurances are understood quite bluntly in the literature. It is the assurance to the party being threatened that if they comply, the hurt will either stop or not be acted on.[49] Quite simply, credible reassurance means a sanctioned state will see them lifted if it complies with the coercive demands. In the case of the threat of the use of force, it means force will not be used. For example, a coercive threat by state A would be to move troops in a contested territory with, or at the border of, state B and demand it leaves the contested territory. Reassurances are the promise of disengagement and/or troops removal by state A if state B complies. Actual promises are positive inducement offering either some part of the territory or some economic benefits as part of the bargain to seek compliance by state B.

The example of the North Korean nuclear programme is illustrative of this point. The United States has sought for over thirty years to stop the nuclearization process of Pyongyang. Now that it has achieved nuclear status, it has sought to denuclearize the country. The situation escalated in September 2016 when Pyongyang performed an underground nuclear test. It was followed in September 2017 with another test, this time to demonstrate it had acquired a multistage hydrogen bomb.[50]

In early 2018, however, the crisis de-escalated. In late March Secretary of State Mike Pompeo met with Kim Jung-Un to plan and discuss a US-North Korean summit. Concurrently, the two Koreas agreed to participate in an Inter-Korean Summit in April of that year. The discussions focused on the nuclear issues and the possibility to formally end the Korean War. President Trump and Kim Jung-Un met on 12 June 2018, in Singapore in what was the first meeting between a sitting US President and the head of the North Korean regime. As concessions, Pyongyang dismantled the Punggye-ri nuclear site. While Washington did not agree to remove or ease the sanctions on the regime until denuclearization was under way, it still agreed to freeze the joint military exercises with South Korea. Security guarantees for Pyongyang were discussed, and a joint statement released reaffirming previous commitments to work on the denuclearization of the Korean Peninsula.[51] The Singapore Summit was followed by the Hanoi Summit in February 2019. The second summit ended abruptly in large part due to the refusal by the United States to end sanctions on the North Korean regime prior to full denuclearization.

There are multiple issues with the two US-North Korean Summits. Chief among them are the profound differences in understanding what the statement 'complete denuclearization of the Korean Peninsula' actually means. For the United States, it means the dismantlement of the North Korean nuclear arsenal. For North Korea, it means the complete military retrenchment by the United States from the Korean Peninsula. Such a gap is particularly difficult to breach.

More fundamental for this chapter, however, is the recent history of US coercive diplomacy and its promises. In 2003, the Clinton administration was successful in having Muammar Gaddafi forgo the Libyan nuclear program. In 2011, however, Gaddafi's regime was toppled by insurgents who were backed by the US government. Pyongyang specifically referred to Libya when justifying its nuclear program and its continuation.[52] We can also imagine that the fate of Saddam Hussein was not too far from Kim Jung-un's mind as well. Iraq is a potent reminder of what can happen to relatively weaker powers who are adversaries of the United States, and who do not possess nuclear weapons. Washington could promise Pyongyang it would respect its territorial integrity even if denuclearized, but recent history paints a different story, which assuredly influenced how the North Korean leadership received US coercive diplomacy.

Additionally, the fate of the Joint Comprehensive Plan of Action (JCPOA) with Iran was decided concurrently. The JCPOA, or the Iran nuclear deal, was negotiated by the Obama administration to stifle Tehran's nuclear ambitions. Despite all indications that the Iranian government were making good on its commitment,[53] President Trump and the Republican Party remained sceptical. The focal point was the sunset clauses found in the agreement which would over time remove the limitations on the enrichment levels Iran could achieve, the lifting of restriction on the type of centrifuge it could buy (and its monitoring), and the mining of uranium. Hawks argued that, all told, by 2040 Iran would be at the doorstep of a nuclear bomb if it so desired and there would be nothing the United States could do. With this and other factors in mind, the United States exited the agreement on 8 May 2018.

It is relevant to ask how much of an impact this decision had on the negotiations with North Korea. The Trump administration's rejection of commitments made by previous American administrations was detrimental to its ability to make a credible commitment on the issue, and for the foreseeable future.[54] In the case of North Korea, there are little incentives for the regime to engage in an agreement that could simply be ignored by a later administration, especially if the agreement meant it put its territorial, and leadership, status at risk.

But competent coercive diplomacy in this case goes further. It requires some empathy and the ability to place oneself in the shoes of the adversary to understand the motivations guiding their decisions.[55] In the case of nuclear acquisition, the motives are generally a mixture of demands for increased security, international status and recognition, and domestic pressures and demands.[56] Understanding why a state sought, or acquired, nuclear weapons is essential to understand what it might be willing to accept in return of either forgoing its program or decommissioning it altogether. Coercive diplomacy in this case can work only if it takes the context of proliferation into account when devising its reassurances and promises to achieve the identified objective.[57]

On the other hand, states like Pakistan and North Korea who sought nuclear weapons for security purposes, against a relatively stronger conventional adversary in the case of Pakistan, and as a way to ensure territorial integrity for a reduced price tag in the case of North Korea, are less likely to agree to put an end to their program or to denuclearize. A successful coercive diplomacy campaign in these cases must rely on especially strong security guarantees to be efficient. The United States provided conventional weapons and so on to Pakistan to try and forestall its nuclear program, but never extended the nuclear umbrella to Islamabad as it did to other allies.[58] In this case, the best Washington was able to achieve was a tacit agreement with Pakistan that it would not test its nuclear capability,[59] a promise it would renege on in 1998. In the case of North Korea, the United States was never able to reach a negotiated settlement and Pyongyang became nuclear in 2006.

Competent coercive diplomacy is about being clear as to what one expects to see behaviour-wise, but it is also understanding what the other side is ready to accept. If one understands the former but ignores the latter, we may well end up in an escalating conflict. With the North Korean negotiations, it was clear from the onset it sought sanctions relief and/or removal, but it was also clear to most they had no intentions of dismantling its nuclear arsenal. Once negotiations stalled Pyongyang continued to use belligerent tactics to seek more compromises from Washington while demonstrating it could deter US aggression given the technology it had acquired.

Since 2018 Pyongyang has completed eleven missile tests. This situation is not without danger. The possibility of the United States engaging in a limited attack against Pyongyang missile facilities surfaced in late 2017, early 2018. It is speculated that the attack would be meant as a compellent threat to force Pyongyang to seriously consider the US offers, but also to remind it of US might.[60] This would have been incredibly risky. The likelihood of North Koreans doing nothing following such an attack would be slim. Additionally, any escalation runs the risk to eventually become nuclear. At the same time, if the United States is not ready to send additional troops on the Korean Peninsula to show some resolve, it would have run the risk to embolden the Kim regime in the region. This potential scenario was entirely the result of a US administration unable to wield coercive diplomacy in a competent and realistic fashion.

Conclusion

The argument this chapter has developed is that the necessity for hard power is not going away, especially when it comes to coercive diplomacy. However, issues arise when states seek to achieve objectives through coercive threats with no intentions of following through with them. Additionally, coercive diplomacy is best used when it takes into consideration context and provides measures of compliance that are realizable for the state on the receiving end of the coercive diplomacy.

But the future is not looking particularly good. There is a definite move away from the use of conventional military campaigns as part of statecraft and foreign policy. The drone revolution and the current technological improvement in automated warfare is evidence of this.[61] Unfortunately, recent work has shown that coercive diplomacy works best when boots are put on the ground.[62] Due to the possibilities of cheap victories, states with larger hard power capabilities will likely continue to bluff in its use to support coercive diplomacy. The result should be increased tensions and unintended escalation as challengers will get wise to the tactic and continuously push the boundaries of how far they can go.

Notes

1 Thomas C. Schelling, *The Strategy of Conflict* (Cambridge: Harvard University Press, 1960); James D Fearon, 'Rationalist Explanations for War', *International Organization* 49, no. 3 (Summer 1995): 379–414; Dan Reiter, 'Security Commitments and Nuclear Proliferation', *Foreign Policy Analysis* 10, no. 1 (January 2014): 61–80.

2 Paul Huth and Bruce Russett, 'Deterrence Failure and Crisis Escalation', *International Studies Quarterly* 32, no. 1 (March 1988): 29; Paul Huth and Bruce Russett, 'Testing Deterrence Theory: Rigor Makes a Difference', *World Politics* 42, no. 4 (July 1990): 466–501.

3 Frank C. Zagare and D. Marc Kilgour, *Perfect Deterrence* (New York: Cambridge University Press, 2000).

4 Jan Ludvik, 'Closing the Window of Vulnerability: Nuclear Proliferation and Conventional Retaliation', *Security Studies* 28, no. 1 (2019): 87–115.

5 Daniel Sobelman, 'Learning to Deter: Deterrence Failure and Success in the Israel-Hezbollah Conflict, 2006–16', *International Security* 41, no. 3 (January 2017): 151–96; Jean-Francois Belanger and T. V. Paul, 'Asymmetrical Deterrence: Examining the Coercive Power of the Weak', *Working Paper*, May 2020.

6 Michael Kofman, 'The Expensive Pretzel Logic of Deterring Russia by Denial', *War on the Rocks*, 23 June 2016, https://warontherocks.com/2016/06/the-expensive-pretzel-logic-of-deterring-russia-by-denial/ (accessed 30 May 2020).

7 Zhen Han and Jean-François Bélanger, 'Balancing Strategies and the China-India Rivalry', in *The China-India Rivalry in the Globalization Era* (Washington, DC:

Georgetown University Press, 2018), 95–116; 'Military Tensions Mount on the India-China Border', *The Economist,* 29 May 2020, https://www.economist.com/asia/2020/05/29/military-tensions-mount-on-the-india-china-border (accessed 30 May 2020).

8   Jean-François Bélanger, *Why Competence Matters: Counter-Proliferation and Deterrence* (Manuscript, Yale University, May 2020).

9   Vincent Pouliot, *International Security in Practice: The Politics of NATO-Russia Diplomacy* (Cambridge: Cambridge University Press, 2010); Emanuel Adler and Vincent Pouliot, *International Practices* (Cambridge and New York: Cambridge University Press, 2011).

10 Vincent Pouliot, *International Pecking Orders: The Politics and Practice of Multilateral Diplomacy* (New York: Cambridge University Press, 2016).

11 This discussion is adapted from Thomas Schelling's differentiation between deterrence and compellence. See Thomas C. Schelling, *Arms and Influence* (New Haven, CT: Yale University Press, 2008).

12 Tami Davis Biddle, 'Coercion Theory: A Basic Introduction For Practitioners', *Texas National Security Review* 2, no. 2 (Spring 2020), https://tnsr.org/2020/02/coercion-theory-a-basic-introduction-for-practitioners/ (accessed 29 May 2020).

13 Joel S. Wit, Daniel B. Poneman, and Robert L. Gallucci, *Going Critical: The First North Korean Nuclear Crisis* (Washington, DC: Brookings Institution Press, 2005); Tom Sauer, 'Coercive Diplomacy by the EU: The Iranian Nuclear Weapons Crisis', *Third World Quarterly* 28, no. 3 (April 2007): 613–33; Farhad Rezaei, 'The American Response To Pakistani And Iranian Nuclear Proliferation: A Study In Paradox', *Asian Affairs* 48, no. 1 (2 January 2017): 27–50.

14 On the coercive diplomacy employed by the United States against South Korea see Alexandre Debs and Nuno P. Monteiro, *Nuclear Politics: The Strategic Logic of Nuclear Proliferation* (New York: Cambridge University Press, 2016); Jiyoung Ko, 'Alliance and Public Preference for Nuclear Forbearance: Evidence from South Korea', *Foreign Policy Analysis*, 11 December 2018; Gene Gerzhoy, 'Alliance Coercion and Nuclear Restraint: How the United States Thwarted West Germany's Nuclear Ambitions', *International Security* 39, no. 4 (April 2015): 91–129.

15 For a general discussion on the United States and coercive diplomacy see Robert J. Art and Patrick M. Cronin, eds., *The United States and Coercive Diplomacy* (Washington, DC: United States Institute of Peace, 2003). On coercive punishment see Richard K. Betts, 'The Lost Logic of Deterrence: What the Strategy That Won the Cold War Can – and Can't – Do Now', *Foreign Affairs* 92, no. 2 (2013): 87–99. On coercive denial, see Robert A. Pape, *Bombing to Win: Air Power and Coercion in War* (Ithaca, NY: Cornell University Press, 1996).

16 For a rapid survey of the literature, see Paul K. Davis and Brian Michael Jenkins, *Deterrence and Influence in Counterterrorism: A Component in the War on al Qaeda* (Santa Monica, CA: Rand Corporation, 2002); Robert F. Trager and Dessislava

P. Zagorcheva, 'Deterring Terrorism: It Can Be Done', *International Security* 30, no. 3 (Winter 2005/2006): 87–123; Alex S. Wilner, 'Deterring the Undeterrable: Coercion, Denial, and Delegitimization in Counterterrorism', *Journal of Strategic Studies* 34, no. 1 (February 2011): 3–37; Andreas Wenger, ed., *Deterring Terrorism: Theory and Practice* (Stanford: Stanford University Press, 2012); Alex S. Wilner, *Deterring Rational Fanatics* (Philadelphia: University of Pennsylvania Press, 2015).

17 Dale C. Copeland. *Economic Interdependence and War* (Princeton: Princeton University Press, 2014); Erik Gartzke, 'The Capitalist Peace', *American Journal of Political Science* 51, no. 1 (2007): 166–91; Erik Gartzke and J. Joseph Hewitt, 'International Crises and the Capitalist Peace', *International Interactions* 36, no. 2 (2010): 115–45.

18 David A. Koplow, *Death by Moderation: The U.S. Military's Quest for Useable Weapons* (Cambridge: Cambridge University Press, 2009).

19 Richard J. Regan, *Just War: Principles and Cases* (Washington, DC: The Catholic University of America Press, 1996).

20 Stuart N. Soroka, 'Media, Public Opinion, and Foreign Policy', *Harvard International Journal of Press/Politics* 8, no. 1 (2003): 27–48; Ole R. Holsti, 'Public Opinion and Foreign Policy: Challenges to the Almond-Lippmann Consensus', *International Studies Quarterly* 36, no. 4 (1992): 439–66; Ole R. Holsti, *Public Opinion and American Foreign Policy* (Ann Arbor: University of Michigan Press, 2004); Thomas Risse-Kappen, 'Public Opinion, Domestic Structure, and Foreign Policy in Liberal Democracies', *World Politics* 43, no. 4 (1991): 479–512.

21 Robert Jervis, *The Meaning of the Nuclear Revolution : Statecraft and the Prospect of Armageddon* (Ithaca, NY: Cornell University Press, 1989).

22 This could be referred to as a form of self-deterrence, where states have the means to make good on a threat because of their relative superiority but refrain from engaging due to an internal, not external, decision. See TV Paul, 'Self-Deterrence: Nuclear Weapons and the Enduring Credibility Challenge', *International Journal: Canada's Journal of Global Policy Analysis* 71, no. 1 (March 2016): 20–40.

23 'Remarks by the President to the White House Press Corps', *The White House*, 20 August 2012, https://obamawhitehouse.archives.gov/the-press-office/2012/08/20/remarks-president-white-house-press-corps (accessed 29 May 2020).

24 113th Congress (2013–14), 'S.J.Res.21 – Authorization for the Use of Military Force Against the Government of Syria to Respond to Use of Chemical Weapons', *Congress.Gov*, 10 September 2013, https://www.congress.gov/bill/113th-congress/senate-joint-resolution/21 (accessed 29 May 2020).

25 For the argument that US coercive diplomacy in Syria was a success, see Frank P. Harvey and John Mitton, *Fighting for Credibility: US Reputation and International Politics* (Toronto: University of Toronto Press, 2016). For the role played by President Putin in getting the Syrian to give up.

26 James Rogers, 'The Origins of Drone Warfare', *History Today* 68, no. 4 (2018): 8–22.

27 Examples include 'National Security Strategy of the United States', *The White House*, 1988, 1990, 1991, 1993, 2000, 2002, 2006, 2010, 2015, 2017.
28 'National Security Strategy of the United States', *The White House*, December 2017.
29 'French White Paper: Defence and National Security 2013', République Française, 2013.
30 'National Security Strategy and Strategic Defence and Security Review 2015: A Secure and Prosperous United Kingdom', *HM Government*, November 2015, 23–4.
31 'China's National Defense in the New Era', *The State Council Information Office of the People's Republic of China*, July 2019, 13.
32 Condoleezza Rice, in her memoir, points specifically to the earlier use of chemical weapons by Saddam Hussein to argue that he could not be taken at his words. See Condoleezza Rice, *No Higher Honor: A Memoir of My Years in Washington* (New York: Crown, 2011), chapter 12.
33 Sarah E. Kreps and Matthew Fuhrmann, 'Attacking the Atom: Does Bombing Nuclear Facilities Affect Proliferation?' *Journal of Strategic Studies* 34, no. 2 (April 2011): 161–87.
34 Hans Blix, *Disarming Iraq* (New York: Pantheon, 2004); Lawrence Freedman, 'War in Iraq: Selling the Threat', *Survival* 46, no. 2 (June 2004): 7–49; Frank P. Harvey, *Explaining the Iraq War: Counterfactual Theory, Logic and Evidence* (New York: Cambridge University Press, 2011).
35 Point 13 of the resolution has generated a lot of controversy. The paragraph reads, '*Recalls*, in that context, that the Council has repeatedly warned Iraq that it will face *serious consequences* as a result of its continued violations of its obligations [.]' Emphasis added by the author. Many US decision makers have argued that serious consequences meant the use of force, whereas decision makers elsewhere such as in France rejected this interpretation. See United Nations Security Council, 'Resolution 1441 (2002)', 8 November 2002, 5; See also Harvey, *Explaining the Iraq War*.
36 Adam J. Berinsky, *In Time of War: Understanding American Public Opinion from World War II to Iraq* (Chicago: University of Chicago Press, 2009).
37 Amatzia Baram, 'Deterrence Lessons from Iraq', *Foreign Affairs* 91, no. 4 (July/August 2012): 82.
38 Shawn Woodford, 'Assessing the 1990–1991 Gulf War Forecasts', *Dupuy Institute*, 17 May 2016, http://www.dupuyinstitute.org/blog/2016/05/17/assessing-the-1990-1991-gulf-war-forecasts/ (accessed 17 August 2019).
39 Micheal Clodfelter, *Warfare and Armed Conflicts: A Statistical Reference to Casualty and Other Figures, 1618–1991* (Jefferson, NC: McFarland Publishing, 1992); William A. Boettcher and Michael D. Cobb, 'Echoes of Vietnam?: Casualty Framing and Public Perceptions of Success and Failure in Iraq', *Journal of Conflict Resolution* 50, no. 6 (December 2006): 831–54.
40 Betts, 'The Lost Logic of Deterrence: What the Strategy That Won the Cold War Can – and Can't – Do Now'.

41 Schelling, *Arms and Influence*, 55–6.
42 Gregory D. Miller, *The Shadow of the Past: Reputation and Military Alliances before the First World War* (Ithaca, NY: Cornell University Press, 2012).
43 Anne E. Sartori, 'The Might of the Pen: A Reputational Theory of Communication in International Disputes', *International Organization* 56, no. 1 (1 February 2002): 121–49.
44 Harvey and Mitton, *Fighting for Credibility*.
45 Alex Weisiger and Keren Yarhi-Milo, 'Revisiting Reputation: How Past Actions Matter in International Politics', *International Organization* 69, no. 2 (2015).
46 Paul K. Huth, 'Reputations and Deterrence: A Theoretical and Empirical Assessment', *Security Studies* 7, no. 1 (1 September 1997): 72–99.
47 Branislav L. Slantchev, *Military Threats: The Costs of Coercion and the Price of Peace* (New York: Cambridge University Press, 2012).
48 Robert Jervis, 'Deterrence Theory Revisited', *World Politics* 31, no. 2 (January 1979): 289–324.
49 Schelling, *The Strategy of Conflict*; Michael Howard, 'Reassurance and Deterrence: Western Defense in the 1980s', *Foreign Affairs* 61, no. 2 (1982): 309–24; Schelling, *Arms and Influence*.
50 The claim is still disputed. North Korea claimed they now have the capability to manufacture thermonuclear weapons, whereas observers have argued it is possible that the design used by North Korea is a boosted fission bomb where fusion fuel is used to increase the fission reaction.
51 'Joint Statement of President Donald J. Trump of the United States of America and Chairman Kim Jong Un of the Democratic People's Republic of Korea at the Singapore Summit', *The White House*, 12 June 2018, https://www.whitehouse.gov/briefings-statements/joint-statement-president-donald-j-trump-united-states-america-chairman-kim-jong-un-democratic-peoples-republic-korea-singapore-summit/ (accessed 30 May 2020).
52 Malfrid Braut-Hegghammer, 'Giving Up on the Bomb: Revisiting Libya's Decision to Dismantle Its Nuclear Program', *Wilson Center*, 23 October 2017, https://www.wilsoncenter.org/blog-post/giving-the-bomb-revisiting-libyas-decision-to-dismantle-its-nuclear-program (accessed 30 May 2020)
53 Kelsey Davenport, 'IAEA Says Iran Abiding by Nuclear Deal', *Arms Control Today*, April 2019, https://www.armscontrol.org/act/2019-04/news/iaea-says-iran-abiding-nuclear-deal (accessed 30 May 2020).
54 Stephen M. Walt, 'The United States Will be Shocked by Its Future', *Foreign Policy*, 16 April 2019, https://foreignpolicy.com/2019/04/16/the-united-states-will-be-shocked-by-its-future/ (accessed 30 May 2020).
55 Barbara Keys and Claire Yorke, 'Personal and Political Emotions in the Mind of the Diplomat', *Political Psychology* 40, no. 6 (2019): 1235–49.

56 Scott D. Sagan, 'Why Do States Build Nuclear Weapons? Three Models in Search of a Bomb', *International Security* 21, no. 3 (1997): 54–86.
57 See Etel Solingen, *Nuclear Logics: Contrasting Paths in East Asia and the Middle East* (Princeton: Princeton University Press, 2007). The United States has generally approached all cases of nuclear proliferation as if the dominant cause of nuclearization was prestige and status concerns and not important security issues. See Jean-Francois Belanger and Wes Hutto, 'When the Causes of Proliferation Meet Counter-Proliferation Strategies: Examining the Agreed Framework and the JCPOA'. Working paper.
58 Feroz Khan, *Eating Grass: The Making of the Pakistani Bomb* (Stanford: Stanford Security Studies, 2012).
59 Or Rabinowitz, *Bargaining on Nuclear Tests: Washington and Its Cold War Deals* (New York: Oxford University Press, 2014). For a dissenting view, see Jeffrey W. Taliaferro, *Defending Frenemies: Alliances, Politics, and Nuclear Nonproliferation in US Foreign Policy* (New York: Oxford University Press, 2019).
60 Michael O'Hanlon and James Kirchick, 'A "Bloody Nose" Attack in Korea Would Have Lasting Consequences', *Brookins*, 26 February 2018, https://www.brookings.edu/blog/order-from-chaos/2018/02/26/a-bloody-nose-attack-in-korea-would-have-lasting-consequences/ (accessed 30 May 2020).
61 James Der Derian, *Virtuous War: Mapping The Military-Industrial-Media-Entertainment Network* (Boulder, CO: Westview Press, 2001); Caroline Kennedy and James I. Rogers, 'Virtuous Drones?' *The International Journal of Human Rights* 19, no. 2 (17 February 2015): 211–27.
62 Melanie W. Sisson, James A. Siebens, and Barry M. Blechman, eds., *Military Coercion and US Foreign Policy: The Use of Force Short of War* (New York: Routledge, 2020).

3

Intelligence and diplomacy: Changing environment, old problems

Dr Daniel W. B. Lomas

In June 2013, journalists from *The Guardian* newspaper met an unnamed source in a central Hong Kong hotel. Their source – introducing himself only as 'senior member of the intelligence community' – had requested the meeting, and to prove his credentials sent the journalists selected secret files from the US signals intelligence organization, the National Security Agency (NSA).[1] The official, a contractor named Edward Snowden, blew the lid on the operations of the NSA and its allies, with the eventual number of stolen files totalling an estimated 1.7 million – only a fraction ever published.[2] Snowden's claims and the subsequent story led to debate on privacy and intelligence oversight, and resulted in condemnation from the US government and others. Speaking to the US Senate Intelligence Committee in 2014, Director of National Intelligence James Clapper said the revelations caused 'profound damage … [the US] is less safe and its people less secure'.[3] But Snowden's leaks served to lift the lid on modern-day intelligence work, reminding us – with the growing focus on counter-terrorism – that states continue to spy on each other and that intelligence is important to modern diplomacy.

James Der Derian once referred to intelligence as part of the 'antidiplomacy',[4] suggesting espionage and intelligence broke 'traditional' foreign policy norms. In reality, diplomacy – a process of 'dialogue and negotiation' allowing states to pursue aims 'short of war'[5] – and intelligence have had a long relationship. 'Good diplomacy goes hand-in-hand with good intelligence,' writes Michael Rubin.[6] Diplomats and intelligence officers both seek to collect and process information to shape policy but, since the emergence of permanent intelligence agencies in the late nineteenth and early twentieth centuries, the covert collection of information has increasingly been separated from the overt collection that forms part of normal diplomatic activity. Today, diplomats work to a set of international rules and are reliant on normal relations with other countries for their work, while the collection of secret information by agencies – or the conduct of 'covert action' to shape events – can often disrupt this function. Nonetheless, intelligence remains as vital to statecraft as it has always been, and many of the problems faced by diplomats today are timeless – something this chapter shows. Historical lessons can be important in understanding the issues facing modern-day diplomats, but this chapter also shows how contemporary intelligence and security have evolved and how the twenty-first century offers some change for an era of 'new' diplomacy.

Intelligence: What is it?

Throughout history the relationship between formal diplomacy and intelligence can be accurately summarized as one of love-hate. For some time, the making of foreign policy has been 'entangled in webs of intrigue and suspicion'.[7] Although today's formalized relationship between diplomats and agencies can be traced to the late nineteenth and early twentieth centuries, intelligence support for diplomacy is far older. 'The spy is as old as history,' wrote journalist Phillip Knightley.[8] Indeed, the title of Knightley's 1986 book *The Second Oldest Profession* was borrowed from former CIA Assistant General Counsel Michael J. Barnett's quip that espionage was 'the world's second oldest profession and just as honourable as the first'.[9] If intelligence is the second oldest profession – to borrow the cliché – then diplomacy 'might rate as the third-oldest', suggests former State Department official Robert V. Kelly.[10] David Reynolds dates the origins of diplomacy to at least the Bronze Age; documents from Babylon show a fledging diplomatic system with neighbouring states, and the exchange of envoys for trade and averting conflict.[11] Likewise, ancient leaders were also reliant on espionage for information on enemies and friends alike. Much later, the city states of Renaissance Italy in the fifteenth and sixteenth centuries marked the beginnings of resident ambassadors, spreading quickly across the rest of Europe.[12] By the seventeenth and eighteenth centuries, European statesmen were becoming increasingly adept at using intercepted correspondence to shape diplomacy, while spies and cryptography proved useful for their nineteenth-century equivalents. But much of what we would now call 'intelligence' was ad hoc and it was not until the late nineteenth and early twentieth centuries that the institutionalization of intelligence or development of permanent peacetime organizations took hold.

In the twentieth century, intelligence has shaped diplomacy at important moments. During the First World War, the interception and decryption of the 'Zimmerman Telegram', promising Mexico territory in the United States if she supported Germany, was one factor behind America's formal declaration of war in April 1917. 'No other single cryptanalysis has had such enormous consequences,' wrote intelligence historian David Kahn, though few intelligence successes are as decisive.[13] During the Second World War, while much has been made of Britain's success against Germany's Enigma machine, GC&CS's diplomatic section was just as important in winning the diplomatic war against the Axis powers, producing large numbers of reports on German and Japanese traffic. Intelligence generally would become an important strand of international relations during the Cold War, allowing East and West to understand the intentions and capabilities of the other side.[14] For Gordon Barrass, a former Chief of the Cabinet Office's Assessments Staff, intelligence had a 'powerful impact, because each side had time to check whether its judgements were well founded'. Intelligence generally helped stabilize relations at moments of crisis and reassured policymakers that the Third World War was not about to break out. In giving insights into Moscow and Washington's thinking, Barrass argues that intelligence made a significant contribution to the 'peaceful ending of the Cold War'.[15] Such conclusions should be caveated, however; Western Cold War intelligence was especially good at estimating Eastern Bloc capability, but less effective at understanding 'intentions'. Cold War specialist Mark Kramer points out that intelligence effectiveness varied depending on circumstances. 'It would be ... incorrect to say either that foreign intelligence *always* had a large impact or that it *never* had much of an impact,' he suggests.[16]

But what exactly is intelligence? American academic Michael Warner writes that the term is 'defined anew by each author who addresses it', and there remain challenges to finding a concise, all-encompassing definition. Governments and organizations have outlined intelligence according to functionality – what their agencies do, and definitions change from country to country. Sherman Kent saw intelligence as simply 'knowledge' acquired by government to ensure 'national welfare',[17] while, more recently, former CIA Inspector General Lyman Kirkpatrick described it as 'the knowledge – and, ideally, the foreknowledge – sought by nations in response to external threats'.[18] Warner himself went on to define intelligence as a 'secret, state activity to understand or influence foreign entities'.[19] Although intelligence is not just restricted to the study of 'things foreign' and is increasingly a non-state activity, it can be argued that intelligence in its purest sense is the end result of a process of collection and analysis of information, with the final product or 'intelligence' shared to those who need to use it – a process called the 'intelligence cycle'. The collection of intelligence is usually done by dedicated agencies, employing a variety of specialist methods, including human intelligence (HUMINT), signals intelligence (SIGINT) and imagery intelligence (IMINT), to access mostly 'secret' sources. 'We steal secrets,' said CIA Director George Tenet, a view echoed by a Chief of Britain's Secret Intelligence Service (SIS or MI6): 'Everything we do is secret – if it's not secret we shouldn't be doing it.'[20]

Is this any different from diplomacy? Former US diplomat Robert V. Kelly suggests the formal difference between spying and diplomacy is that intelligence is a 'tactic used in political rivalry or actual military warfare', whereas diplomacy is for 'conflict resolution'.[21] Diplomats are also the 'front door' representing their countries, while intelligence officials, with the exception of avowed representatives, work in secret.[22] Nevertheless, diplomats are just as important to intelligence formulation, as suggested by John Ferris, official historian of British signals intelligence. Although secrets are often linked to intelligence, non-secret sources are also vital – and this is why diplomats are essential. For Ferris, 'open sources, such as diplomats' form a key role as do 'secret ones, including agents and codebreaking'.[23] Equally, Lord Butler's report on UK intelligence and Iraqi WMD observes that government decision-making is based on 'many types of information', the majority 'openly available or compiled, much is published, and some is consciously provided by individuals, organizations or other governments in confidence', supplemented by 'secret sources'.[24] Often intelligence and diplomacy will interact. In his study of British foreign policy, Geoffrey McDermott explained a diplomat's first job was to gain 'accurate and full information about other countries'.[25] While much emphasis goes on 'secret' information, diplomats and officials have their own confidential or open sources from local news, contacts with friendly politicians and traditional diplomatic sources that often feed into the same process as the secret sources – a process known as 'all-source' analysis.[26]

Intelligence and diplomacy in practice

Intelligence and diplomacy work in tandem to understand the world around us. But the proportion of secret and non-secret information going into intelligence assessments is hard to estimate. Diplomats and other open sources will provide intelligence analysts with the context they need to properly evaluate the secret information collected. Sir Reginald Hibbert, who joined the Foreign Office in

1946, and enjoyed a long career, including a period as FCO Political Director, estimated that as much as half of all the information obtained by diplomatic posts drew on 'overt published sources – newspapers, radio and TV broadcasts, journals, books, pamphlets and lectures'. Hibbert estimated a further 30 per cent came from 'confidential' sources open to diplomatic missions, suggesting that as little as 10 per cent could be truly classed as 'secret'.[27] Hibbert questioned the overriding reliance on 'secret' material, complaining of a 'culture where secrecy comes to be confused with truth'.[28] More recently, US intelligence academic Loch Johnson suggests as much as 90 per cent of all intelligence assessments are made up of OSINT – including diplomatic sources, with questions raised about the budgets devoted to secret intelligence.[29] In 2016, the US State Department had a budget of $50.3 billion, while the US intelligence community's funds – combining the national (NIP) and military (MIP) programmes – hit $70.7 billion. The UK picture also shows a similar pattern; while the Foreign and Commonwealth Office budget totalled an estimated £1.2 billion in 2018, spending on UK intelligence via the Single Intelligence Account was over double at £2.7 billion.[30] Even though the FCO's core budget was protected, forecasts suggested a cut of £62 million by 2020 with funds for UK diplomacy 'precarious'[31] – at a time Whitehall sources suggest UK intelligence agencies could receive increased investment as part of a wide-ranging defence review, a trend likely to continue with demands for investment into new technology and resources.

Given the growing imbalance in the funding of traditional diplomacy and secret intelligence, it seems valid to ask whether secret sources are as significant as the figures suggest. As history tells us, although secret intelligence carries significant benefits for diplomacy, we need to be cautious. Intelligence can provide answers to wider policy questions. 'Policymakers' lives are dominated by their "in boxes" and the crises of the moment,' writes Richard N. Haas, a former Director of Policy Planning for the US State Department, and intelligence can often lessen the uncertainty for policymakers and officials alike.[32] Adda Bozeman observes that secret information is a 'component of statecraft', of considerable importance, she argued, as 'knowledge or intelligence is valuable because it can provide information as well as foresight in policy-making and tactics'.[33] Intelligence can be particularly useful during summit diplomacy, finding out the bargaining position of opposing officials.[34] It was alleged that GCHQ intercepted the communications of foreign leaders and officials during the G20 summit in London in 2009, according to leaks by Edward Snowden.[35] But there are limits to what you can do with this knowledge; if true, intelligence on the private views of G20 diplomats could help educate policy, yet acting on the intelligence could give away sources and tradecraft – an important lesson that generations of officials have found out to their cost. Nevertheless, secret intelligence is just part of a much wider range of sources. 'NSA [National Security Agency] can point to things they have obtained that have been useful,' said former State Department official Herbert Levin, 'but whether they're worth the billions that are spent, is a genuine question in my mind.'[36] Another former senior State Department official questioned the growing emphasis on secret information: 'Today we are relying more on the CIA for information at a time when clandestine sources are in most cases needed less ... the availability of open source information has grown exponentially.'[37]

Mostly, diplomatic intelligence is educational. 'More often than not, intelligence provides first-rate information on third rate issues, or knowledge which one cannot appl[y] to policy,' writes Ferris.[38] In effect, eavesdropping on another country's communications might provide items of interest to regional specialists, but do little to answer the bigger questions of the day. As Ferris also warns, the most dangerous assumption is that of intelligence's 'influence'. Just because secret sources were available does not mean 'it must have affected his [or her] decisions; or because intelligence provided invaluable information, access to its records must transform our understanding of events'.[39] In reality, officials (and policymakers generally) receive, as suggested earlier, more than just intelligence reports – a pattern likely to continue as alternative information sources grow. In his experience, Robert Kelly suggests that too much emphasis went on information classified 'secret' which could have been obtained by other means, while the JIC's former chair and an Ambassador to Moscow Sir Rodric Braithwaite is equally dismissive, comparing intelligence to the work of the UK Inland Revenue. 'To glamorize or mystify intelligence,' he told an audience in 2003, 'is not in anyone's real interests.'[40] Braithwaite later added that intelligence 'was in any case only ever one part of the picture, of varying importance in different cases. The judgements of individual political leaders were usually far more important'.[41]

Although billions go into collecting secret information – as the figures earlier cited show – the irony is that much intelligence is ignored. Uri Bar Joseph's observation that the intelligence–policy relationship is essentially 'an ongoing obstacle race' where 'both sides express dissatisfaction with the actions taken by the other' is accurate. For policymakers intelligence needs to meet three important criteria, according to Loch Johnson: it needs to be timely, relevant and accurate. History is littered with many so-called failures where intelligence communities have 'failed' to provide the necessary information at the right time.

While intelligence officials can certainly point to significant successes, agencies across the world face criticism for their shortcomings. Lack of warning about the Islamic Revolution in 1979, the dramatic collapse of Soviet communism in the late 1980s, Al-Qaida's attacks on 9/11, the Arab Spring and the toppling of Middle Eastern regimes, and US and South Korean agencies' lack of reporting on the death of North Korean leader Kim Jong-II in 2011 can be cited as examples of agencies being caught out. Yet talk of intelligence failure is too simplistic. While agencies are not immune from mistakes, many 'failures' result from the breakdown in intelligence–policy relations and should, on reflection, be called 'policy' failures. Many more can be classed as inevitable given what US Defense Secretary Donald Rumsfeld once called the 'unknown unknowns', 'unexpected or unforeseeable' events. Those studying intelligence or diplomacy often forget that foreign policy is not separate from other actions in government. As Gill Bennett rightly observes, 'Even in cases where a foreign policy issue is handled by a small group of ministers, they must bear in mind other considerations, whether it be the views of their constituency and party, or the current electoral position or budgetary restrictions on their department, not to mention what might be going on elsewhere.'[42]

Intelligence and diplomacy: Some problems

In theory, the closely aligned roles of diplomats and intelligence officials necessitate close collaboration. However, this is not always the case, as the UK and US examples show. In Britain, the Foreign Office (from 1968 the FCO) has enjoyed tight control over the UK's foreign intelligence agencies, even if initially, the department had wanted to stay far removed from the work of the agencies; from 1919, the Foreign Office took responsibility for SIS as the 'only Government Department in a position to decide whether such operations may or may not conflict with the general foreign policy of H.M. Government'; two years later, in 1921, it gained control of the national SIGINT agency, the Government Code and Cipher School (renamed the Government Communications Headquarters from 1946).[43] The importance of the Foreign Office's political input was reflected in the chairmanship of the Joint Intelligence Sub-Committee (later the Joint Intelligence Committee), first created in 1936. The Foreign Office's chairing of the committee ended only after the Falklands War in 1982, when a report by Lord Franks recommended future chairs should be independent prime ministerial appointees, though many still enjoyed a diplomatic background. At lower levels, staff from the Foreign Office's Research Department (now Research Analysts) – effectively the FCO's all-source analysis department – also regularly attended meetings of the JIC's Current Intelligence Groups (CIGs) and wider Cabinet Office Assessments Staff feeding into the intelligence process, inputting diplomatic sources with the secret intelligence coming from the agencies.[44]

In the United States, the situation is different; the Department of State has traditionally had less control and influence over intelligence thanks to the Department of Defense's power. Initially, proposals to put US foreign intelligence under the State Department were rejected and, as the Church Committee report identified, while responsible for shaping policy, State had 'no command over intelligence activities essential to its mission except the Foreign Service' – with the exception of the Bureau of Intelligence and Research (INR), the oldest and smallest member of the US intelligence community, responsible to the State Department. In their 2004 report on pre-war intelligence on Iraq, Senators found that INR's analysis of Foreign Service reports got it 'least wrong' and took a 'second, harder look' at worst-case assessments.[45] Beyond INR, America's diplomats essentially competed 'with the Clandestine Service in the production of … intelligence'.[46] Nonetheless, the US intelligence community still provides significant support for US policy. State Department officials also, like their UK counterparts, have input to debates on intelligence operations or 'covert action' that may upset work overseas.[47] For US diplomats, the degree of control over CIA operations in their assigned country was a touchy subject. Initially, the CIA had complete autonomy on operations, shielding them from diplomats. In 1961, President John F. Kennedy ruled that ambassadors should be kept fully informed of the CIA's activities in their countries.[48] President Carter tried to strengthen the influence of the diplomats by requiring CIA Station Chiefs to disclose information about sources the ambassador was likely to meet – a practice handled with 'exceptional flexibility'. Some Station Chiefs surrendered the information only after the ambassador had asked the 'right question'.[49]

Despite these natural tensions, diplomatic establishments continue to be vital to foreign intelligence collection. Although Article 3 of the 1961 'Vienna Convention on Diplomatic Relations' maintained that diplomats should collect and report information on 'conditions and developments' in a host state only by 'lawful means'[50] – ruling out the use of official diplomats as intelligence officers, diplomatic missions host a range of intelligence activities. For HUMINT agencies, diplomatic posts provide the necessary 'cover' – the special protection afforded to diplomats, so they enjoy diplomatic immunity. Without this, and caught carrying out illegal activity, intelligence officers face imprisonment or death. Embassies also host military or defence attachés, uniformed personnel who develop links to other militaries while gathering intelligence in the process. Diplomatic missions also provide the necessary secure communications and support technical intelligence collection such as SIGINT. In 1960s Moscow, the US and British Embassies housed secret intercept sites codenamed BROADSIDE and TRYST collecting valuable intelligence from the mobile phones used by the Soviet leadership in their official vehicles, codenamed GAMMA GUPPY.[51] By the 1970s, tipped off about the US-UK success by newspaper reports, the Soviets responded by bombarding the missions with microwave signals.[52] Similarly, Soviet intelligence developed a network of SIGINT sites; by 1989 the KGB and GRU had covert posts in up to 62 countries.[53] Until it was closed in September 2017, Russia's Consulate in San Francisco was a hub for stealing tech developed and produced in Silicon Valley.[54]

But using diplomatic establishments as bases for intelligence work can be risky. Robert E. White, a US Ambassador to Paraguay and El Salvador, went so far as to suggest that intelligence and covert action were alien to the open aims of the State Department, betraying values and undermining the 'trust and confidence with foreign governments'.[55] Similarly, Robert Kelly writes that intelligence causes 'a host of problems, mostly to the detriment of our professional diplomats'.[56] China's Ministry of State Security viewed foreign diplomats as 'open spies' – a view partly attributable to Beijing's suspicion of outsiders.[57] In effect, diplomatic missions can fall into a siege mentality as rival intelligence and security agencies try and penetrate missions or compromise staff. Sir Brian Crowe, serving as a junior diplomat in 1960s Moscow, recalled the 'restrictions' imposed, especially regarding relationships for fear of 'blackmail' or *kompromat*. In the 1950s, at least a dozen US diplomats were sent home having admitted sexual encounters with Russian agents, and in 1989 State Department official Felix Bloch was found passing secrets to the Soviets having been blackmailed for his love of sadomasochistic sex. He was not the last to be caught out. In July 2009, a four-minute video was posted online showing a UK diplomat with two Russian prostitutes, and a month later a US official was caught in a similar 'honeytrap'.[58] In 2012, Canada's Security Intelligence Service warned the 'clandestine recording of an intimate encounter' would be used 'to blackmail or publicly embarrass the victim'.[59] Embassies are also a common target for technical intelligence. Famously, the Soviet Union presented the US Embassy in Moscow with a carved wooden plaque of the Great Seal of the United States as a 'gesture of friendship', secretly containing a listening device (known as 'The Thing'), accidentally found in 1952, while State Department officials stationed in China and Cuba have complained of alleged 'sonic attacks' – a claim denied by the Cuban and Chinese governments. Despite supposedly being on the same side, in 2004 Pakistan's Inter-Service Intelligence viewed the CIA station in Islamabad as a 'hostile intelligence presence', tapping the phones of US diplomats and CIA operatives, with even locally recruited maids, cooks and porters believed to be on the ISI's payroll, with inevitable consequences for US-Pakistan diplomatic relations.[60]

Such activities get in the way of day-to-day diplomacy, undermining the trust diplomacy needs to thrive. 'Foreign officials, ordinary citizens, and all other potentially useful contacts or interlocutors for a diplomat,' Robert Kelly wrote, 'are likely to be wary of dealing with someone they think may be a spy.'[61] Another danger of affording diplomatic cover to intelligence officials is that legitimate diplomats are often targeted. A staple on the diplomatic scene has always been the reciprocal expulsions of diplomats following scandals. The poisoning of former Russian double agent Sergei Skripal and his daughter, Yulia, in Salisbury in March 2018, provoked a wave of expulsions as the UK's allies responded to the incident, resulting in a Russian response. A combined total of 342 diplomats – 189 from the United States, the United Kingdom, Canada, Ukraine and elsewhere, plus an additional 153 Russian officials – were expelled in April. In the worst cases, intelligence operations can undermine foreign policy. In June 2010, the arrest of a network of ten Russian 'illegals' – deep undercover agents – took place just seventy-two hours after President Obama and Russia's Dmitry Medvedev had met at the White House to help reset US-Russia relations with fears for the future relationship. For Obama the arrests were unwelcome; CIA Director Leon Panetta recalls the White House was more concerned it would 'undermine' efforts to 'work with the Russians because it would be so embarrassing'.[62]

Intelligence as diplomatic power

As well as its centrality in advising policy, intelligence can be just as significant as a form of diplomatic 'power'. The People's Republic of China's (PRC) dramatic political, economic and military ascendancy is underwritten by the growing reach of her spying agencies. In the twenty-first century, China's agencies have a significant global reach, supplementing Beijing's growing 'soft power', in a concerted effort to expand its economic and security interests, stealing economic and military information to allow Beijing to grow in the fastest and cheapest way. As China's economy has expanded, so too has her spy network. Now China's operations are increasingly sophisticated, using a blend of traditional and tech-driven approaches, part of President Xi Jinping's vision for the 'Chinese Dream'. In 2015, the FBI announced it had seen an alarming 53 per cent increase in economic espionage against US companies.[63] Analysis by former CIA and Defense Intelligence Agency official Nicholas Eftimiades reveals nearly half of all Chinese espionage against the United States targeted military and space technology, with almost 25 per cent targeting sensitive commercial interests to advance Beijing's military and economic growth in a 'vacuum cleaner'-like approach to intelligence work.[64] In 1999, the 'Cox Report' identified China's goal of obtaining information on battlefield communications, space weapons, nuclear weapons, submarine technology, advanced weapons systems and guided munitions as on the PRC's shopping list of information – and the situation remains the same today, even if China's methods are more sophisticated.[65] As the US National Counterintelligence and Security Centre noted in 2018, the PRC's cyber operations target 'engineering, telecommunications, and aerospace industries', including companies 'Google, Microsoft, Intel, and VMware'.[66] Additionally, China makes extensive use of students, expats and official diplomats to collect the information with the PRC's overseas operations going from a fairly amateurish start, with the Chinese intelligence agencies now larger than their long-established counterparts, equalling, if not rivalling, the US and Russian services for their sophistication, particularly on SIGINT and the cyber operations.[67]

Intelligence has been used as a bargaining chip with mixed results, especially in the case of the UK's exit from the European Union. In her formal letter triggering the Brexit process, Prime Minister Theresa May had warned that a failure to agree a comprehensive deal would weaken the UK-EU 'fight against crime and terrorism', leading EU figures to warn against using security as 'blackmail'. For the European Parliament's Brexit coordinator Guy Verhofstadt, security was 'far too important' to be an opening bargaining chip, with another source saying it was 'outrageous to play with people's lives … This was not a smart move'.[68] Equally, efforts by the UK to use security and intelligence as a negotiating tool during the European Council summit in June 2018 did not go down well, and the issue of future security ties is a major sticking point for negotiators.[69] In part, Britain is 'Europe's leader' on intelligence – a point made by former SIS Chief Sir Richard Dearlove, and much intelligence is shared at a bilateral, rather than a multilateral, level, but the loss of access to Europe's intelligence databases would be problematic. UK national security has come to rely on institutions such as Europol, with its focus on law enforcement intelligence.[70] Equally, loss of access also lessens influence; in 2014 then Europol Director Rob Wainwright said the UK was 'one of the most influential Members States in shaping European internal security legislation'.[71] As the example also shows, although the sharing of intelligence is not new, international cooperation and intelligence liaison is increasingly important as threats such as terrorism, serious organized crime and other global issues cross national boundaries. While former MI5 Director-General Sir Stephen Lander suggested that intelligence agencies and collection were 'manifestations of individual state power and of national self-interest', he rightly observed that intelligence was increasingly a multinational activity where the risks of sharing national information were 'outweighed by the benefits of access to others'.[72] Indeed, cooperation is now at the heart of intelligence activity, bringing significant benefits in terms of access to information and tradecraft, underlying the argument that intelligence can be seen as a form of power supplementing diplomacy.

Although intelligence can be a form of power, supplementing economic, military and diplomatic power, intelligence officers can sometimes be unofficial diplomats in their own right – a form of 'parallel diplomacy' – as several historical and contemporary examples show.[73] During 'The Troubles' in Northern Ireland the UK government maintained a backchannel to the Republican movement, hidden away from overt political discourse. More recently, documents unearthed in Tripoli in 2018 revealed that UK intelligence officials played an important role in developing a growing relationship with Muammar Gaddafi's Libya, previously a pariah state in the international community. In February 2004, after Gaddafi had written to Prime Minister Tony Blair, the then head of SIS, Sir Richard Dearlove, met with Libyan officials to discuss counter-terrorism, followed by FCO and Downing Street officials, with intelligence links providing an opening for a wider UK-Libyan détente lasting until the Arab Spring.[74] Other examples include the contribution of Israeli intelligence in promoting peace initiatives with Egypt and Jordan, the CIA's links to the Palestine Liberation Organization and SIS's ties to Hamas. 'Depending upon our political assumptions and values,' writes Len Scott, 'many would conclude that this role is intrinsically worthwhile.'[75]

More generally, the sharing of intelligence between states can reinforce existing diplomatic relationships, sustaining relationships even at times of stress, as former GCHQ and JIC official-turned-academic Michael Herman has suggested. For Herman, intelligence does more than just inform. Over longer periods, working with close allies, it helps produce a hidden 'international cooperative system, rather like the other "expert" intergovernmental relationships which develop on the fringes of diplomacy'.[76] In many ways, these links cement existing diplomatic relationships, and gather their own momentum with the exchange of liaison officers, arrangements for the handling and processing of reports, divisions of responsibility against geographical targets or the sharing of assessments forming, what Herman calls a 'professional community'.[77] Equally, as with the trading of economic commodities or providing political good will, intelligence is a tool that can be bartered in exchange for favours elsewhere. The most significant of these intelligence alliances has been the Anglo-American intelligence 'special relationship' that first emerged in 1941 and matured during the Cold War. Creating these alliances has their own benefits. For Britain, close collaboration with the United States ensured access to American financial and technological support, maintaining the UK's global presence and influence at the 'top table'. For the United States, Britain's overseas imperial territories and her links to the Commonwealth gave unrivalled access to a chain of facilities serving 'US foreign policy interests'. Even today, the geography of intelligence, especially SIGINT, ensures these relationships continue, as the access to fibre optic cables, revealed by Edward Snowden, demonstrates. But beyond the mutual benefits come the role of intelligence in maintaining or re-establishing strained diplomatic relationships. For Herman, who experienced first-hand the benefits to US-UK liaison, intelligence relationships have their 'own momentum; once well established, considerable political weight is needed to disrupt them', with intelligence also 'compartmentalized' or insulated from wider political differences – even twenty-first-century Twitter spats with President Donald Trump.[78]

The new diplomacy: New problems?

Despite the changing environment of modern diplomacy, many of the issues raised earlier will continue. The need for diplomats and intelligence officials to work side by side means that tension is inevitable. Nonetheless, the networked world and the environment the 'new diplomacy' operates in exacerbate age-old problems. Zakia Shiraz and Richard J. Aldrich observe that globalization has already accelerated a 'wide range of sub-military transnational threats', with international borders 'increasingly porous'. Like their governments, intelligence agencies 'cannot meet the improbable demands for omniscience'. In effect, intelligence failure becomes ever more likely as events are harder to predict.[79] While global communications have made it easier and cheaper to communicate, the security of diplomatic communications is challenging; the proliferation of new technology makes it possible for countries such as Iran to conduct their own offensive SIGINT operations. Another problem is the communications security (COMSEC), especially in an age when government no longer holds a monopoly on communications. The decision taken by the UK's National Security Council to allow Chinese telecommunications company Huawei to help develop 5G networks in non-critical parts of the network provoked condemnation from Washington and other UK allies, fearing that Huawei offers a backdoor into critical national infrastructure. Huawei, founded in 1987, has enjoyed major growth to become one of the world's leading telecommunications companies, helped by a 'gigantic business intelligence apparatus', and finds itself locked in an economic struggle between Washington and Beijing over its links to Chinese intelligence operations, with knock-on effects for UK diplomacy. Although Britain's National Cyber Security Centre, an arm of GCHQ, maintained the threat could be mitigated, the White House was said to be 'apoplectic' while Secretary of State Pompeo urged an urgent rethink, citing intelligence-sharing concerns.

Huawei is a perfect illustration of modern-day concerns about communications security in a globalized world. Although the making and breaking of codes and ciphers are nothing new, the growing capabilities of rival states, non-state actors and even individuals to compromise communications and leak secrets have proven to be embarrassing, especially when states are found to be spying on friends and allies. Although diplomacy often relies on trust, secret intelligence operations can undermine it, as several contemporary examples show. The publication of State Department cables by WikiLeaks in 2010 and 2011, a leak referred to as *Cablegate*, included over 251,000 diplomatic cables. They revealed the work of over 270 US embassies and consulates, showing unguarded comments on foreign diplomats, intelligence and security activity and much more, in one of the largest dumps of information ever.[80] WikiLeaks led many officials, including former UK Ambassador to Lebanon, Tom Fletcher, to argue that the new threat came from 'modern-day Kim Philbys, [sic] information anarchists motivated not by creed or crusade but by a desire to get back at the system'.[81] The effect was to make diplomats 'more cautious'.[82] In July 2019, the leak of diplomatic cables by Britain's ambassador to the United States Sir Kim Darroch criticizing Trump as 'inept', 'insecure' and 'incompetent' proved just as damaging.[83] Worse still were the Snowden leaks, revealing the exploitation of fibre-optic cables and use of 'big data' by NSA and GCHQ. Both WikiLeaks and Snowden showed what many had already guessed – that allies spy on each other. In 2015, WikiLeaks revealed that NSA had run a 'decade-long policy of economic espionage against France', spying on 'the French Finance Minister, a

French Senator, officials within the Treasury and Economic Policy Directorate, the French ambassador to the United States'.[84] Leaks also revealed US officials spied on three French presidents, while the Snowden claims suggested other allies were monitored. German Chancellor Angela Merkel's phone had been tapped, according to files. Merkel later told President Obama that 'spying between friends just isn't on'.[85] In November 2013, Britain's Ambassador to Berlin was also called to Germany's Foreign Ministry to explain allegations that GCHQ ran a secret post from the UK embassy, reportedly targeting German politicians.[86] More widely, claims that the United States and the United Kingdom spied on friends provoked condemnation and unwelcome investigations. Ironically, it later emerged that Germany's foreign intelligence agency had spied on Poland, Denmark, Croatia and the Vatican.[87] In each example, intelligence activity undermined traditional diplomatic ties and trust that diplomacy needs to thrive.

Equally challenging is the new environment that intelligence officials and diplomats operate in today. The end of the Cold War marked the changing nature of international relations and the end of the bipolar order that had existed since 1945. As CIA Director James Woolsey remarked in 1993, 'We live now in a jungle filled with a bewildering variety of poisonous snakes.'[88] The proliferation of non-state threats presented a paradigm shift, with terrorism rising up the international agenda following the 9/11 attacks and the subsequent 'War on Terror', forcing a rethink in how most Western intelligence agencies operated in the new era. Although it remains true that much intelligence work still involves the collection and analysis of information, intelligence activity is moving beyond Michael Herman's belief that intelligence is just 'information and information gathering'. Writing in 2004, Herman saw intelligence and covert action – the secret use of propaganda, economic sabotage, paramilitary operations and assassination – as separate functions.[89] Now, the dividing lines are increasingly blurred, although the history of some agencies has always included such activity. The CIA has always used paramilitary activity in South America, the Middle East and Asia, while Soviet intelligence conducted similar actions, especially the use of targeted assassination, otherwise known as 'wetwork'. Even Britain, despite Herman's view, has carried out 'special operations' – admittedly on a smaller scale.[90] Traditionally, intelligence officials and diplomats have diverged over what happens with the intelligence; only in a small number of cases would intelligence officials ever have to act on the information and implement policy through 'covert action'. Now, what Marc Sageman memorably called the 'leaderless jihad' – groups of small, local, self-organized groups linked by the internet – requires a global approach, and, for some, drastic responses.[91]

In 2004, former CIA officer Charles 'Chuck' Cogan argued officials in the twenty-first century needed to 'become hunters, not gatherers', calling for a sea change far beyond just sitting back and gathering 'information that comes in, analyse it, and then decide what to do about it'. Cogan went on to argue that future officials 'will have to go and hunt out intelligence that will enable them to track down or kill terrorists. This will involve sending operatives into countries with which we are not at war'.[92] The growing reliance on assassination, Special Forces raids and remote killing through drone strikes can muddy diplomatic relations even with friendly states, as such activities infringe territorial boundaries, international laws and cross ethical red lines. The CIA's programme of 'extraordinary rendition' – the illegal transfer of terrorist suspects to black sites around the globe – led to extensive condemnation at home and overseas. Indeed, even US allies such as the UK came under fire as it was alleged that intelligence officials and diplomats were 'complicit' in torture. Equally, long-established norms of international diplomacy are now challenged; Russia's 'active measures' or 'hybrid warfare', combining military and non-military means to influence events, are just one example.[93] Currently, writes Mark Galeotti, Russia's spies are 'active, aggressive, and well-funded' having 'considerable latitude in their methods, unconstrained by the concerns of diplomats or the scrutiny of legislators'.[94] Of all the Russian agencies, the GRU ('Main Intelligence Directorate') has been particularly active, gaining a reputation as a 'swashbuckling and risk-taking organization', most notably with the poisoning of Sergei Skripal.[95] The changed nature of international affairs also tells us that activities often easily hidden in the past now have global implications; the Mossad killing of Hamas's Mahmoud Abdel Rauf al-Mabhouh in a Dubai hotel in January 2010, while a tactical success, was a 'strategic failure' after it was revealed that the assassins had used falsified Western passports, with the UK launching a 'full investigation' and Australia expelling a senior Mossad official.[96] Events once hidden under a shroud of 'plausible deniability' are now an open secret (described as 'implausible deniability') as states brazenly deny operations in a web of lies, half-truths and competing narratives.[97] The killing of US-based Saudi dissident Jamal Khashoggi at a Saudi consulate in Istanbul drew widespread condemnation, but did little to impact long-term Western policy towards Riyadh.

Conclusion

This chapter has argued that intelligence officials and diplomats will continue to face the same age-old problems, exacerbated by the context of the 'new' diplomacy. Diplomats and intelligence officials will always have to work together to achieve their common goals. Intelligence officials will provide information that supplements the overt material gathered by diplomatic establishments and other open sources, guaranteeing some degree of influence on foreign policy. By their very nature, intelligence agencies will always have a monopoly on secret information. Equally, intelligence officials will always have to rely on the diplomats for overseas cover and the provision of hubs for technical forms of collection, and intelligence analysts will always need the wider context provided by diplomats to understand the 'secret' information from specialized agencies. Yet although much intelligence is not secret, traditional diplomacy – other than being challenged by the wider proliferation of information in the internet age – faces budget demands and cuts, while intelligence funding is on the increase as new security threats emerge and new technologies are needed on the intelligence frontline. Although history tells us that diplomats and intelligence officials have always fallen out, it can be suggested that the era of the 'new' diplomacy exacerbates age-old problems, while presenting news ones. Now, intelligence agencies are increasingly asked to implement policy rather than stand by and collect and analyse information as they had done in the past. While covert action and special operations have always gone on, calls for modern-day agencies to increasingly 'become hunters, not gatherers' challenge traditional diplomacy as intelligence operations cross national boundaries and breach legal and ethical red lines, problems that diplomats will often have to solve. WikiLeaks and Snowden show that the leaking of confidential diplomatic communications or secret intelligence activity can undermine the trust needed for diplomats to work, especially when allies are involved. In future, then, intelligence and diplomacy will continue to be two sides of the same coin.

Notes

1   Luke Harding, *The Snowden Files* (London: Faber & Faber, 2014).
2   Mark Mazzetti and Michael S. Schmidt, 'Officials Say US May Never Know Extent of Snowden's Leaks', *The New York Times*, December 2013.
3   'Clapper: Snowden Caused "Profound Damage"', *BBC News*, 29 January 2014.
4   Derian referred to the 'three forces challenging traditional diplomacy … *spies* (intelligence and surveillance), *terror* (global terrorism and the national security culture), and *speed* (the acceleration of pace in war and diplomacy'). See James der Derian, *Antidiplomacy: Spies, Terror, Speed, and War* (Cambridge, MA: Blackwell, 1992), 4.
5   Adam Watson, *Diplomacy: The Dialogue between States* (Taylor & Frances, 2005), xvi.

6 Michael Rubin, 'The Temptation of Intelligence Politicisation to Support Diplomacy', *International Journal of Intelligence and CounterIntelligence* 29, no. 1 (2016): 1.
7 Keith Hamilton and Richard Langhorne, *The Practice of Diplomacy: Its Evolution, Theory and Administration* (London: Routledge, 1995), 195.
8 Phillip Knightley, *The Second Oldest Profession: The Spy as Bureaucrat, Patriot, Fantasist and Whore* (London: Andre Deutsch, 1986), 3.
9 Ibid.
10 Robert V. Kelly, 'CIA-Foreign Service Relations', in *National Insecurity: US Intelligence after the Cold War*, ed. Craig Eisendrath (Philadelphia: Temple University Press, 2000), 61.
11 David Reynolds, *Summits: Six Meetings That Shaped the Twentieth Century* (London: Allen Lane, 2007), 11.
12 Christopher Andrew, *The Secret World: A History of Intelligence* (London: Allen Lane, 2018), 121.
13 David Kahn, *The Codebreakers* (New York: Scribner, 1997). Read also Thomas Boghardt, *The Zimmermann Telegram: Intelligence, Diplomacy and America's Entry into World War I* (Annapolis, MD: Naval Institute Press, 2012).
14 Michael Herman, *Intelligence Services in the Information Age* (London: Frank Cass, 2005), 159.
15 Gordon S. Barrass, *The Great Cold War: A Journey through the Hall of Mirrors* (Stanford: Stanford University Press, 2009), 389, 396.
16 Mark Kramer, 'The Soviet Bloc Perspective on Intelligence during the Cold War', in *Out of the Cold: The Cold War and Its Legacy*, ed. Michael Fitzgerald (London: Bloomsbury, 2013), 107–8.
17 Michael Warner, 'Wanted: A Definition of Intelligence', *Studies in Intelligence* 46, no. 3 (2002): 15–16.
18 Ibid., 16.
19 Ibid., 21.
20 Andrew, *The Secret World*, 2; Duncan Gardham, 'Real "James Bond" Revealed in MI6 Archives', *The Telegraph*, September 2010.
21 Kelly, 'CIA-Foreign Service Relations', 61.
22 Michael Herman, 'Diplomacy and Intelligence', *Diplomacy & Statecraft* 9, no. 2 (1998): 6.
23 John Ferris, *Intelligence and Strategy: Selected Essays* (Oxon: Routledge, 2005), 99.
24 HC 898, *Review of Intelligence on Weapons of Mass Destruction* (London: The Stationary Office, 2004), 7.
25 McDermott Geoffrey, *The New Diplomacy and Its Apparatus* (London: Plume Press, 1973), 136.
26 Peter Davies, *The Authorised History of British Defence Economic Intelligence: A Cold War in Whitehall, 1929–1990* (Oxon: Routledge, 2019), 149.

27 Reginald Hibbert, 'Intelligence and Policy', *Intelligence & National Security* 5, no. 1 (1990): 112.
28 Ibid.
29 Loch Johnson, *National Security Intelligence* (London: Polity, 2012), 44.
30 On intelligence funding see 'Security and Intelligence Agencies: Financial Statement 2018–19' (July 2019), 17 and HC. 1692, 'Annual Report, 2017–18' (November 2018). For FCO figures, read Patrick Wintour, 'Foreign Office Overseas Staffing Cut By 1,000 in 30 Years, Say Diplomats', *The Guardian*, June 2019.
31 'Key Takeaways from the Foreign Office's 2018–19 Departmental Accounts', https://bfpg.co.uk/2019/07/key-takeaways-from-the-foreign-offices-2018-19-departmental-accounts/
32 Richard N. Haas, 'Supporting US Foreign Policy in the Post-9/11 World', *Studies in Intelligence* 46, no. 3 (2002): 1.
33 Adda Bozeman, *Strategic Intelligence & Statecraft: Selected Essays* (Washington: Brassey's, 1992), 1, 233.
34 John Ferris, 'Communications Intelligence and Conference Diplomacy', in *Exploring Intelligence Archives: Enquiries into the Secret State*, ed. R. Gerald Hughes, Peter Jackson and Len Scott (Oxon: Routledge, 2006), 45–6.
35 'GCHQ Intercepted Foreign Politicians' Communications at G20 Summit', *The Guardian*, 17 June 2013.
36 Matthew Aid, *The Secret Sentry: The Untold History of the National Security Agency* (New York: Bloomsbury Press, 2009), 304–5.
37 Kelly, 'CIA-Foreign Service Relations', 66.
38 Ferris, 'Communications Intelligence', 45.
39 John Ferris, 'Intelligence', in *The Origins of World War Two: The Debate Continues*, ed. Robert Boyce and Joseph A. Maiolo (Houndmills: Palgrave Macmillan, 2003), 309.
40 Dan Lomas and Christopher Murphy, *Intelligence & Espionage: Secrets and Spies* (Oxon: Routledge, 2019), 94.
41 Rodric Braithwaite, *Armageddon and Paranoia: The Nuclear Confrontation* (London: Profile Books, 2017), 236.
42 Gill Bennett, *Six Moments of Crisis: Inside British Foreign Policy* (Oxford: Oxford University Press, 2016), 5.
43 Keith Jeffery, *MI6: The History of the Secret Intelligence Service, 1909–1949* (London: Bloomsbury, 2010), 146.
44 Robert Longmire and Kenneth C. Walker, *Herald of a Noisy World – Interpreting the News of All Nations: The Research and Analysis Department of the Foreign and Commonwealth Office*, Foreign Policy Document (Special Issue), No. 263, London: Foreign & Commonwealth Office, 1995, 30. Philip H. J. Davies, *Intelligence and Government in Britain and the United States: A Comparative Perspective, Vol. 2: Evolution of the UK Intelligence Community* (Santa Barbara: Praeger, 2012), 254.

45 Douglas Jehl, 'The Reach of War: Intelligence: Tiny Agency's Iraq Analysis Better than Big Rivals', *The New York Times*, 2004.
46 Church Committee Report, 305, 308.
47 Philip H. J. Davies, *Intelligence and Government in Britain and the United States: Vol. 1: Evolution of the US Intelligence Community* (London: Praeger, 2012), 154.
48 John Prados, *Safe for Democracy: The Secret Wars of the CIA* (Chicago: Ivan R. Dee, 2006), 292.
49 Kelly, 'CIA-Foreign Service Relations', 65.
50 Vienna Convention on Diplomatic Relations, 1961, https://legal.un.org/ilc/texts/instruments/english/conventions/9_1_1961.pdf
51 Aid, *The Secret Sentry*, 152.
52 Ibid., 153.
53 Berridge, *Diplomacy: Theory and Practice*, 157–8.
54 Zach Dorfman, 'How Silicon Valley Became a Den of Spies', *Politico*, July 2018.
55 Robert E. White, 'Too Many Spies, Too Little Intelligence', in Eisendrath, *National Insecurity*, 45.
56 Kelly, 'CIA-Foreign Service Relations', in ibid., 61.
57 Nicholas Eftimiades, *Chinese Intelligence Operations* (Oxon: Routledge, Kindle Edition, 2017).
58 Will Stewart, 'US Diplomat "Caught on Video in a New Russian Honeytrap"', *Daily Mail*, August 2009.
59 Connor Simpson, 'No "Honey Traps" Will Dupe a Canadian Spy!', *The Atlantic*, July 2013.
60 Matthew Aid, *Intel Wars: The Secret History of the Fight Against Terror* (New York: Bloomsbury Press, 2012), 106.
61 Kelly, 'CIA-Foreign Service Relations', 61.
62 Gordon Corera, *Russians Among Us* (London: William Collins, 2020), 240.
63 James M. Olsen, *To Catch a Spy: The Art of Counterintelligence* (Georgetown: Georgetown University Press, 2019), 3.
64 Nicholas Eftimiades, 'Uncovering Chinese Espionage in the US', *The Diplomat*, November 2018.
65 Lomas, 'Report of the Select Committee on US National Security and Military/Commercial Concerns with the People's Republic of China', May 1999.
66 'Foreign Economic Espionage in Cyberspace: National Counterintelligence and Security Centre', p. 7, file:///F:/Articles/Intelligence%20and%20Diplomacy%20-Chapter/20180724-economic-espionage-pub.pdf.
67 Roger Faligot, *Chinese Spies: From Chairman Mao to Xi Jinping* (London: Hurst & Company, 2019), 401. See also Eftimiades, *Chinese Intelligence Operations*.
68 'Don't Blackmail Us over Security, EU Warns', *The Guardian*, March 2017.
69 Charlie Cooper, 'Theresa May Plays Brexit Security Card at EU Summit', *Politico*, June 2018.

70 Frederic Ischebeck-Baum, 'Anglo-German Relations and Brexit', *Journal of Intelligence History* 16, no. 2 (2017): 99.
71 Claudia Hillebrand, 'With or Without You? The UK and Information and Intelligence Sharing in the EU', *Journal of Intelligence History* 16, no. 2 (2017): 94.
72 Stephen Lander, 'International Intelligence Co-operation: An Insider Perspective', in *Secret Intelligence: A Reader*, ed. Christopher Andrew et al. (Oxon: Routledge, 2008), 140, 151.
73 For example, read Hesi Carmel, ed., *Intelligence for Peace: The Role of Intelligence in Times of Peace* (London: Frank Cass, 2002).
74 Ian Cobain and Owen Bowcott, 'Extent of UK Cooperation Gaddafi Revealed', *The Guardian*, 2018.
75 Len Scott, 'Secret Intelligence, Covert Action and Clandestine Diplomacy', *Intelligence & National Security* 19, no. 2 (2004): 331.
76 Michael Herman, *Intelligence Power in Peace and War* (Cambridge: Cambridge University Press, 1996), 200.
77 Ibid., 209.
78 Ibid., 215. See also Lomas and Murphy, *Intelligence and Espionage: Secrets and Spies*, 64–6.
79 Zakia Shiraz and Richard J. Aldrich, 'Globalisation and Borders', in *Routledge Companion to Intelligence Studies*, ed. Robert Dover et al. (Oxon: Routledge, 2013), 264.
80 Read *The Wikileaks Files: The World According to the US Empire* (London: Verso Books, 2016) and David Leigh and Luke Harding, *Wikileaks: Inside Julian Assange's War on Secrecy* (London: Faber, 2013).
81 Tom Fletcher, *The Naked Diplomat: Understanding Power and Politics in the Digital Age* (London: William Collins, 2017), 120.
82 Ibid., 121.
83 Dan Lomas, 'Donald Trump's Reaction to Kim Darroch's Criticism Reeks of Double Standards', *The Conversation*, July 2019.
84 'Espionnage Élysée', https://wikileaks.org/nsa-france/
85 'Snowden NSA: Germany Drops Merkel Phone-tapping Probe', *BBC News*, 12 June 2015.
86 'Revealed: Britain's "Secret Listening Post in the Heart of Berlin"', *The Independent*, November 2013.
87 'Germany Spied on Friends and Vatican', *Spiegel International*, 7 November 2015, https://www.spiegel.de/international/germany/german-bnd-intelligence-spied-on-friends-and-vatican-a-1061588.html.
88 Stephen Grey, *The New Spymasters: Inside Espionage from the Cold War to Global Terror* (London: Viking, 2015), 82.
89 Michael Herman, 'Ethics and Intelligence after September 2001', *Intelligence & National Security* 19, no. 2 (2004): 342.

90 See Rory Cormac, *Disrupt and Deny: Spies, Special Forces and the Secret Pursuit of British Foreign Policy* (Oxford: Oxford University Press, 2018).
91 Marc Sageman, *Leaderless Jihad: Terror Networks in the Twenty-First Century* (Philadelphia: University of Pennsylvania Press, 2008), 143.
92 Charles Cogan, 'Hunters not Gatherers: Intelligence in the Twenty-First Century', *Intelligence & National Security* 19, no. 2 (2004): 304.
93 Mark Galeotti, 'Hybrid, Ambiguous, and Non-Linear? How New Is Russia's "New Way of War"', *Small Wars & Insurgencies* 27, no. 2 (2016): 287.
94 Mark Galeotti, 'Putin's Hydra: Inside Russia's Intelligence Services', *European Council on Foreign Relations*, Policy Brief 169 (2016): 1–2.
95 Galeotti, 'Hybrid, Ambiguous', 290.
96 Ronen Bergman, *Rise and Kill First: The Secret History of Israel's Targeted Assassinations* (London: John Murray, 2019), 610.
97 Rory Cormac and Richard J. Aldrich, 'Grey is the New Black: Covert Action and Implausible Deniability', *International Affairs* 94, no. 3 (2018): 477–94.

4

The power of describing identity in diplomacy: Writing subjects, territory, time and evil at the end of Gaddafi's Libya

Dr Pablo de Orellana

Demande d'agréation: The role of identity in diplomacy

How do diplomatic practitioners inform policymakers as to whom they are talking to and their motivations? In writing, of course. Specifically, through one of the oldest set of practices in modern diplomacy: reporting, assessment and analysis of information. These practices involve many individual agents, from diplomats on mission, through summaries, reports, analysis and assessments, some of which make their way to the desks of policymakers. Their objective was, and remains, to understand whom we are talking to as well as the contexts and interests that animate them. These are as limited as the language into which they are written. Language is the principal means by which information gathered in missions is reported, assessed, summarized, quoted in further reports and analysis if considered relevant, forgotten if not. The construction of knowledge in language is one of the least researched aspects of diplomacy. This is not because there has been no awareness of the relevance of language to diplomacy.[1] Rather, the problem has long been a conceptual and analytical one: it is difficult to research how diplomacy constitutes depictions, descriptions and assessments.

Studying the *how* of diplomacy's constitution of knowledge opens two new perspectives on diplomatic practice and policymaking. The first concerns the constitution of identity in diplomatic knowledge production, an analytical application of great relevance to questions of how a state came to believe that an actor was an existential threat. This perspective opens analysis to a far greater understanding of the role played by representation of identity in international relations.[2] This is because understanding the interlocutor is a key precursor to establishing most formal diplomatic relations based on perceptions of alignment, which can result in relations based on alliances, enmity, partnership, stigma, securitization or protection. The second perspective concerns diplomacy itself, laying bare the dynamics of an institution, revealing how some information is prioritized while some is not, and explaining how self-deception can occur as well as how, on certain occasions, other actors can be persuaded of specific representations. In this way, practices of knowledge production are opened to critique, evaluation and improved utilization.

Concern about the effectiveness of knowledge production practices is as old as diplomacy itself.[3] Diplomatic pioneers like Machiavelli, Botero, Callieres and Guicciardini were particularly concerned about the possibility of misidentifying actors, intentions and events in 'speculative' analytical efforts.[4] They were aware, furthermore, of the potential benefits of persuading foreign powers of a certain interpretation of events. This has remained a grey area, however, covered in Realist assumptions of diplomatic communication as an instrumental tool of a grand strategist who can see reality.[5] In response to the methodological challenge of analysing how diplomacy constitutes knowledge,[6] my research draws on post-structuralist concepts to design a method that retrieves how diplomacy constitutes representations of subjects and their contexts.

The following section conceptualizes diplomacy as a textual enterprise of knowledge production at the heart of how states read the political identity of international actors and themselves. Diplomacy's descriptive products are treated as more complex and nuanced than 'identity' might denote. This is why from here this chapter refers to 'representations': a more complex conceptualization that refers to the identity of subjects as well as the descriptions of spatial, temporal and normative contexts that work towards constituting it. The third section develops the concepts and methods necessary to research diplomacy's constitution of representations of the identity of subjects and their contexts within an actor's diplomatic institutions and across the diplomacy of several actors. The fourth and fifth sections apply this method to how US diplomacy reported to Washington from Libya during the 2010s, discerning the dynamics and conditions of the 2011 shift in representation of Libya from an ally in the War on Terror to genocidal danger. The final section discusses the relevance of these findings and the perspectives opened up by paying attention to how diplomacy produces knowledge.

Tour d'horizon: Diplomacy as mediation of identity

Whether intentional or accidental, representation of an actor's identity and context wields significant power over diplomatic events. Diplomatic practices observe, research and analyse an actor, producing complex, ideationally contextual, discursively located inscriptions that articulate what is known of an actor and its identity: representations.[7] Representations are the end of the line when making policy: information is delivered in language, and these products are the evidence against which decisions must be made. This is why the manner in which they constitute subjectivity is of vital importance to understanding diplomacy and policy decisions.

Post-structuralist scholarship has drawn attention to how identity constitutes international political subjects, showing how constructions of identity (representations) inform considerations of security, threats and conflict. Connolly conceptualized identity as a living text, evolving through articulations, contradictions categorizations and interventions that are not based on an underlying reality but political subjectivity.[8] Constructions of identity and difference are mutually constitutive, and security policy is informed by the articulation of a threatening Other.[9] The discursive identification of an actor's political identity locates it in relation to other better-known actors, situating it in an intersubjectively comprehensible position.[10] Representation of identity can then enable a 'discourse of exclusion implicated in the legitimation of violence' categorizing the subject as the excluded Other and a security concern.[11] The constitution of an actor's political identity can thus unlock mechanisms of security, global governance, or enable alliances and support.[12]

Under a post-structuralist lens, diplomacy is revealed as a practice that both constitutes and mediates identity.[13] Its communicative practices establish Self and Other when they 'recognize', describe and analyse other actors while contemporarily establishing a discourse of Self.[14] This is a political act that occurs in communication and can be analysed as textual production using Foucauldian analytics.[15] To do this, discourse analysis retrieves where subjects are inscribed in temporal, spatial and ethical dimensions – key parts of identity-formation – and the linguistic and ideational means that achieve this. For our purposes, this entails firstly analysing how constructions of identity are constituted in diplomatic knowledge and retrieving how they are implicated in particular conflicts by mapping their presence in policy discourses and events.[16]

The state's understanding of itself and other actors is constituted in diplomatic text and sustained by the continuity of bureaucratic knowledge production. Research drawing on critical perspectives based on anthropology, Bourdieusian sociology, Latourian Actor-Network theory and de Certeau has highlighted that its practices depend on material assemblages, technology, bureaucratic structures and norms, personal performances and social capital.[17] The capacity to exercise influence (on representatives of other actors as well as one's own superiors) emerges from the deployment of personal resources, skills and competences.[18] Non-representative and non-textual practices, competences, strategies, limitations and resources are, however, deployed into channels where they are necessarily crystallized into text: a démarche, vote, resolution or declaration.

In bilateral and multilateral negotiations, for instance, diplomats invest their competences into influencing the drafting of a text. The 2011 Security Council resolutions authorizing a no-fly zone in Libya (UNSCR 1970 and 1973) necessitated an agreed-upon inscription of subjects: Gaddafi's government, the opposition and their contexts. This instance is circumscribed by cultures of practice, hierarchy and most of all by the fate of the diplomat's dispatch: after submission, it is bound to be rewritten, summarized, analysed, translated, shared with foreign diplomats or ignored. Her descriptions might be ignored or thrive, launching influential discursive trends like Kennan's Long Telegram. They might even cross over to the diplomacy of another actor, potentially influencing its knowledge production.[19]

Aide mémoire: Retrieving how diplomacy writes subjects, space, time and conflict

Diplomatic practices are invested in the textual representation of subjects and their contexts, raising the question of how to systematically analyse it. This challenge is addressed by developing a version of post-structuralist discourse analysis adapted to the conditions of diplomatic knowledge. Such a native approach to textual analysis is necessary because diplomacy produces knowledge across thousands of documents involving many authors, drafts, institutions and practices. Consequently, analysis needs to capture how knowledge is produced across an entire *body* of texts, which requires large-scale systematization of single-texts analysis and mapping of how representations evolve in and across them.

This analytical challenge is addressed in three distinct interlocking steps that form a theory-powered analytical methodology. The first tightens conceptualization of what a diplomatic text is, allowing for rigorous data selection. The second examines how a diplomatic document describes subjects and their spatial, temporal and normative contexts. The third systematizes analysis of representations across hundreds of texts to follow their development and chart the emergence of a dominant representation. This determines how certain representations are constituted, why some are more influential and whether and when they cross to the diplomacy of another actor.

The first methodological step establishes who speaks on behalf of an international actor. This is resolved through consideration of the instance of practice, for '[w]hich expression of identity dominates or prevails is dependent on the degree of control different social groups exercise over discursive and institutional practices'.[20] Focus on practice is therefore crucial.[21] What makes a communication distinctly 'diplomatic' is its conditioning by the knowledge that it represents sovereignty. This 'delegation of presence' is the key condition of possibility for diplomatic practice and is the very core of the diplomatic condition.[22] Since this delegation does not take place at the foreign ministry alone, this methodology includes diplomatic cables and communication by actors in instances where they represent the state: leaders, politicians and their formally recognized agents. Its textual practices are empirically sited at an instance I call *the diplomatic moment*: when a diplomat's work is submitted and becomes part of bureaucratic knowledge production. Evidence for analysis is, therefore, selected in relation to the claim of sovereign representation and institutional submission of diplomatic writing: the *diplomatic text*.

This chapter analyses over 500 cables, memoranda and other documents available thanks to the 2010 leak of over 300,000 US State Department documents and Secretary Clinton's emails in 2016, as well as publicly available documents. Sources include State Department cables to and from the mission in Tripoli (for the period 2008–10),[23] the cache of over 30,000 emails and attachments to and from Secretary Clinton (2009–11),[24] as well as official press releases from governments and the UN.[25] The chronological extent of data collection is determined by the policy decision being studied and the representations it was based on, which in practice means including documents that carry that representation, tracing its presence backwards until reaching its earliest first iteration. In this manner, to avoid historical determinism, it is the very presence of representations in texts that determines the extent of data collection.

The second methodological step analyses how a diplomatic text represents actors and their contexts. It draws on Foucauldian archaeology which, beyond linguistic analysis of how words suggest meaning, 'retrieves' or identifies and examines the modes, rules and references that make the expression of identity discursively meaningful and subjectively operational.[26] To structure systematic analysis, this method draws on Barthian literary commentary.[27] Literary commentary systematically organizes analysis from the outside in: form (structure), textual context (location within an opus), the stanza (or paragraph), the verse (or articulation) and words (vocabulary and musicality). Form is the 'expected' structure: diplomatic documents draw on very old and consistent forms (cables, communiques, updates, reports) and diplomats have flexibility within them. Within form, its immediate (literary) context explains relational features and links to other texts. Deeper, paragraphs organize content and categorize hierarchy or causality, while literary devices create and locate objects and relations among them. In phrases, grammatical devices construct relations among objects and order hierarchy; subjugate clauses and word order construct action-based verbal relations; orthographical choices can highlight foreignness; and punctuation can frame hierarchy. Finally, word choice is powerful as specific items of diplomatic vocabulary have significant categorization effects.

Demonstrated in the next section, this analysis reveals how identity works in specific texts, and additionally retrieves textual markers, called topoi in literary studies, that signpost the presence of the specific aspects and architectures of normative representation.[28] They allow the next analytical step to follow representations of political identity across time and texts. All texts researched are analysed in this way, but for publications it is practical to select a representative sample that contains the main representations involved, particularly the link between a representation ('you are a communist danger') and the logic of the policy event being researched ('contain you because you are communist').

The third step accounts for how a representation evolved. In this chapter, we take the 2011 decision to impose a no-fly zone in Libya and, in a chronologically reverse genealogy, research the history of the representations that enabled it. Analysis stops itself when the first iteration of that representation is found. The approach traces how a representation emerged dominant over others, retrieving who promoted it, when, in which context, and enabling research to map its evolution. This reveals a representation's relationship to the local and global context, the practices that promoted or stifled it through various intertextual incarnations from a mission report to the brief handed to policymakers, and the instructions that determined its journey. It is through this detail that we discover how a representation comes to dominate understanding of international actors and their contexts, revealing bureaucratic, ideological and other subjective dynamics.

This method can be applied to the diplomacy of one or more actors. In this chapter we research how the US State Department came to see the Libyan civil

The power of describing identity in diplomacy 83

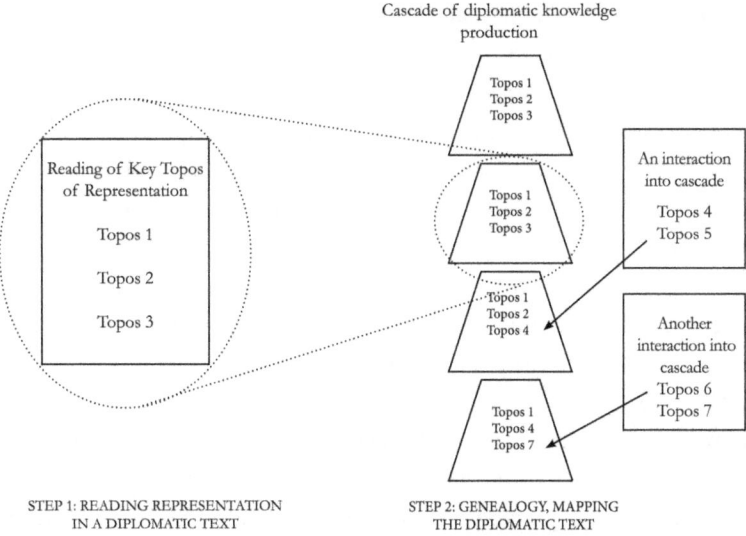

Figure 1 Diagram summarizing the method. Arrows denote the crossover of representations – signposted by their topoi – from one text to another. Credit: Tally de Orellana, Philadelphia Museum of Art.

war in a specific light. It is also possible to collect data, analyse single texts and carry out a genealogy for how several states came to see a situation or actor and potentially even how they influenced each other's views. This makes it possible to follow the journey of a representation when it crosses over to the diplomacy of another actor, revealing when an actor persuades another of its understanding of events.[29] The above diagram (Figure 1) summarizes the two-step method executed in Parts IV and V of this chapter.

The second step, on the left, analyses the constitution of representation in single texts and individuates the topoi that denote their presence. On the right is the third step, the genealogy of these representations across time and texts. As illustrated in the diagram, the method identified which representations cross over (signposted by Topoi 4 and 7) and those that do not (Topoi 5 and 6) from another source, be it another agency, individual or country. The following sections apply this method to the 2011 US decision to support Libyan rebels' 'promise of freedom' against the 'genocidal' Gaddafi regime.

Cables from the Jamahiriya: Analysing representations

In US diplomacy, the Gaddafi regime transformed in 2011 from 'key ally in the war on terror' to a 'genocidal' regime run by a 'madman'. As Obama explained in his 28 March speech, this was because Gaddafi was repressing democrats and planned to massacre dissenters. This section analyses texts in detail to understand the structure and functionality of these policy-influencing descriptions. To demonstrate a representative analysis, this section explores how Gaddafi's regime was described at the time of the diplomatic moves that led to the 2011 intervention in UN Security Council Resolutions 1970 and 1973, as well as President Barack Obama's 28 March speech announcing intervention.

Reaching agreement on these texts was very difficult. Diplomats strained their personal and institutional influence to affect the language of UN Security Council Resolutions 1970 (26 February 2011, imposing sanctions on the regime) and 1973 (17 March 2011, imposing a no-fly zone).[30] This highlights the efforts states make to have their preferred description of events, actors, their motives and context sanctioned by the Security Council, NATO and the EU. This is why the first analytical step involves analysing in detail the texts that determined policy on the basis of descriptions.

Resolutions 1970 and 1973 consecrated a description of the Gaddafi regime that sealed its fate. Their text posed an urgent normative binary pitting genocidal regime employing mercenaries against citizens 'with legitimate demands'. The actions demanded by the resolutions make sense *only* when 'deploring' human rights violations is combined with 'expressing concern' that they might worsen (see Figure 2 above). This is because these opposing representations are mutually constitutive and depend on one another to be discursively coherent. That is, action was predicated on the contrast between protestors and Gaddafi. This is the binary representation of the conflict that underpinned US policy on Libya – what was it made of?

The first representation categorizes Gaddafi as a would-be perpetrator of genocide. The assumption that Gaddafi would kill and 'massacre' all dissenters is present in both resolutions, Obama's speech and Clinton's explanations, which posit a 'tyrant' 'madman', committed to 'genocide', who has perpetrated 'war crimes', and employed mercenaries. While violations had become self-evident by February 2011, the assumption of Gaddafi's genocidal intentions stemmed from his own statements 'that he would show "no mercy" '. This is a thin basis for such an important policy assumption, particularly considering Gaddafi's record of overblown statements and the lack of evidence. Yet it is present in justifications for the 2011 intervention championed by Secretary Hillary Clinton, British Prime Minister David Cameron and French President Nicolas Sarkozy.[31]

The second representation posits an unarmed protest movement with 'legitimate demands'. Vaguely in the UNSC Resolutions, but explicitly in

Security Council

Distr.: General
17 March 2011

Resolution 1973 (2011)

Adopted by the Security Council at its 6498th meeting, on 17 March 2011

The Security Council,

Recalling its resolution 1970 (2011) of 26 February 2011,

Deploring the failure of the Libyan authorities to comply with resolution 1970 (2011),

Expressing grave concern at the deteriorating situation, the escalation of violence, and the heavy civilian casualties,

Reiterating the responsibility of the Libyan authorities to protect the Libyan population and *reaffirming* that parties to armed conflicts bear the primary responsibility to take all feasible steps to ensure the protection of civilians,

Condemning the gross and systematic violation of human rights, including arbitrary detentions, enforced disappearances, torture and summary executions,

Further condemning acts of violence and intimidation committed by the Libyan authorities against journalists, media professionals and associated personnel and *urging* these authorities to comply with their obligations under international humanitarian law as outlined in resolution 1738 (2006),

Considering that the widespread and systematic attacks currently taking place in the Libyan Arab Jamahiriya against the civilian population may amount to crimes against humanity,

Recalling paragraph 26 of resolution 1970 (2011) in which the Council expressed its readiness to consider taking additional appropriate measures, as necessary, to facilitate and support the return of humanitarian agencies and make available humanitarian and related assistance in the Libyan Arab Jamahiriya,

Expressing its determination to ensure the protection of civilians and civilian populated areas and the rapid and unimpeded passage of humanitarian assistance and the safety of humanitarian personnel,

Recalling the condemnation by the League of Arab States, the African Union, and the Secretary General of the Organization of the Islamic Conference of the serious violations of human rights and international humanitarian law that have been and are being committed in the Libyan Arab Jamahiriya,

Taking note of the final communiqué of the Organisation of the Islamic Conference of 8 March 2011, and the communiqué of the Peace and Security Council of the African Union of 10 March 2011 which established an ad hoc High Level Committee on Libya,

Taking note also of the decision of the Council of the League of Arab States of 12 March 2011 to call for the imposition of a no-fly zone on Libyan military aviation, and to establish safe areas in places exposed to shelling as a precautionary measure that allows the protection of the Libyan people and foreign nationals residing in the Libyan Arab Jamahiriya,

Taking note further of the Secretary-General's call on 16 March 2011 for an immediate cease-fire,

Recalling its decision to refer the situation in the Libyan Arab Jamahiriya since 15 February 2011 to the Prosecutor of the International Criminal Court, and *stressing* that those responsible for or complicit in attacks targeting the civilian population, including aerial and naval attacks, must be held to account,

Reiterating its concern at the plight of refugees and foreign workers forced to flee the violence in the Libyan Arab Jamahiriya, *welcoming* the response of neighbouring States, in particular Tunisia and Egypt, to address the needs of those refugees and foreign workers, and *calling on* the international community to support those efforts,

Deploring the continuing use of mercenaries by the Libyan authorities,

Considering that the establishment of a ban on all flights in the airspace of the Libyan Arab Jamahiriya constitutes an important element for the protection of civilians as well as the safety of the delivery of humanitarian assistance and a decisive step for the cessation of hostilities in Libya,

Expressing concern also for the safety of foreign nationals and their rights in the Libyan Arab Jamahiriya,

Welcoming the appointment by the Secretary General of his Special Envoy to Libya, Mr. Abdel-Elah Mohamed Al-Khatib and supporting his efforts to find a sustainable and peaceful solution to the crisis in the Libyan Arab Jamahiriya,

Reaffirming its strong commitment to the sovereignty, independence, territorial integrity and national unity of the Libyan Arab Jamahiriya,

Determining that the situation in the Libyan Arab Jamahiriya continues to constitute a threat to international peace and security,

Acting under Chapter VII of the Charter of the United Nations,

1. *Demands* the immediate establishment of a cease-fire and a complete end to violence and all attacks against, and abuses of, civilians;

2. *Stresses* the need to intensify efforts to find a solution to the crisis which responds to the legitimate demands of the Libyan people and *notes* the decisions of the Secretary-General to send his Special Envoy to Libya and of the Peace and Security Council of the African Union to send its ad hoc High Level Committee to Libya with the aim of facilitating dialogue to lead to the political reforms necessary to find a peaceful and sustainable solution;

Figure 2 Screenshots of UNSCR 1973, pp. 1–2. Available at https://www.un.org/securitycouncil/content/resolutions-0

Obama and Clinton's descriptions, it is assumed that these demands are democratic, particularly as their ambitions are described by association with other democratic movements in the so-called Arab Spring. Emphasis lies on being unarmed, legitimate, 'heavy civilian casualties' – avoiding all mention of an armed rebellion. Crucially, and this is evident in Obama's speech, it was assumed that this 'promise of freedom' would establish a democratic pro-Western administration. The lack of detail on the rebels highlights that this representation depended almost entirely on its binary opposition to Gaddafi's.

These representations follow a discursive architecture that promotes binary opposition between them. On the one hand, the regime is firstly categorized as criminal, which is directly tied to assertions of Gaddafi's war crimes and human rights abuses, which in turn serve as evidence of Gaddafi's intention to massacre Benghazi. This is opposed by 'peaceful protesters', normatively inscribed in terms of their 'legitimate demands', which are described as such but never specified beyond being anti-Gaddafi. Protesters are constituted as innocently vulnerable by assertions of being unarmed and inserted into a Western context by linking their demands to Western values and democracy. This is evident in Obama's speech: 'Born as we are of a revolution by those that longed to be free [...] wherever people long to be free they will find a friend in the United States.'

This architecture constitutes specific conditions of discursive possibility. Protesters are not only legitimate, close to Western values and vulnerable, but are also in danger from the regime's extreme violence. This is vital to 2011 US representation of the conflict as a struggle for freedom among very unequal sides rather than as a civil war. Thanks to Gaddafi's evil the rebels could be described by their opposition to Gaddafi rather than their participants, intentions or affiliations. This architecture papers over inconsistencies, the fragility of some assumptions (particularly Gaddafi's intentions) and contradictions. Crucially, the reliance of this representation on Gaddafi being a 'madman' bent on 'genocide' obscured comparisons with similar events, particularly in Bahrain, Morocco and Egypt, who also ended protests with military force under the cover of internet blackouts.

To examine how these specific representations evolved it is necessary to identify the topoi markers that signpost their presence. The first is found in the use of terms indicating legality/illegality such as 'legitimate' or 'righteous' combined with slurs ('madman', 'bloodthirsty') that indicate the presence of this specific representation. Secondly, this violence is signposted by language referencing 'war crimes' and dramatic terms like 'bloodbath'. The third signposts rebel intentions with Western democratic terms like 'democratic', 'aspirations' and failure to 'fulfil the legitimate demands'. The urgent vulnerability of the rebels is indicated by the use of 'protesters' (rather than 'rebels' or 'insurgents'), emphasis on 'unarmed' or 'undefended' while consistently avoiding of the rebels' organization, armament, politics or Islamist links.

That text sealed Gaddafi's fate on the basis of its description of the regime as genocidal. Only six months before, however, the gravest issue in US-Libyan relations concerned the release for health reasons of Lockerbie bomber Abdelbaset al-Megrahi by the Scottish Government. US diplomats protested the release and requested that Libya abstain from giving Megrahi a 'hero's welcome' to avoid fallout in US public opinion.[32] Until January–February 2011, despite Megrahi, the United States and Libya experienced a rapprochement driven by Libya having become 'an important ally in the war on terrorism' (see Figure 3, for example).[33]

This is very different from the representation of the Gaddafi regime that emerged in early 2011, which overwhelmed the earlier rapprochement. How did this description, carrying the assumption of a Gaddafi-led genocide, come to have such prominence?

```
MUATASSIM MEETING SECURITY FOCUSED

3. (C) Characterizing the overall pace of the bilateral
relationship as excellent, CODEL McCain opened its August 14
meeting with National Security Advisor Muatassim al-Qadhafi by
noting the drastic change that the relationship had undergone
over the last five years. "We never would have guessed ten
years ago that we would be sitting in Tripoli, being welcomed by
a son of Muammar al-Qadhafi," remarked Senator Lieberman. He
stated that the situation demonstrated that change is possible
and expressed appreciation that Libya had kept its promises to
give up its WMD program and renounce terrorism. Lieberman
called Libya an important ally in the war on terrorism, noting
that common enemies sometimes make better friends. The Senators
recognized Libya's cooperation on counterterrorism and conveyed
that it was in the interest of both countries to make the
relationship stronger. They encouraged Libya to sign the Highly
Enriched Uranium transfer agreement by August 15 in order to
fulfill its obligation to transfer its nuclear spent fuel to
Russia for treatment and disposal. [Note: The Libyan Government
subsequently informed us of its intent to sign the agreement on
August 17 and has begun taking good-faith steps to do so (ref
B). End note.]
```

Figure 3 Screenshot of a paragraph reporting on Senators McCain and Lieberman's August 2009 visit to Libya in 19/8/2009 Tripoli to State, 09TRIPOLI677.

Démarches to ourselves: Understanding knowledge production at the Ministry

Having determined with precision how US diplomacy represented Libya in 2010, this section seeks to understand how it had changed so radically by March 2011. It follows the topoi textual markers identified in the previous section to map the history of the representations that led to this policy shift. This is achieved by applying the third step of the method to trace the shift from representation of Libya from 'key ally in the war on terror' to a 'genocidal' regime run by a 'madman'. This analysis specifically looks to understand which reports were influential and were widely disseminated, which did not, what contingencies determined the rise of one representation over another and the effect of feedback and instructions. This section begins with the texts analysed in the previous section and traces in reverse chronological order the life, twists, development, conflicts with other representations and origins of the vital policy-changing representations they featured.

The two main representations of the conflict analysed in the previous section were dominant at Foggy Bottom around April–March 2011 (just before and after the UN resolutions). However, in the privacy of diplomatic reporting these were challenged by two representations that reveal conflicts at the State Department over how to understand events in Libya. The first was characterized by a growing concern that the rebel National Transitional Council (NTC) and particularly its thirty or so militias included Islamists seeking to establish an anti-American Islamic state in Libya, challenging representation of the rebels as a democratic civilian 'government in waiting'. Secondly, this period saw the emergence of a more complex representation of the conflict as a civil war involving East–West rivalry, Al-Qaida-linked Islamists, tribes and anti-Gaddafi factions supported by various international actors. In this representation Gaddafi is not portrayed as the most dangerous actor, and it is possible that it drew on the previously dominant representation of Gaddafi as a convenient counterterrorism ally.

As Obama declared support for the rebels, the role of Islamists in NTC militias, particularly Al-Qaeda linked Libyan Islamic Fighting Group (LIFG), was being examined by State Department analysis. It highlighted links to Islamist groups and the background that 'Libya was the next [after Saudi Arabia] most common country of origin [of foreign fighters] in Iraq'.[34] Backtracking to the day before Obama's speech, reporting suggested that French President Sarkozy, despite enthusiastically supporting the NTC, also shared these concerns.[35] In 2009 diplomats already knew that Islamists wanted to topple Gaddafi, corroborating that Bin Laden lieutenant 'al-Zawahiri urged AQ fighters to topple the Government of Libya'.[36] Why did these warnings go unheeded?

Clinton and her trusted former campaign advisor Sidney Blumenthal, acting in a personal capacity, argued that 'rebel "ranks" may contain people who fought us in Iraq? Probably, but we do not actually know that except on the word of Qathafi'.[37] A few days earlier, Blumenthal offered Clinton analysis from the blog of W Patrick 'Pat' Lang, a retired intelligence officer highly rated by Blumenthal who felt that '[t]he chance that Islamist parties are likely successors in power in any of the present disputed countries is minimal'.[38] Backtracking to early March 2011, the Islamist link to the rebels is reduced to 'Q[addafi]'s trick'. Meanwhile, NTC chairman Mustafa Abdul Jalil 'is convinced that one of his most important tasks is to convince these Western governments that the rebels are not supported by al-Qai'da, as Gaddafi regularly claims'.[39] The best argument to disbelieve allegations of Islamist involvement in the NTC was that Gaddafi claimed so, and Blumenthal was vital in delivering it to Clinton. This is why Jalil's claims about NTC appeared believable. In terms of diplomatic knowledge production, the collapse of this vital nuance demonstrates Blumenthal's influence on Clinton and how simple binary representations undermine the believability of contradictory evidence.

Representation of the conflict as a complex civil war also failed to make a policy impact. There was concern that rebels 'continue to summarily execute all foreign mercenaries captured' and were sharply divided.[40] While regularly updated on these concerns, Clinton rarely asked for further details.[41] Blumenthal too supplied intelligence and analysis suggesting that the conflict was 'a protracted civil war with various nations backing opposing sides',[42] featuring 'serious rifts' among rebels', and a crisis of local credibility.[43] Even before the UN Resolutions, State Department officials wondered how to 'mitigate the potential for Islamic extremists and al-Qaeda to exploit the transition'.[44] Three days earlier, we find the origin of Clinton's preferred representation of the conflict. In an email titled 'quick note on vocabulary re Libya', Anne-Marie Slaughter, State Department Director of Policy Planning until January 2011, encourages Clinton to 'support [the rebels] by pushing back against the idea that this is anything other than a popular revolt'. This was clearly influential, as from this point Clinton *only* referred to the conflict by these terms which, furthermore, featured heavily in Obama's subsequent 28 March speech.[45]

The most widespread representation posited Gaddafi as a genocidal madman. During negotiations over the UN resolutions, Blumenthal suggested that genocide was likely as Gaddafi 'has already conducted widespread murders in the areas he has retaken'.⁴⁶ Top State Department officials refrained from such assertions, specifying instead that 'Q[addafi] may qualify for war criminal status'.⁴⁷ Likewise, Clinton received evidence against the certainty of genocide, particularly intelligence detailing that the regime's 'planes have virtually run out of high-quality jet fuel', there was 'no evidence of the presence of weaponized chemical material', Libyan overtures to Italy and the UK, and that regime figures (including Gaddafi's son Saif al-Islam) were 'calling for negotiations'.⁴⁸

Certainty as to Gaddafi's genocidal intentions originated with few and mostly unofficial sources. Blumenthal provided the most, selecting pieces of official intelligence, unofficial intelligence from long-time loyalists like Bill Clinton 'fixer' Cody Shearer,⁴⁹ and mixing them with advice from media pundits like retired general Jack Keane,⁵⁰ as well as 'unconfirmed' intelligence and analysis.⁵¹ Blumenthal put a lot of stock on Gaddafi's own statements about Benghazi, and linked these to equally overblown speculation on how 'Qaddafi and his sons are prepared to carry on this struggle as an all-out civil war',⁵² using weapons of mass destruction and even bombing 'the barracks of any troops or police who go over to the anti-government forces'.⁵³ Certainty of genocide was heavily reinforced by meetings with French President Sarkozy's staff,⁵⁴ although State officials warned that Sarkozy wanted an intervention to 'rebuild the reputation of the French military' and, as suggested by Saif al-Islam Gaddafi, conceal financial relations with the regime.⁵⁵

Representing the rebels as a democratic 'civil government-in-waiting' depended on Gaddafi being seen as genocidally insane.⁵⁶ The most avid readers will notice in the cable citations that descriptions of Gaddafi 'the madman' were frequently written alongside and in contrast to those of liberal rebels seeking democracy. It lacks detail, hollowed out by the above-discussed collapse, in Clinton's eyes at least, of the nuances concerning the Islamist insurgents that constituted the rebellion's backbone. It is likely that these were vital in persuading Obama, as Clinton appears to have led the charge on the president and was congratulated by Slaughter for 'Turning POTUS around on this is a major win for everything we have worked for'.⁵⁷ These details were replaced by the assumption that the rebels were democratic and that the conflict 'gives the US a hand in reform and development' in North Africa.⁵⁸ A vital factor, 'fulfilling' policymakers' hope as to rebel intentions, was the diplomatic campaign of NTC leader Mahmood Jibril, who consistently described the conflict as a 'battle for democracy'.⁵⁹ This appears to have convinced informal Clinton aid Cody Shearer, a journalist who met Jibril in early March 2011 and was the first to describe the rebels as a 'reformist government-in-waiting', an articulation consistently repeated for months.[60]

Tracing the origin of the representations analysed above reveals three key sources that advised Clinton over the previous fortnight. On 24 February former British Prime Minister Tony Blair wrote to Clinton with an update on the conflict, explaining that rebels were 'working very hard on legal and structural formations for a transitional government' while 'Misrata completely in the hands of the free, and already made civil government arrangements'.[61] Tony Blair's communications to Clinton form the earliest occurrence of the linguistic formulas that from that moment were used to describe the rebels. Though it has been widely reported that Samantha Power, National Security Council member and Presidential Special Advisor, was key to the decision to intervene,[62] the method here expounded reveals how this occurred. On 21 February she discussed with Clinton the defection to the rebels of the Libyan UN diplomatic mission and presented their credentials as simply: '[t]hey made a plea to the international community to save their country, and said they (in representing Libya) were planning to take steps to bring the situation in Libya to the Security Council. They sided with the protesters and opposition, called for ICC involvement, asked that a no-fly zone be declared'.[63] This formula validates Libyan diplomatic defectors in terms of their links to the rebels, and then by the same token validates their request for military intervention. Crucially, this link worked only because well-documented concerns about the rebels were wilfully ignored.

None of these representations were present before February 2011. Reporting and analysis focused on reengaging with Libya after the Blair-brokered resolution of the Lockerbie bombing, which represented Gaddafi as ready, willing and able to collaborate with the West.[64] There was a clear idea that 'Qadhafi's more inflammatory rhetoric belies a fair amount of common interest and cooperation with the United States'.[65] US diplomacy reported stress over issues remaining from Libya's 1980s terrorism campaign and monitored Libyan nuclear and chemical research to ensure disarmament and non-proliferation.[66] The main issue, however, was treatment of Lockerbie bomber Megrahi after his release on humanitarian grounds, with exasperation that he was given a hero's welcome, which kept it in the US 'election cycle'.[67] This was considered eminently resolvable, as was minor stress over collaboration at the UN to impose sanctions on North Korea.[68]

Before 2011, American diplomats and policymakers were keen to involve Libya in counterterrorism,[69] and it became 'a critical ally […] one of our primary partners in combating the flow of foreign fighters'.[70] US-Libyan collaboration focused on African security,⁷¹ including US counterterrorism initiatives, diplomatic endeavours like Darfur, the 2008 Mauritanian coup⁷² and the Chad–Sudan conflict in which Libya was an influential mediator.⁷³ Slower engagement proceeded in economic development,⁷⁴ education and civil society issues.⁷⁵ US diplomats warned that the only clear opposition to Gaddafi consisted of hardline Islamists led by LIFG,⁷⁶ and encouraged gradual human rights engagement, including a regime-supported public Human Rights Watch 'public forum for discussion of Libya's past abuses' and a bilateral dialogue.⁷⁷ Gaddafi apparently had great hopes for Obama, expressing that he could work with 'the new America without reservation' and was keen to meet in person.⁷⁸ Even as the regime crumbled, the dictator pleaded to Obama that 'you will always remain our son'.⁷⁹

Memorandum: Perspectives on diplomatic knowledge production

Key lessons emerge for the practice, analysis and understanding of diplomacy. This section summarizes findings and discusses their relevance. It focuses on lessons concerning diplomatic knowledge production practices, how this knowledge is used, lessons that emerge for making policy on its basis and finally the relevance of this perspective to study of diplomacy and international relations.

In Section IV, this chapter analysed in detail how key US diplomacy represented Libya in 2011. It determined that the 2011 policy shift hinged on understanding Gaddafi as a genocidal madman repressing defenceless protestors. Representation of the rebels was almost entirely subsumed into the vague category of defenceless freedom-loving civilians. These representations depended on and constituted one another, to the extent that contradictions concerning the rebels were papered over by an ever more diabolical representation of Gaddafi. This was successful because it linked both representations more solidly through their alterity,⁸⁰ which was exacerbated to divert from the fissures in the construction of the Self, in this case the specific rebel Self supposedly similar to the American revolutionaries. The 2011 representations overwhelmed previous representations of US-Libyan rapprochement, especially antiterrorist collaboration, discarding previously detailed understanding that anti-regime opposition included Al-Qaeda-linked militants.

Mapping the evolution of these representations focused on the collapse of nuances in understanding Libyan rebel groups and the civil war. It showed how this amplified NTC chairman Jibril's message that rebels wanted democratic freedom, but also how this was most of all facilitated by the dominant view of events in Washington – which energetically chose to see the rebels as liberal democrats. This view was not the product of NTC communicative prowess as much as selective reading of the situation against diplomatic evidence policymakers had ample access to. Mapping the evolution of these representations showed how, in practice, a government can see only what it wants to see.

Examining knowledge production revealed the gatekeepers and facilitators of information. Sidney Blumenthal was revealed as the key distributor of reports and analysis and Clinton engaged with his submissions more than anyone else's. Even when he submitted less than one-sided selections of reports, his opinion that rebels would not turn to Islamism was influential and Clinton adhered to that representation. A year later, following the Benghazi consulate attack, she insisted on attributing the attack to extremist 'elements' or Gaddafi loyalists, unpersuaded that much of the NTC Free Libyan Army was in fact a Salafist operation.[81]

The key lesson is to take diplomatic knowledge production seriously. Sadly, Libya stands as a case study in how not to do this. Representations are powerful: they make sense of and order knowledge about events, which is why they should be continually questioned, substantiated and never simplified. Simplicity in understanding the Libyan conflict made the dual representation of Gaddafi as genocidal maniac and the rebels as liberal democrats sustainable. These representations obscured understanding of the situation to the extent that it mired Libya in a still-ongoing civil war (because rebels never united); sabotaged policy (democracy remains unlikely); made Libya the centre of Salafism, Al-Qaeda and ISIS in the Sahel (due to long-established Libyan precursors) and caused catastrophic regional destabilization (because, as appreciated in pre-2011 US diplomacy, Gaddafi played a key role in North Africa). These representations needed to be questioned critically: would rebel niceness have remained believable without Gaddafi's evil?

This case raises questions as to who participates in diplomatic knowledge production and the extent to which policy depends upon their work. For example, the sources behind the flow of information, intelligence and analysis provided by Blumenthal remain obscure. This method substantiates concerns that much of the information Blumenthal forwarded to Clinton came from private firms, not to mention the supplies of intelligence and advice provided by Tony Blair so Clinton could do the 'Lord's Work'.[82] In 2011 the State Department did not have a Libya desk officer and the Near Eastern Maghreb Bureau only counted two staffers, limiting capacity to assess the validity of this stream of intelligence and analysis. This method's close reading approach furthermore shows that it would have been difficult for Clinton and other policymakers to distinguish between government-produced reports and others since Blumenthal did not respect reporting conventions.

For interpretive analyses of international relations this method lays bare how diplomacy transmits and constructs representations, contributing to and substantiating research on the international role of discourses of violence. Studying the applications of power that govern representations as they evolve reveals the effects of institutional hierarchy and power relations explored by the Practice Turn, particularly the dynamics of 'the bureaucratic mode of knowledge production' explored by Neumann.[83] The power of the representations studied here substantiates their role in constituting the subjects of securitization. By tracing how actors see the world, this method contributes to the study of phenomena like stigmatization that depend on shared representation of a transgressor.[84]

Beyond post-structuralist concerns, this contribution addresses one of the oldest questions of diplomacy and international politics: how international actors see one another. Its analytical yield is widely applicable, for instance to international history approaches focusing on practice and institutional relations,[85] and raises questions in novel fields of diplomatic research. For example, the above-analysed interventions by Anne-Marie Slaughter raise questions about the role of emotion in the normatively committed attachment felt by the Obama administration to the Libyan rebel cause.[86] This method's focus on large volumes of diplomatic correspondence and its empirical focus allows for analytical claims relevant to scholars of other IR traditions, from Realists like Kissinger that saw diplomacy's power as embedded in its communicative functions, to English School theorists who would find substantiation of polysemy – conflicts over definition of an institution's norms – in this method's treatment of representations competing for supremacy.[87]

The core concern of the approach here expounded counts among the oldest questions of international relations. In the early 1500s Secretary of State Niccolò Machiavelli, in charge of Florentine foreign affairs, wrote to their ambassador in Spain demanding that he write more accurate and helpful descriptions. Poor reporting, he complained, made for poor policy at a time when he needed to understand what Spain wanted.[88] He was right: application of this method to study diplomatic intercourse conceptually reiterates and empirically substantiates the power of representations in diplomacy. For the contemporary theorist, analyst and student of diplomacy, it brings representation and knowledge production to the forefront of understanding diplomacy. Such is the power of knowing who we and the other are and the role of diplomacy in producing this knowledge.

Notes

1. See, for instance, the classics Ernest Mason Satow, *A Guide to Diplomatic Practice* (Neully Sur Seine: Ulan Press, 1917); Harold George Nicolson, *Diplomacy*, Institute for the Study of Diplomacy Ed. (Georgetown University Press, 1998); Adam Watson, *Diplomacy: The Dialogue between States* (London: Routledge, 1984).
2. See previous applications of this method in Pablo de Orellana, 'Struggles over Identity in Diplomacy: "Commie Terrorists" Contra "Imperialists" in Western Sahara', *International Relations* 29, no. 4 (1 December 2015): 477–99; 'When Diplomacy Identifies Terrorists: Subjects, Identity and Agency in the War on Terror in Mali', in *The Palgrave Handbook of Global Counterterrorism Policy*, ed. Scott Romaniuk, Francis Grice, and Stewart Webb (London: Palgrave Macmillan, 2016); '"You Can Count on Us": When Malian Diplomacy Stratcommed Uncle Sam and the Role of Identity in Communication', *Defence Strategic Communications* 3, no. 1 (November 2017): 99–170; *The Road to Vietnam* (I.B. Tauris, 2020).
3. See Machiavelli's memoranda to his ambassadors ('notule') in Niccolò Machiavelli, *Le opere di Niccolò Machiavelli* (Rome: Tipografia Cenniniana, 1877); Bruno Figliuolo and Francesco Senatore, 'Per un ritratto del buon ambasciatore: regole di comportamento e profilo dell'inviato negli scritti di Diomede Carafa, Niccolò Machiavelli e Francesco Guicciardini1', in *De l'ambassadeur : Les écrits relatifs à l'ambassadeur et à l'art de négocier du Moyen Âge au début du xixe siècle*, ed. Stefano Andretta, Stéphane Péquignot, and Jean-Claude Waquet, Collection de l'École française de Rome (Rome: Publications de l'École française de Rome, 2016); François de Callières, *De la manière de négocier avec les souverains* (Paris: Michel Brunet, 1716); Francesco Guicciardini, *Ricordi* (Scotts Valley: CreateSpace Independent Publishing Platform, 2012); Giovanni Botero, *Relations of the Most Famous Kingdoms and Common-Weales thorough the World* (London: Iohn Iaggard, 1611).
4. Machiavelli, *Le opere di Niccolò Machiavelli*, 378.
5. H. Kissinger, *Diplomacy* (New York: Simon and Schuster, 1994); H. J. Morgenthau, *Politics among Nations: The Struggle for Power and Peace* (New York: Knopf, 1966); S. M. Walt, *The Origins of Alliances* (Ithaca, NY: Cornell University Press, 1987); S. M. Walt, 'Testing Theories of Alliance Formation: The Case of Southwest Asia', *International Organization*, 1988, 275–316; S. M. Walt, 'Why Alliances Endure or Collapse', *Survival* 39, no. 1 (1997): 156–79.
6. I. B. Neumann, 'Returning Practice to the Linguistic Turn: The Case of Diplomacy', *Millennium: Journal of International Studies* 31, no. 3 (2002): 627; *Diplomatic Sites:*

A Critical Enquiry, 2013; 'The English School on Diplomacy: Scholarly Promise Unfulfilled', International Relations 17, no. 3 (9 January 2003): 341–69; '"A Speech That the Entire Ministry May Stand for," or: Why Diplomats Never Produce Anything New', International Political Sociology 1, no. 2 (1 June 2007): 183–200.
7   See the seminal M. J. Shapiro, The Politics of Representation: Writing Practices in Biography, Photography, and Policy Analysis (Madison, WI: University of Wisconsin Press Madison, 1988).
8   William E. Connolly, Identity\Difference: Democratic Negotiations of Political Paradox (Minneapolis: University of Minnesota Press, 2002).
9   David Campbell, Writing Security: United States Foreign Policy and the Politics of Identity, 2nd revised edition 1998 (Manchester: Manchester University Press, 1992).
10 William E. Connolly, 'Identity and Difference in Global Politics', in International/Intertextual Relations (Lexington, MA: Lexington Books, 1989).
11 Vivienne Jabri, Discourses on Violence: Conflict Analysis Reconsidered (Manchester: Manchester University Press, 1996), 131.
12 V. Jabri, 'Cosmopolitan Politics, Security, Political Subjectivity', European Journal of International Relations, no. 18 (2011); V. Jabri, 'War, Security and the Liberal State', Security Dialogue 37, no. 1 (2006): 47; Michael C. Williams, 'Words, Images, Enemies: Securitization and International Politics', International Studies Quarterly 47, no. 4 (2003): 511–31; Michael C. Williams and Iver B. Neumann, 'From Alliance to Security Community: NATO, Russia, and the Power of Identity', Millennium – Journal of International Studies 29, no. 2 (6 January 2000): 357–87; Iver B. Neumann, Russia and the Idea of Europe: A Study in Identity and International Relations (London: Routledge, 1996); Barry Buzan, Ole Wæver, and Jaap De Wilde, Security: A New Framework for Analysis (Boulder, CO: Lynne Rienner Publishers, 1998); L. Hansen and O. Waever, European Integration and National Identity: The Challenge of the Nordic States (London: Routledge 2002); Pinar Bilgin, Regional Security in the Middle East: A Critical Perspective Vol. 18, No. 4 (London: Routledge, 2004).
13 J. Der Derian, Antidiplomacy: Spies, Terror, Speed, and War (Cambridge, MA: Blackwell, 1992); J. Der Derian, On Diplomacy: A Genealogy of Western Estrangement (Oxford: Oxford University Press, 1987).
14 C. M. Constantinou, On the Way to Diplomacy (Minneapolis: University of Minnesota Press, 1996); C. M. Constantinou, O. P. Richmond, and A. Watson, Cultures and Politics of Global Communication: Volume 34, Review of International Studies (Cambridge: Cambridge University Press, 2008); Costas M. Constantinou, Pauline Kerr, and Paul Sharp, The SAGE Handbook of Diplomacy, 1st edition (Los Angeles: Sage, 2016).
15 M. J. Shapiro, 'Textualising Global Politics', in International/Intertextual Relations, ed. James Der Derian and M. J. Shapiro (Lexington, MA: Lexington Books, 1989).
16 See the extensive discussion in L. Hansen, Security as Practice: Discourse Analysis and the Bosnian War (London: Routledge, 2006), 18–54.

17 Jason Dittmer, *Diplomatic Material: Affect, Assemblage, and Foreign Policy* (Durham: Duke University Press Books, 2017); Tobias Wille, 'Diplomatic Cable', in *Making Things International 2*, ed. Mark B. Salter (Minneapolis: Minnesota University Press, 2016); Tobias Wille, 'Representation and Agency in Diplomacy: How Kosovo Came to Agree to the Rambouillet Accords', *Journal of International Relations and Development* 22, no. 4 (1 December 2019): 808–31; Iver B. Neumann, *At Home with the Diplomats: Inside a European Foreign Ministry* (Ithaca, NY: Cornell University Press, 2012); Vincent Pouliot, *International Pecking Orders: The Politics and Practice of Multilateral Diplomacy* (Cambridge: Cambridge University Press, 2016).

18 Rebecca Adler-Nissen and Vincent Pouliot, 'Power in Practice: Negotiating the International Intervention in Libya', *European Journal of International Relations* 20, no. 4 (1 December 2014): 889–911; Emanuel Adler and Vincent Pouliot, eds., *International Practices* (Cambridge: Cambridge University Press, 2011); Neumann, *Diplomatic Sites*; Cynthia Enloe, *Bananas, Beaches and Bases: Making Feminist Sense of International Politics* (New York: University of California Press, 2014); Iver B. Neumann, 'The Body of the Diplomat', *European Journal of International Relations* 14, no. 4 (12 January 2008): 671–95.

19 For a more extensive theoretical discussion on the unique importance of text in diplomacy see Pablo de Orellana, 'Retrieving How Diplomacy Writes Subjects, Space and Time: A Methodological Contribution', *European Journal of International Relations* 26, no. 2 (1 June 2020): 469–94.

20 Jabri, *Discourses on Violence*, 131.

21 Neumann, 'Returning Practice to the Linguistic Turn'.

22 Constantinou, *On the Way to Diplomacy*, 31.

23 WikiLeaks US Embassy Cables, cited by date, sender/recipient and original State Department reference (for example: 25/8/09 State to Tripoli, 09STATE88783). These can be searched, using provided references, at the searchable database available at https://search.wikileaks.org/plusd/ (accessed May 2020).

24 Hilary Clinton Email Archive, email threads cited by date and subject where available (1/4/11 Memo to State: Info on Libya and AQ) or date author/recipient (27/7/10 Clinton to JJ Sullivan). These can be searched at https://wikileaks.org/clinton-emails/ (accessed May 2020) and https://foia.state.gov/Search/Results.aspx?collection=Clinton_Email (accessed May 2020).

25 French Presidency documents, speeches, press releases and communiques: https://bnf.libguides.com/c.php?g=659907&p=4659910 and https://www.elysee.fr/toutes-les-actualites?categories%5B%5D=communique-de-presse (accessed May 2020); US Presidential speeches, press releases and statements: https://obamawhitehouse.archives.gov/briefing-room/statements-and-releases; British Government and Ministerial statements: https://www.gov.uk/search/news-and-communications and https://www.gov.uk/government/people/david-cameron (accessed May 2020). Note

on spelling conventions: unless spelled otherwise in citations, معمر القذافي is Latinized as Muammar Gaddafi. For this notorious spelling controversy see 'Rebel Discovers Qaddafi Passport, Real Spelling of Leader's Name – The Atlantic', https://www.theatlantic.com/international/archive/2011/08/rebel-discovers-qaddafi-passport-real-spelling-of-leaders-name/244077/ (accessed 13 May 2020).

26 Michel Foucault, 'The Order of Discourse', in *Language and Politics*, ed. Michael Shapiro (Oxford: Blackwell, 1984); Michel Foucault, *The Archaeology of Knowledge* (London: Tavistock Publications, 1972).
27 Roland Barthes, *Image Music Text*, new edition. (London: Fontana Press, 1977); Roland Barthes, *S/Z* (Oxford: Blackwell, 1990).
28 Topoi (τοποι) are the 'seats of arguments', referents that act as markers for arguments or issues at a textual or oratorical level – shorthands for arguments. Marcus Tullius Cicero, *De Inventione; De Optimo Genere Oratorum* (Cambridge, MA: Loeb, 1989); Marcus Fabius Quintilianus, *M. Fabi Quintiliani institutionis oratoriae liber decimus*, ed. William Peterson, 2007, http://www.gutenberg.org/ebooks/21827; Sara Rubinelli, *Ars Topica: The Classical Technique of Constructing Arguments from Aristotle to Cicero* (Berlin: Springer Science & Business Media, 2009); Ernst Robert Curtius, *European Literature and the Latin Middle Ages* (Princeton: Princeton University Press, 1953).
29 This is executed on a huge scale (enabled by historical full archival declassification) in my book *The Road to Vietnam*.
30 Adler-Nissen and Pouliot, 'Power in Practice'.
31 'Prime Minister David Cameron's Statement on Libya', *BBC News*, 2011, http://www.bbc.com/news/av/uk-12786786/prime-minister-david-cameron-s-statement-on-libya; Brian Wheeler, 'David Cameron Defends Libya Decisions', *BBC News*, 15 January 2016. UK Politics, http://www.bbc.com/news/uk-politics-35300667; 'David Cameron Meets Libya Rebel Leader at Number 10', *BBC News*, 2011, http://www.bbc.com/news/av/uk-politics-13374560/david-cameron-meets-libya-rebel-leader-at-number-10.
32 25/8/09 State to Tripoli, 09STATE88783.
33 19/8/2009 Tripoli to State, 09TRIPOLI677.
34 1/4/11 Memo to State: Info on Libya and AQ, links to Iraq Islamic insurgency.
35 27/3/11 Blumenthal to Clinton.
36 22/12/09 Tripoli to State 09TRIPOLI1030.
37 30/3/11 Blumenthal to Clinton.
38 27/3/11 Blumenthal to Clinton; see also 'Sic Semper Tyrannis', Sic Semper Tyrannis, at https://turcopolier.typepad.com/sic_semper_tyrannis/ (accessed 20 February 2020).
39 10/3/11 Blumenthal to Clinton.
40 27/3/11 Blumenthal to Clinton; 25/3/11 Blumenthal to Clinton.

41 This is most evident in her correspondence with advisors such as Deputy Chief of Staff Huma Abedin. See, for example, 21/3/11 Clinton & Abedin email thread.
42 3/3/11 Blumenthal to Clinton.
43 28/2/11 Blumenthal to H 'up to minute detailed state of play politically and militarily'.
44 27/2/11 State Department briefings for Clinton.
45 24/3/11 Slaughter to Clinton.
46 19/3/11 Blumenthal to Clinton; 18/3/11 Blumenthal and Clinton exchange; 13/3/11 Blumenthal to Clinton.
47 21/2/11, JJ Sullivan and Jeff Feltman exchange.
48 16/3/11 Blumenthal to Clinton; 27/2/11 Blumenthal to Clinton; 24/2/11 Blumenthal to Clinton.
49 7–6/3/11 Shearer to Clinton via Blumenthal.
50 23/3/11 Jack Keane to Clinton via Blumenthal.
51 23/2/11 Blumenthal to Clinton.
52 1/3/11 Blumenthal to H to Sullivan.
53 25/2/11 Blumenthal to Clinton; 6/3/11 Blumenthal to Clinton; 21/2/11 Blumenthal to Clinton.
54 20/3/11 Blumenthal to Clinton; 26/2/11 William J Burns to Clinton.
55 20/3/11 Blumenthal to Clinton; 18/3/11 Blumenthal to Clinton. Sarkozy is currently on trial for this, see 'Financement libyen de la campagne de 2007 : Nicolas Sarkozy est mis en examen', *Le Monde.fr*, 21 March 2018, https://www.lemonde.fr/politique/article/2018/03/21/financement-libyen-de-la-campagne-de-2007-fin-de-la-garde-a-vue-de-nicolas-sarkozy_5274484_823448.html; Kim Willsher, 'Gaddafi "Gave Nicolas Sarkozy €50m for 2007 Presidential Campaign,"' *The Guardian*, 15 November 2016, sec. World news, https://www.theguardian.com/world/2016/nov/15/muammar-gaddafi-allegedly-gave-nicolas-sarkozy-50m-euros-2007-presidential-campaign.
56 27/3/11 Blumenthal to Clinton.
57 19/3/11 Slaughter to Clinton via Abedin.
58 17/3/11 Memorandum to Clinton.
59 22/3/11 Cody Shearer to Clinton via Blumenthal.
60 7–6/3/11 Shearer to Clinton via Blumenthal.
61 [underlined in the original] 24/2/11 from Tony Blair to Clinton.
62 'Samantha Power Brought Activism Inside to Sway Obama on Libya', *Bloomberg. Com*, 25 March 2011, https://www.bloomberg.com/news/articles/2011-03-25/samantha-power-brought-activist-role-inside-to-help-sway-obama-on-libya.
63 21/2/11 Samantha Power to State.
64 18/6/09 Libya to State 09TRIPOLI492.
65 20/2/09 State to Tripoli, 09STATE16169.
66 17/7/09 State to Tripoli 09STATE74778; 9/11/09 State to Tripoli 09STATE115619.

67 19/8/2010, Clinton and JJ Sullivan on Megrahi, 27/7/10 huge discussion with officials; 27/8/09 Tripoli to State, 09TRIPOLI695; 25/8/09 Tripoli to State, 09TRIPOLI689; 25/8/09 State to Tripoli, 09STATE88783; 21/8/09 Tripoli to State 09TRIPOLI685; 20/8/09 Tripoli to State 09TRIPOLI683.
68 17/4/09, State to Tripoli, 09STATE38608.
69 25/5/09, Tripoli to State 09TRIPOLI415; 18/5/09 Tripoli to State and AFRICOM 09TRIPOLI401; 6/5/09 Tripoli to State 09TRIPOLI371.
70 10/8/09 Tripoli to State 09TRIPOLI648; 11/4/09 State to Tripoli and all NA missions, 09STATTE35882.
71 11/2/09, Tripoli to State, 09TRIPOLI134; 3/2/09, State to Tripoli, 09STATE9857; 4/1/2010 State to Tripoli, 10STATE284.
72 17/3/09 State to Tripoli, 09STATE25557.
73 10/8/09 Tripoli to State 09TRIPOLI648; 13/7/09 Libya to State 09TRIPOLI564; 6/7/09 Libya to State 09TRIPOLI535.
74 11/5/09 Tripoli to State 09TRIPOLI386; 26/1/10, Tripoli to State, 10TRIPOLI74.
75 14/9/09 Tripoli to State, 09TRIPOLI739.
76 20/8/2009 Tripoli to State and CIA 09TRIPOLI678.
77 20/12/09 Tripoli to State 09TRIPOLI1021; 12/8/09 Tripoli to State and NSCouncil 09TRIPOLI657; 27/7/09 Tripoli to State and AFRICOM 09TRIPOLI599.
78 10/8/09 Tripoli to State 09TRIPOLI648; 20/7/09 Libya to State and USmissionUN 09TRIPOLI583; 26/5/09, Tripoli to State 09TRIPOLI417; 21/7/09 Tripoli to State and CIA.
79 'Libya: Col Gaddafi's Letter to Barack Obama in Full', 6 April 2011, sec. World, https://www.telegraph.co.uk/news/worldnews/africaandindianocean/libya/8433367/Libya-Col-Gaddafis-letter-to-Barack-Obama-in-full.html.
80 See Connolly, *Identity, Difference*.
81 See 12–15/12/2012 Blumenthal-Clinton thread.
82 Jeff Gerth, 'Private Emails Reveal Ex-Clinton Aide's Secret Spy Network', text/html, ProPublica, 27 March 2015, https://www.propublica.org/article/private-emails-reveal-ex-clinton-aides-secret-spy-network.
83 Neumann, 'A Speech That the Entire Ministry May Stand For'.
84 Rebecca Adler-Nissen, 'Stigma Management in International Relations: Transgressive Identities, Norms, and Order in International Society', *International Organization* 68, no. 1 (January 2014): 143–76.
85 Th W. Bottelier, '"Not on a Purely Nationalistic Basis": The Internationalism of Allied Coalition Warfare in the Second World War', *European Review of History: Revue Européenne d'histoire* 27, no. 1–2 (3 March 2020): 152–75, https://doi.org/10.1080/13507486.2019.1705251.
86 Barbara Keys and Claire Yorke, 'Personal and Political Emotions in the Mind of the Diplomat', *Political Psychology* 40, no. 6 (2019): 1235–49.

87 Filippo Costa-Buranelli, '"Do You Know What I Mean?" "Not Exactly": English School, Global International Society and the Polysemy of Institutions', *Global Discourse* 5, no. 3 (3 July 2015): 499–514.
88 Machiavelli, *Le opere di Niccolò Machiavelli*.

5

The Beijing and Moscow 1972 summits: Strengths and limits of two iconic diplomatic breakthroughs

Dr Barbara Zanchetta

Summits as potential diplomatic transformations?

The word 'summit' was first coined by Winston Churchill. During the dark days of the Cold War, speaking in Edinburgh in February 1950, he called for 'another talk with the Soviet Union at the highest level', adding that he could not see how 'matters could be worsened by a parley at the summit'. He again called for 'a conference on the highest level' in May 1953, appealing for peace 'at the summit of nations'. As pointed out by David Reynolds, it is interesting to note that Churchill chose to apply the term 'summit' to diplomacy just as the expression was dominating British newspapers, since expeditions to Mount Everest, the world's highest peak, had resumed in the late 1940s. The metaphor was thus powerful, suggesting dangerous and risky endeavours. The choice of the word 'parley' was equally significant. An archaic word, much used by Shakespeare, it evoked a hazardous encounter between enemies in order to broker terms. At its origin, therefore, Churchill's reference to a 'diplomatic parley at the summit' was associated with an adventurous, risky and perilous encounter between adversaries.[1] Yet, as summits multiplied in later decades and took on different forms and modalities, becoming a permanent characteristic of diplomacy, the adversarial component has been progressively lost. Contemporary studies on

---

This chapter is based on primary documents from the Nixon administration consulted at the US National Archives and draws from portions of my book *The Transformation of American International Power in the 1970s* (New York: Cambridge University Press, 2014), Chapters 2 and 3. It is also based on extensive discussions with my students on the impact of these summits in my class *Diplomacy and Foreign Policy Crises*, which I have been teaching at KCL since 2016.

summits and summit diplomacy, in fact, have moved away from the association with an adversarial relationship, and have instead focused on summits as an ordinary practice of diplomacy.[2] Summits between allies, for example, as the publicized meetings between Tony Blair and George W. Bush in the lead-up to the Iraq War of 2003, or multilateral summits, such as the G7/8, are, obviously, diplomacy at the highest level and are thus considered summits. But the stakes in these cases are relatively low, as the amicable relationship between participants is *not* in question. These meetings are more of a forum for discussion and exchange of – however important – views, rather than authentic negotiations. In contrast, in summits between adversaries, such as the meeting between John F. Kennedy and Nikita Khrushchev in Vienna in 1961, or between Anwar Sadat and Menachem Begin in 1978, the stakes were much higher. The issues on the table required more than discussion; they were the subject of often painful negotiation, in search of difficult compromises. Sometimes, as in the case of Vienna, the compromises were not found, and the summit resulted in failure to deliver any breakthrough. While acknowledging the existence of other types of summits, this chapter will focus on summits between adversaries and thus return to the 'original' notion coined by Winston Churchill in the 1950s.

Generally, the term 'summit' accurately applies only to meetings between incumbent heads of government or state, or political leaders and the highest representative of an international organization.[3] A summit also requires agreement on the time and location of the meeting. In summits between allies, this is most often uncontroversial, but in meetings between adversaries, particularly during the Cold War, even the agreement on a location could be a matter of contention. For example, in the midst of the crisis of US-Soviet détente, Leonid Brezhnev and Jimmy Carter decided to meet in Vienna to sign the Strategic Arms Limitation Talks (SALT) II, and Reagan and Gorbachev chose neutral Geneva, almost equidistant from their respective capitals, for their first tentative summit in 1985. While the definitions of summitry are limited to the time that the leaders actually spend together, it is important to underline that summits – as the emblematic case of the Reagan–Gorbachev summits show – are not isolated events. As Hans Morgenthau pointed out, 'As instruments for the negotiated settlement of outstanding issues, summit meetings are a supplement to ordinary diplomatic procedures … they follow ordinary diplomatic negotiations as they are followed by them, each laying the groundwork for the other.'[4] As will emerge in the case of the opening to China, at times the process is not 'ordinary' in the sense outlined above, but the significance of the process and of the preparatory work is crucial notwithstanding.

Moreover, the broader context in which summit meetings take place is essential to understanding the meaning and impact of the negotiations. In the cases analysed in this chapter, the broader context of the Cold War had created a profoundly adversarial relationship between both the United States and China, and the United States and the Soviet Union. In the early 1970s, détente gradually mitigated such antagonism, but in radically different ways. While as a consequence of the 1972 summit, China slowly but inexorably moved into a tacit alliance with the United States, the renewed relationship with the Soviet Union only lasted a few years, soon replummeting into hostility in the early 1980s. If diplomacy, as has been widely recognized, has the capacity to mitigate conflicts between adversaries,[5] why did it yield such different results in these two cases? In other words, what role did the specific summits of 1972 – and the processes behind them – have in triggering, or not, a long-term positive shift in the bilateral relationship?

Less scholarly attention has, in fact, has been dedicated to the specific role of summit diplomacy in diffusing conflict and, going a step further, in potentially ameliorating an adversarial relationship. In short, do summits have the potential to *transform* an adversarial relationship? Interestingly, Nicholas J. Wheeler provides the link between the general practice of diplomacy and summits through the concept of trust. The precondition, he writes, for the growth of trust at 'the highest level of diplomacy' is a capacity to understand and empathize with the other sides' security fears or, as he puts it, their ability to develop 'security dilemma sensitivity'. If this occurs, meetings at the highest levels between policymakers, what Martin Wight called 'moments of maximum communication,' may have the potential to transform conflicts because they can become venues for the establishment of trust between key actors. While obviously the leaders alone cannot transform the entire relationship, according to Wheeler, summits can trigger broader processes of diplomatic transformation if and when the following indicators are present: the key decision makers no longer impute malevolent motives and intentions to each other; both recognize the role that past actions have played in making the other side insecure; cooperative moves that promote reassurance are reciprocal.[6]

This chapter will seek to validate Wheeler's claim and establish whether summits are, indeed, able to build trust and thus transform adversarial relationships. It will analyse two iconic Cold War summits that took place in 1972: the Beijing summit, the final act of the American opening to the People's Republic of China, and the climax of what US President Richard Nixon labelled 'the week that changed the world'; and the Moscow summit, during which the first nuclear arms control agreement between the United States and the Soviet Union was signed, thus representing the generally recognized high point of US-Soviet détente.

The first section will outline the motivations of the US opening to China, and assess the secret negotiations conducted by National Security Adviser Henry Kissinger in 1971 and the actual summit meeting, which took place in February 1972. It will then evaluate the results of the summit in the longer term. The second part will outline the motivations behind the first meeting between President Richard Nixon and Soviet leader Leonid Brezhnev in May 1972, with particular emphasis posed on the negotiations that led to the signing of the Strategic Arms Limitation Treaties. It will also assess the importance of the summit for the evolution of the Cold War. The final section will compare the two summits, the processes behind them and their results in order to ascertain whether these summits may be considered 'transformative' on the basis of Wheeler's indicators outlined above. While acknowledging that summitry plays a broader role in international relations – with a wide range of summits and of multilateral fora – the scope of this chapter is to analyse the particular role of summitry in the context of adversarial relationships. Specifically, it will assess the importance of summits, rather than of diplomacy in general, in mitigating conflict and in transforming a relationship from adversarial to amicable.

From a 'flight of fancy' to the 'week that changed the world': the Beijing summit of 1972

The creation of the People's Republic of China in October 1949 'sent tremors throughout the American political landscape'.[7] The transformation of the most populous Asian country into a communist state had caused a huge psychological shock for the United States. This was further aggravated the following year, with the support lent by the newly born Republic to North Korea during the Korean War. The perception in Washington was one of a huge Communist monolith, as the Soviet Union and China aligned against the West. Originally rooted in the division of Europe, the Cold War dramatically spread to the Asian continent. China thus openly became, together with the Soviet Union, the enemy to confront. Consequently, and for the next two decades, the United States refused to grant legitimacy to the People's Republic. American policy aimed at isolating Beijing through the stubborn recognition of Chiang Kai-shek's regime, exiled in Taiwan, as the sole government of China.[8]

Until the late 1960s, this was the policy endorsed by Richard Nixon, a staunch anticommunist, who, as Vice President under Eisenhower, had supported the US involvement in Vietnam against the communist influence. Nixon had also been a member and promoter of the so-called China lobby, which advocated a return of the nationalist government of Taiwan to mainland China. Yet, in 1972 President Nixon became the first US president to visit Communist China and to meet with Chairman Mao. How did this personal and, most significantly, diplomatic turnabout occur?

Early in the Nixon administration, China had not been a priority. The Vietnam War had dominated the American foreign policy agenda for more than a decade. It had triggered profound domestic opposition to US foreign policy choices, deeply dividing both the American political landscape and the civil society. Vietnam, therefore, remained the central preoccupation for the incoming president in 1968. The theoretical importance of an opening to China was acknowledged in Washington – already in 1967 Nixon had written: 'Taking the long view, we simply cannot afford to leave China forever outside the family of nations ... There is no place on this small planet for a billion of its potentially most able people to live in angry isolation.' But, in practice, reconciliation did not seem possible.[9] Decades of enmity, and of complete absence of relations, together with the staunch opposition to any opening from the right wing of the Republican Party that remained loyal and committed to recognizing Taiwan as the legitimate Chinese government, made a breakthrough seem pure fantasy. Despite this, in early February 1969, Nixon asked his National Security Advisor Henry Kissinger to explore the possibility of an opening and, consequently, an internal review of US-China policy was initiated.[10] But Kissinger was far from enthusiastic. In fact, he told his top aide Colonel (and later General) Alexander Haig that the president had just ordered him to 'make this flight of fancy come true'.[11]

Events well beyond US control made it possible to transform Nixon's abstract intuition into concrete policy. The military clashes between China and the Soviet Union along the Ussuri river border, and the consequent realization of a definitive breach between the two Communist giants, opened new prospects and possibilities for American policy. The US leadership became convinced that the Soviet Union was the more aggressive actor in the context of the Sino-Soviet rivalry. When assessing the potential ramifications of the clashes, Nixon declared that he would never tolerate a Soviet attack on China. Therefore, as Kissinger put it: the United States 'had a strategic interest in the survival of a major communist country, long an enemy, and with which we had no contact'.[12]

As threat perceptions were shifting in Washington, the same occurred in Beijing. Chinese Chairman Mao had become convinced that Soviet power was growing and that it would be inevitable that sooner or later the Soviet Union would attack China. After 1969, Mao's entire foreign policy would be based on this premise and, consequently, on the need to engage in an alliance with the United States against the rise of Soviet power.[13] As he reportedly told his doctor in 1969, 'didn't our ancestors counsel negotiating with faraway countries while fighting those that are near?'[14]

In other words, Beijing and Washington had a major incentive for rapprochement even before having established any form of contact; they needed only to find a pursuable line of action, a task which evolved with surprising rapidity. To start the process, President Nixon signalled the intention to shift course on China by initiating a secret channel of communication through Pakistan and by reactivating the only remaining thin line of communication between Washington and Beijing via the diplomatic meetings in Warsaw (that existed since the Korean War for the purpose of exchanging information on prisoners of war). While the two sides initiated a secret dialogue for the first time since the 1950s, the world became aware that something was, indeed, changing with the so-called 'Ping Pong diplomacy'. During the table tennis World Championship held in Japan in late March 1971 the Chinese (considered the best team worldwide) and American players exchanged friendly gestures and gifts (reportedly a scarf and a T-shirt). A few days later, the Chinese team invited – an order issued by Mao himself – the American team to visit Beijing, and was received by Premier Zhou Enlai.[15] The White House reciprocated and instructed the American team to invite the Chinese team to the United States. Only hours after the players' meeting with Zhou, the White House lifted the trade embargo against China that had lasted for twenty-two years.[16]

Ping pong diplomacy captured world attention and, on the wave of this enthusiasm, the secret communications via Pakistan accelerated. Between April and May 1971, an agreement was reached for Kissinger's secret visit to China, which took place in July 1971. During these meetings Kissinger was able to ascertain that, indeed, a rapprochement between the United States and China was considered an utmost priority also in Beijing. The problematic issue of Taiwan – i.e. that the United States formally still supported the exiled government of Chiang Kai Shek and did not recognize the People's Republic of China – could be momentarily set aside in order for the opening to take place. Moreover, the support for opposite factions in the Vietnam War, which had been considered a second unsurmountable obstacle in relations, was sidelined. In fact, and this is the crucial point, during his secret trip Kissinger was able to verify that the potent force behind the realignment was the common objective of containing potential Soviet expansionism.

During the high-level conversations of July 1971, the Soviet Union was the central topic of conversation. For example, Zhou underlined the fear of a Soviet invasion of Chinese territory, given the aggressiveness demonstrated by Moscow in the border clashes, and claimed that the construction of shelters for the protection of the population against aerial bombings had already begun.[17] On the American side, Kissinger repeatedly reassured Zhou on Washington's readiness to support China in its dispute with the Soviet Union. Referring to the long-term Soviet goal of creating cooperation between states targeted against China, the United States, stated Kissinger, not only would never share such objectives, but would also try to dissuade any other country from pursuing them. Kissinger went as far as declaring openly that President Nixon did not consider the People's Republic a threat to American security. In order to build trust, Kissinger added that the United States was prepared to discuss any initiative that might affect China's interests. In particular, he was authorized to reveal the essence of the agreements being negotiated with China's 'neighbors' – a clear reference to the talks with the Soviet Union.[18] The following day, Kissinger directly mentioned the Soviet Union and the ongoing Strategic Arms Limitation Talks.[19]

Overall, therefore, the discussions on the Soviet Union were extremely significant. On the one hand, Zhou explicitly described the Chinese fears and concerns regarding a Soviet attack. On the other, Kissinger repeatedly underlined the US willingness to support China's integrity and respect its interests. In this way, both sides clearly identified the common perception of the Soviet threat as the main driving force of the Sino-American rapprochement.

These indications were confirmed at the February 1972 summit, during the conversations between Nixon and the Chinese leadership, and then further, with the inclusion of a particularly significant clause in the text of the Shanghai Communiqué. In his meeting with Chairman Mao, Nixon pointed to their parallel foreign policy interests and underlined that the United States and China did *not* threaten each other. Mao went a step further, specifying that China threatened neither Japan nor South Korea, thus offering an important reassurance to Washington's allies and an implicit guarantee of non-interference in America's defence of its commitments.[20] To Nixon's long analysis on which of the superpowers represented a major threat for China, Mao responded by underlining that no major issue divided the United States and the People's Republic: 'At the present time, the question of aggression from the United States or aggression from China is relatively small; that is, it could be said that this is not a major issue.'[21]

In general, therefore, the American long-term objective of redefining the global balance of power was shared by the Chinese[22] and inserted in the Shanghai Communiqué, issued at the end of 'the week that changed the world'.[23] Particularly significant was the pledge that 'neither side would seek hegemony in the Asia-Pacific region' and both 'opposed efforts by any other country or group of countries to establish such hegemony'.[24] With this commitment the United States and the People's Republic accepted to set limits to their actions in Asia and, most importantly, formally agreed to oppose any expansionist and hegemonic ambitions of other countries. The reference to Soviet foreign policy was indisputable. As Kissinger later stated, 'Alliances have been founded on far less ... the enemies of a little more than six months earlier were announcing their opposition to any further expansion of the Soviet sphere. It was a veritable diplomatic revolution.'[25]

The opening to China was a triumph for Nixon's and Kissinger's foreign policy. They had successfully taken advantage of the rupture within the communist camp and demonstrated that it was possible to create a tacit alliance with a country that had been a fierce adversary and that still proclaimed ideological enmity. For both sides, the realignment was crucial in order to balance and oppose the Soviet Union. There were little doubts, in fact, that the shared perception of the Soviet Union had been the main motivation for the rapprochement. This had shaped both the process that triggered the opening and the discussions at the summit itself. Their shared perception provided the basis for the building of trust between Beijing and Washington, and this element outweighed all other aspects of the relationship. Elements of animosity of course remained, but they were no longer assessed as important determinants in their newly forged relationship.

Détente with the Soviet Union: The Moscow summit of 1972

'After a period of confrontation, we are entering an era of negotiation. Let all nations know that during this administration our lines of communication will be open,' declared President Nixon during his Inaugural address of 1969. There is no doubt that by 1972 this call had translated into a spectacular realignment of policies towards the two largest Communist countries. Closely after the February summit in Beijing, Nixon in fact visited Moscow and held a summit with Soviet leader Leonid Brezhnev. Although, as will be outlined below, negotiations with the Soviets had been ongoing since 1969, the US opening to China had a huge impact on Moscow, triggering fears of isolation and betrayal, which led to questioning the whole basis of détente with the United States. Was Washington playing the Chinese against them, asked the Soviets? Despite assurances to the contrary, that was, in essence, precisely what the United States was doing. Although this ambiguity did not lead to an abrupt change of course with the Americans, as the Soviets remained committed to détente, it did provide a deep and constant source of suspicion and mistrust. Moreover, it provided a further motivation to want to conclude the negotiations on arms control, considered by Moscow (and by the United States) as the cornerstone of détente.

Immediately after entering the White House in 1969, Nixon had intensified the dialogue with the Soviets, with the creation of the so-called backchannel of negotiations between Kissinger and Soviet Ambassador Anatoly Dobrynin. While these encompassed other crucial aspects of the superpower relationship (such as trade and the Berlin Agreements), it is undeniable that the SALT talks were perceived as the utmost priority.

Following the Cuban missile crisis of 1962, both Washington and Moscow had adjusted their nuclear arsenals. From the standpoint of a widespread perception strength, the United States had focused on maintaining its 'second strike capability', concentrating on the development of very precise silos-based intercontinental ballistic missiles (ICBMs) and of ballistic missiles to be placed on nuclear submarines (submarine-launched ballistic missiles – SLBMs). In the mid-1960s, when a number of nuclear systems deemed able of guaranteeing such a capability had been achieved, the missile production was halted, and only their progressive technological modernization continued.[26] The Soviet Union, instead, reacted to the Cuban humiliation by initiating a program of quantitative growth of its strategic weapons, directing its efforts on the production of land-based, heavy (i.e. with significant throw-weight and payload) ICBMs.[27]

It is important to underline that the United States had established maximum ceilings of missile production when its strategic forces were conspicuously superior to those of the Soviet Union and did *not* modify those ceilings, even when it became evident that Moscow had engaged in a significant build-up. Moreover, the Soviets did not appear to halt their missile production, the approaching of numerical parity with the US notwithstanding. Consequently, by the second half of the 1960s, the Soviet programs started to be a serious preoccupation in Washington. The CIA assessed the Soviet build-up as 'being aimed at narrowing the lead that the US has had' in strategic attack forces, mainly through an 'extensive intercontinental ballistic missile (ICBM) deployment'.[28]

The report then projected the Soviet missile development on a ten-year period (thus well into the 1970s). Although the document considered all types of Soviet strategic systems, the most alarming data referred to the numerical increase of ICBMs. The Soviet Union was expected to be able to field between 1,000 and 1,500 ICBMs by the mid-1970s if, at the same time, it tested the Multiple Independently targeted Re-entry Vehicles (MIRVs) technology. Without this innovation (which the Soviets had not yet experimented), it was likely that the Soviets would exceed 1,500 ICBMs and, by 1977, have more than 1,700 missiles. A force of about 1,100 ICBMs could only result from a Soviet deliberate decision to maintain a level more or less equal to that of the United States.[29] This was the preoccupying situation inherited by Nixon when he entered the White House, which led to the decision to initiate major negotiations with Moscow. The objective was to bring about a political decision in Moscow to halt missile production once parity with the United States had been achieved.

Though himself not a long-time advocate of arms control, these technical motivations were integral to President Nixon's support for SALT. Moreover, the particular domestic context which the administration inherited provided further incentives for the pursuit of a strategic dialogue with the Soviet Union. The public widespread criticism of the Vietnam War involved all aspects of American defence policy and pressures for the reorganization of national priorities translated into demands to reduce the defence budget. Therefore, Nixon faced domestic pressures for unilateral American constraint precisely at a time when the Soviet Union's nuclear force had reached unprecedented strength. Consequently, the dialogue with the Soviets seemed to be the only means to avoid the potential tilting of the strategic balance in favour of Moscow.

If in Washington the time had come to engage in arms limitation talks, their successful outcome was eventually possible only due to the parallel and converging motivations of the Soviet Union. While in the years preceding the Nixon presidency, Moscow had not responded to the reiterated American efforts to begin SALT, in 1969 the Soviet interest in the talks was explicit. Given the position of strength that the Soviets had acquired, the late 1960s seemed like the opportune moment for negotiations for Moscow. A SALT agreement represented the opportunity to finally codify the status of superpower and of strategic equality with the United States, a long-sought objective and an essential element of Soviet foreign policy.

In addition, Moscow had technical motivations. The traditional American lead in technological research and development cautioned the Kremlin against a future competition in anti-ballistic missile systems (this represented a significant change of stance since the Glassboro meeting of 1967 between President Johnson and Premier Kosygin, when the Soviet leader had rebuked the possibility to enter talks on defensive systems).[30] For the same reasons, the Soviets were aware of the need to monitor the MIRV development which, through the multiplication of the warheads, was eventually bound to deprive Moscow of the gains reached through the numerical increase of its missile force. Moreover, and most importantly, the Kremlin realized the necessity of curtailing the potentially destabilizing effect of the combination of the two innovations – a nationwide ABM system coupled with the large-scale deployment of MIRV missiles.[31]

The Soviet broader political objectives and the military-technical motivations were, at the same time, interrelated with the complex world scene of the late 1960s. The process of improved relations between the Soviet Union and Western Europe, especially with the Federal Republic of Germany, would become complicated with US opposition, and the American position (in the context of the Berlin Agreements) was in large part determined by the prospect of strategic arms control. Furthermore, Moscow had to face the deteriorating relationship with the People's Republic of China. The improvement of relations with the United States was thus in Moscow's broader interest and on that path SALT was the central building block.[32]

Therefore, by the late 1960s both superpowers considered the Strategic Arms Limitation Talks as a necessity, and a priority. This enabled the preliminary talks to start in Helsinki in late 1969. The Soviet and American delegations then continued to meet alternatively in Vienna and Helsinki, until the signing of the SALT I agreements at the Moscow summit in May 1972. While at the Moscow summit numerous other agreements were signed (mainly the Basic Principles of Relations between the United States and the USSR, which defined some rules of coexistence between the superpowers, and agreements on scientific cooperation and educational exchanges), and great emphasis was given to the shift from competition to cooperation in US-Soviet relations, the significance of the SALT agreements was, paradoxically, to maintain the Cold War strategic balance.

Since the launching of the nuclear arms race, the deterrent capacity of the superpowers' forces constituted the main feature of the bipolar rivalry, while the logic of mutual assured destruction (MAD) guaranteed strategic stability. However, given the pace of the strengthening and modernization of their arsenals, Washington and Moscow realized that the potential for tilting the equilibrium in favour of one or the other was potentially present – a development which, ultimately, neither considered desirable. Consequently, the SALT process was elaborated as a means to maintain and respect the Cold War equilibrium, or the so-called balance of terror.

A reading of the end results of the three-year SALT negotiations enables the affirmation that the sides, to a large extent, succeeded in their task. In fact, by signing the accords the superpowers recognized and accepted that neither could, nor would, strive for a 'first strike capability'.[33] At the same time, within the limits of the negotiated agreement, the ability to continue the strengthening of their respective forces was assured.

The SALT I package included the ABM Treaty and the Interim Agreement on offensive weapons. The ABM Treaty allowed for two ABM sites, for the defence of the capital and of one ICBM base. With the clear objective of preventing the systems from being expanded to cover the whole national territory, it offered a picture of quantitative and functional symmetry, leaving the credibility of MAD untouched. The Interim Agreement simply stated that the number of allowed ICBMs and SLBMs, for the five-year duration of the freeze, had to be equal to the number of those operational or in construction as of 26 May 1972 for the SLBMs, and as of 1 July 1972 for the ICBMs. The modernization and replacement of the missiles was openly permitted, with the only exception being the ban on further deployment of 'heavy' missiles. In terms of aggregates, the agreement favoured the Soviet Union,[34] but this was more than compensated for in other aspects of the accord. In fact, the extension of the freeze to the missiles in construction substantially limited the potential Soviet advantage, given the pace of the Soviet build-up.[35] And, most importantly, the agreement did not limit in any way the number of intercontinental bombers and of MIRVs, for which the United States clearly maintained superiority.[36]

Contrary to the criticism which gradually emerged around the Interim Agreement and the supposed advantages conceded to the Soviets, its most significant aspect was precisely the fact that it left the United States free to secure its advantage in MIRV development. As the Nixon administration was well aware, the agreement, although codifying a Soviet lead in the number of missiles, did not weaken the American strategic forces in any way. As an internal document assessed, 'We estimate that we will maintain our current substantial lead in strategic warheads for at least the next five years. This lead might even be increased. Since the number of targets we can attack is directly related to the number of warheads in our forces, warheads are a better measure of relative strategic strength than launchers.'[37] In short, Washington was convinced that the agreements protected American security, while leaving open the future possibility to strive for superiority.

However, the signing of the agreements was possible only because the compromise reached satisfied both sides. As Brezhnev put it, 'We are both fully aware, Mr. President, of the immense effort that was required in order to prepare these agreements. I am sure that we are both fully aware of how useful it has been from the standpoint of the direct national interests of our two states and in terms of their influence on the general international climate.'[38]

'Direct national interests' were therefore the key in a process geared towards maintaining strategic stability. Aside from the complexity of the language and the technicalities (throw-weight, payload, tactical and/or strategic), the SALT I agreements ultimately confirmed that nuclear deterrence remained the central vital characteristic of the superpowers' strategic posture. At the time – as noted by historian Robert Schulzinger – Nixon was successful in solidifying his 'public position as a masterful statesman who had grown far beyond this early anti-communism to usher a new era of stability and peace and to dampen the tension of the Cold War.'[39] In reality, however, through the 'era of negotiation' the Nixon administration had simply guaranteed the continued reliance on one of the central aspects of the Cold War.

In contrast to the summit in Beijing, where some of the substance of the nascent relationship was discussed, at the Moscow summit Nixon and Brezhnev were presented with agreements, pre-negotiated by specialists, which they had to merely sign. While SALT was at the time rightly considered a breakthrough, as it initiated the arms control process, its scope was *not* to break down the broader Cold War enmity, or to build trust between the two sides (it is important to note, in fact, that both sides relied on their own national means of verification of the agreements). Both sides potently perceived the agreement to be in their interest, but the broader aspects of the US-Soviet relationship continued to be characterized by animosity, antagonism and mistrust.

A transformative versus a stabilizing relationship?

From this brief snapshot of the Beijing and Moscow 1972 summits it emerges quite clearly that the two summits differed greatly, in practical and organizational terms and, most importantly, in their impact and significance. The opening to China was a secret endeavour, personally led by Henry Kissinger, which can and should be seen as a triumph of his personal backchannel diplomacy. While the US State Department had been involved at the initial stages of the opening, after the demise of the Warsaw meetings, Kissinger took the initiative into his own hands. Very few other than the closest of his advisers were aware of the communications via Pakistan and of the planning of his July 1971 trip to China. Given the uncertainty and the high stakes of the process, this may have been an obligated choice. Shrewd perhaps, but definitely justifiable, especially given its spectacularly successful outcome. When Nixon and Mao met in February 1972, the ground had been prepared by Kissinger and his Chinese counterparts, but the two heads of state still had scope and space in their conversations to define their nascent relationship. In contrast, the path towards the Moscow summit was more conventional diplomatic practice. The lower-level highly technical negotiations on strategic arms limitations talks had been ongoing since 1969, alternating between Vienna and Helsinki. Kissinger did play a vital role also in the context of these negotiations. Through his backchannel with Dobrynin, the May 1971 breakthrough agreement on separating the offensive agreement (which became the interim agreement) and the defence one (which became the ABM treaty) was made possible. Nonetheless, when the two heads of state, Nixon and Brezhnev, met at the summit in May 1972, they merely formally sanctioned agreements that had been already defined.

The two summits also, and most importantly, differed in terms of results achieved and longer-term significance. Based on their realistic assessment of security threats, the Chinese and Americans converged on an authentic realignment of interests. Kissinger and Zhou Enlai first, and then Nixon, Zhou and Mao, had the capacity to empathize with each other's security fears and motivations. Sharing the perception of an aggressive Soviet threat, they developed what Wheeler called a 'security dilemma sensitivity'. This enabled the building of trust between them, which in turn led to a truly transformative diplomatic process. From the offset, Kissinger openly disclosed details on the negotiations with the Soviet Union. This openness and consultation continued during and after the 1972 summit, as China gradually became, de facto while not yet de jure, a tacit American ally. While domestic constraints on both sides – Nixon's dramatic downfall following Watergate and the power struggle in China following Mao's death in 1976 – inevitably caused the stalling of the relationship, its transformative foundations had been laid. Progress continued, albeit slowly, under President Ford. These foundations enabled President Jimmy Carter to pick up the process, which led to the formal diplomatic recognition of the People's Republic of China in 1979. Despite tensions and rivalries that ensued,

China and the United States would never again return to the enmity that existed prior to 1972.

The process that led to the Moscow summit was radically different. In the United States, the Soviet Union was still conceived as the main Cold War adversary, an adversary that had become all the more threatening due to its unprecedented nuclear strength. The motivations for the US pursuit of détente were solidly anchored in an adversarial relationship, and negotiations were seen as a means to control and manage – but definitively *not* – to overcome this rivalry. This is confirmed by the centrality of arms control in the process, and the fact that these negotiations were geared towards maintaining the strategic balance of MAD. While the Soviet Union may have invested more in the alleged transformative aspects of détente – and their reliance on the Basic Principles and the rules of coexistence enshrined in them has been cited as a demonstration of this – the American leadership undoubtedly conceived détente as a means to fight the Cold War. The motivations of the China opening, as well as Nixon's Iran policy and the administration's conduct during the 1973 Middle East War – during which Washington did not hesitate to take advantage of the situation – are tangible demonstrations of this.[40] Moreover, the United States remained secretive of their parallel unfolding of relations with China, rightly arousing suspicions in Moscow as to the scope of the nascent Sino-American dialogue.

In conclusion, summits *do* have the potential to transform adversarial relationships, when perceptions of the security dilemma at the heart of the relationship shift dramatically. This was definitively the case of the opening to China, and of the Beijing 1972 summit, when all three of the preconditions for a diplomatic transformation were met: Nixon and Mao no longer imputed malevolent intentions to the other, they both acknowledged past mistakes and gestures of reassurance were reciprocal. Conversely, in the case of US-Soviet détente and the Moscow summit of 1972, the process – while on surface *seemed* to be transformative – in reality simply crystallized the superpower rivalry. The arms control treaties signed in fact codified the continued reliance on the balance of terror. The US-Soviet antagonism was not fundamentally addressed, both sides still feared each other's motives and intentions, and, most crucially, the lack of trust in each other's outlook continued to dominate their relationship. The more authentic transformation in US-Soviet relations had to wait over a decade, when Ronald Reagan and Michael Gorbachev unleashed their series of summits. By placing the building of trust at the centre of their dialogue, and by addressing some of the sources of their animosity, they did fulfil the conditions for transformative summits, thus setting the basis for the beginning of the end of the Cold War.

Notes

1. David Reynolds, *Summits. Six Meetings That Shaped the Twentieth Century* (New York: Basic Books, 2007). Introduction.
2. For example, see G. R. Berridge, *Diplomacy: Theory and Practice* (Basingstoke: Palgrave, 2002), chapter 10; David Dunn, *Diplomacy at the Highest Level: The Evolution of International Summitry* (Basingstoke: Macmillan, 1996); David Reynolds, 'Summitry as Intercultural Communication', *International Affairs* 85, no. 1 (January 2009).
3. Jan Melissen, *Summit Diplomacy Coming of Age*, Discussion Papers in Diplomacy, Netherlands Institute of International Relations 'Clingendael': 4.
4. Hans Morgenthau, *Politics Among Nations: The Struggle for Power and Peace* (New York: McGraw Hill, 1985), 122.
5. See, for example, Martin Wight, *Power Politics* (Leicester: Leicester University Press, 1978).
6. Nicholas J. Wheeler, 'Investigating Diplomatic Transformations', *International Affairs*, 89, no. 2 (2013): 477–81.
7. Michael Shaller, *The United States and China in the Twentieth Century* (New York: Oxford University Press, 1990), 127.
8. For a history of US-China relations before 1972: *Gordon Chang, Friends and Enemies. The United States, China, and the Soviet Union, 1948–1972* (Stanford: Stanford University Press, 1990). See also Margaret Macmillan, *The Week That Changed the World. Nixon and Mao* (New York: Random House, 2007), 94–109.
9. Henry Kissinger, *White House Years* (London: Phoenix Press, 2000), 163.
10. Raymond Garthoff, *Détente and Confrontation. American-Soviet Relations from Nixon to Reagan* (Washington, DC: The Brookings Institution, 1994), 245.
11. Hanhimäki, *The Flawed Architect. Henry Kissinger and American Foreign Policy* (New York: Oxford University Press, 2004), 32.
12. Kissinger, *White House Years*, 179; Hanhimäki, *The Flawed Architect*, 58.
13. Odd Arne Westad, 'The Great Transformation: China in the Long 1970s', in *The Shock of the Global: The 1970s in Perspective,* ed. Neil Ferguson, Charles S. Maier, Erez Manela, Daniel J. Sargent (Cambridge: Belknap Press, 2010), 76.
14. Quoted in Kissinger, *On China* (New York: Penguin, 2012), 208–9.
15. Ibid., 232.
16. Kissinger, *White House Years*, 709–10; Richard Nixon, *RN: The Memoirs of Richard Nixon* (New York: Touchstone Simon and Schuster, 1990), 548.

17 Memorandum of Conversation, 10 July 1971, National Archives (hereafter NA), Nixon Presidential Materials (hereafter NPM), National Security Council (hereafter NSC) files, box 1032, folder 2.
18 Memorandum of Conversation, 9 July 1971, NA, NPM, NSC files, box 1032, folder 2.
19 Memorandum of Conversation, 10 July 1971, NA, NPM, NSC files, box 1032, folder 2.
20 Memorandum of Conversation, Monday, 21 February 1972, 2.50–3.55 p.m., Chairman Mao's Residence, Peking, NA, NPM, NSC files, HAK Office files, box 91, folder 4.
21 Ibid. Scholars have pointed to the lack of detailed conversations on the Soviet Union between Nixon and Mao, in particular Macmillan, *Nixon and Mao*, 73. The transcript of the conversation, however, shows that while not too much time was dedicated to the topic, and the references were indirect and implicit, they were nevertheless crucial and unequivocal in conveying US and Chinese parallel objectives.
22 'The Soviet Union', Briefing Papers sent to the President for the February '72 China Trip, NA, NPM, NSC files, HAK Office files, box 91, folder 2.
23 Nixon defined his week in China in this way in his memoirs: Nixon, *Memoirs*, 580.
24 'The Shanghai Communiqué' issued at the end of Nixon's visit to China in February 1972.
25 Kissinger, *On China*, 270.
26 William Bundy, *A Tangled Web. The Making of Foreign Policy in the Nixon Presidency* (London: I.B. Tauris, 1998), 84; Henry Kissinger, *White House Years*, 196.
27 The numbers of the Soviet build-up were impressive: in 1965, the Soviets could field 200 ICBMs and little more than 100 SLBMs; in 1968, the ICBMs had increased to 860 and the SLBM to 120; Kissinger, *White House Years*, 197.
28 Memorandum for Recipients of NIE 11-8-67, 'Extreme Sensitivity of NIE 11-8-67 – Soviet Capabilities for Strategic Attack', National Security Archive (hereafter NSA), Soviet Estimate Collection, document se0425, 6. It is interesting to note that CIA Director Richard Helms wrote in the memorandum that the dissemination of the Intelligence Estimate had to be 'carefully limited because of extreme sensitivity of the information therein'. He stressed that there should be 'no reproduction of this Estimate, and that no revelation of its existence be made to unauthorized persons'. The tone of these statements conveys a certain degree of preoccupation concerning the subject of the study: the pace of the Soviet build-up.
29 Ibid., 8.
30 During the June 1967 Johnson–Kosygin meeting in Glassboro, then Secretary of Defense Robert McNamara had tried to convince the Soviets about the risks and costs of an ABM systems competition and had proposed to abandon their development. McNamara's arguments on the future destabilizing effects of ABMs

did not persuade Kosygin, who stated that asking for the abandonment of *defensive* systems was an absurd proposal. Significantly, the consequent realization that defensive systems could upset the strategic balance, while the offensive ones assured MAD and stability, would lead to the negotiating basis of the SALT I package.

31 An operationally effective ABM system could encourage its possessor to assess the advantages of a massive first strike aimed at the destruction of the adversary's missile bases, as the system would protect the country from the retaliatory strike. Furthermore, if the country possessed MIRVs, the incentives for a first strike would be even greater, since multiple warheads had a higher possibility of weakening the opponent's retaliation. Therefore, while in the past the strategic arsenals had been conceived to minimize the advantages of a first strike, guaranteeing an overall stability, it would no longer be the case if these developments remained unlimited; William C. Foster, *Prospects for Arms Control*, 'Foreign Affairs', April 1969, Vol. 47, n. 3.

32 Among other motivations on the Soviet side, Dobrynin cites the enormous burden of military expenditures and Brezhnev's personal incentives, as the improvement of relations with the United States would consolidate his position and prestige within the Soviet Union; Anatoly Dobrynin, *In Confidence. Moscow's Ambassador to America's Six Cold War Presidents* (New York: Random House, 1995), 193.

33 This is the capability of a nuclear power to destroy the opponent's nuclear forces, eliminating the possibility of a retaliatory strike.

34 The Soviet Union had 2,424 offensive missiles, of which 950 were SLBMs. The United States had 1,710 missiles, of which 710 were SLBMs; *The Military Balance 1972–1973*, London, IISS, September 1972, 85.

35 The Soviet Union was capable of a yearly production of around 250 ICBMs and 128 SLBMs. In theory, without the *freeze* Moscow could have produced, in five years, over 1,200 SLBMs and around 2,800 ICBM. The United States, as has been underlined, did not have any program for the production of new missiles and would have remained at 1,054 ICBMs and 656 SLBMs; ibid., 84.

36 Regarding intercontinental bombers: the United States had 455 B-52 (including those held in reserve) versus 140 Tu-95 and Mya-4 (100 were propeller driven) of the Soviet Union. The B-52 could carry a bigger weapons load than the Tu-95 and Mya-4. Theoretically, the American strategic air force could drop on the Soviet territory about 2,000 nuclear weapons versus the 420 of the Soviet bombers. Regarding MIRVs: in 1972, the United States had a very advanced 'mirving' program, with 360 operational missiles. The Soviet Union had begun to deploy multiple, but not independently targeted, warheads on some of its SS-9 and SS-11 ICBMs, but had not yet tested MIRVed warheads. The disparity, in favour of the United States, in terms of number of targets which theoretically could be attacked was therefore evident; ibid., 85.

37 *The Strategic Arms Limitation Agreements and National Security*, NA, NPM, NSC files, box 79, folder 3.
38 Memorandum of Conversation, Monday, 22 May 1972, The General Secretary's Office, The Kremlin, Moscow, NA, NPM, NSC files, box 487, folder 3.
39 Robert D. Schulzinger, 'Détente in the Nixon-Ford Years, 1969–1975', in *The Cambridge History of the Cold War, Volume II*, ed. Leffler and Westad (Cambridge: Cambridge University Press, 2010), 382.
40 On the continuation of the US-Soviet rivalry under the guise of détente, see Zanchetta, *The Transformation of American International Power in the 1970s*, chapters 4 and 5.

6

Empathy and emotional diplomacy

Dr Claire Yorke

There I found Winston and Stalin, and Molotov who had joined them, sitting with a heavily-laden board between them: food of all kinds crowned by a sucking pig, and innumerable bottles. What Stalin made me drink seemed pretty savage: Winston, who by that time was complaining of a slight headache, seemed wisely to be confining himself to a comparatively innocuous effervescent Caucasian red wine. Everyone seemed to be as merry as a marriage bell ...

I think the two great men really made contact and got on terms. Certainly, Winston was impressed, and I think that feeling was reciprocated ... Anyhow, conditions have been established in which messages exchanged between the two will mean twice as much, or more, than they did before.

—Sir Alexander Cadogan, Moscow, 1942[1]

When Britain's wartime Prime Minister Winston Churchill went to Moscow in August 1942, it was his first face-to-face meeting with Joseph Stalin, the leader of the Soviet Union. The meeting was part of 'Operation Bracelet', designed to convey allied intentions for the next phase of the war. At this time the Russians were bearing the brunt of the fighting, and Churchill had an unpleasant task: to inform Stalin that there would be no second front – nothing to ease the pressure on Soviet forces – during 1942. While the first meeting went well, the second was less positive and tensions arose. In an effort to resolve the issues Churchill sought a private meeting with his Soviet counterpart. It was in the early hours of the morning, in Stalin's private rooms, that the Permanent Under-Secretary at the Foreign Office, Sir Alexander Cadogan, found the two men as described in the quote above.[2,3] Whilst the episode reflects the potential power of alcohol as a diplomatic lubricant, it also speaks to a more critical dimension of diplomacy: the power of face-to-face communication, rapport and empathy with one's diplomatic counterpart.

Definitions of diplomacy emphasize the art of negotiation, the skill of human engagement and the importance of dialogue and cultural knowledge.[4] Yet, despite its inherently human nature, few have explored the role and implications of empathy and emotions in the art and practice of diplomacy. Connecting diplomatic theory and practice with the affective turn in international relations, this chapter sheds light on the emotional dynamics of diplomacy and relations between states.[5] Rather than a single case study, it uses diverse examples to reveal how emotions give meaning to diplomatic interactions, provide valuable sources of information to guide decision-making and help public figures connect with audiences and signal their feelings and intent, both at home and abroad.

This chapter begins by outlining the meaning of empathy, its connection to the study of emotions and the significance of these themes in diplomacy. Then it turns to examine what these mean in context. Although there are manifold ways in which empathy and emotions are integral to diplomacy, this chapter focuses on three: interpersonal connections, diplomatic signalling and communications, and diplomatic practice. These provide a snapshot of core aspects of diplomacy. Finally, it reflects on how a better appreciation of emotions can inform the future of diplomacy.

Empathy and emotions in diplomacy

Ideas of the utility of empathy and emotions are implicit in diplomatic theory and practice, yet rarely made explicit. The need for diplomats to connect and gain valuable insights into another country and culture is identified in the Groatian tradition of diplomacy in forms of respect, which encapsulate ideas of sympathy, or empathetic understanding for the interests, ideas and motivations of one's diplomatic counterpart, and the state they represent.[6] Abraham de Wicquefort's work suggested the need for 'someone steeped in a knowledge of the long-term interests of his and other states'.[7] Going further back, in Ancient Greece diplomacy had a system of proxenos: figures of distinction who had an understanding for the culture, society and politics of their adoptive state and would represent this to their sovereign state. These ideas of knowledge, cultural insight, understanding and connection remain central to how diplomacy is conceptualized, yet the role of empathy is under-theorized and often overlooked.

In its simplest form, empathy is an attempt to understand the thoughts, feelings and experiences of another: to view the world through their eyes. Definitions of empathy often make distinctions between affective and cognitive forms. However, rather than a rigid binary, empathy is conceptualized here as both cognitive and affective: accounting for the way that relationships and understanding evolve. It can be a feeling of innate connection with another, where you feel a bond based on shared backgrounds or experiences. Similarly, in its more cognitive form, empathy can be a more conscious attempt to comprehend the thoughts, feelings, lived experiences and perspectives of another. It is not about how you would feel in their place, but a process of understanding how someone else, or another group of people, might experience the world. In so doing, it takes account of context, history, identity and the socio-economic and political backdrop. And, critical to this, is the importance of self-reflection. In a diplomatic context this means awareness of how the words, deeds, behaviours and past policies of the country or community you represent have an impact on how another person or society may perceive your actions.

As a concept empathy is too often conflated with compassion, and its connotations of helping or alleviating suffering. It is therefore dismissed as appealing to normative ideals of human behaviour rather than providing a practical tool for the harder realities of politics and diplomacy. Although empathy can aid compassion, it is not synonymous with it. One can observe and consciously imagine the life, experiences and interests of another without needing to respond to, or alleviate, their situation. Instead, better understood, empathy's utility speaks both to the intrinsic human nature of diplomacy and to the need to realize longer-term strategic objectives.

In international relations, empathy is credited with helping political actors bridge divides, reconcile adversaries and facilitate diplomatic transformations.[8] Yet it can play an integral role in policymaking and inform strategic decision-making. In a speech in 2014, for example, former Secretary of State Hillary Rodham Clinton spoke of its intrinsic value to leverage smart power in American diplomacy.[9]

Empathy is not just something that is felt, or an abstract process of conscious imagination of the other, but a tangible part of diplomatic practice. Indeed, the call to look more at empathy does not rest on a belief that empathy has heretofore been missing from international relations or diplomatic interactions and now needs to be inserted, but, critically, that insufficient attention has been given to where it already exists and how it informs and shapes diplomatic interactions.

Identifying and analysing empathy in this space involves qualitative approaches, such as discourse analysis and behavioural analysis, that interpret the meaning and significance of texts, symbols and interactions. Rather than being neatly conceptualized as something that exists in interpersonal relations alone, empathy is part of dynamic and symbiotic interactions that incorporate the individual and collective, the public and the private, and the wider context within which it operates. As Carolyn Pedwell states, 'It is not just that *discourses and rhetorics* of empathy are strategically mobilized to suit a wide range of political agendas and interests (though they certainly are), but also that the particular social, cultural and geo-political circuits through which emotions and affects are produced are constitutive of how empathy is *felt and materialised*.'[10] This iterative process underlines the importance of context in analysing the role of empathy and its impact.

A focus on empathy is situated in a broader spectrum of emotions. In some ways, empathy serves as a cipher by which to interpret them. A willingness to seek to understand another perspective, and attempt to grasp alternative lived experiences, is a process of divining how other people *feel*, and involves a receptivity to moods. Importantly, it is a tool by which to see how these emotions give meaning to different realities, the stories they tell and their interests, motivations, and context. Critically, emotions are not ancillary to interests, but play a central role in informing the decision-making process, motivating public action or support, and in building more cooperative relations.

This leads to a broader point to be made about the significance of emotions to our understanding and practice of diplomacy. There remains a tendency across the discipline of international relations and diplomacy to reify rationality, as if the world can be measured in an objective, dispassionate manner. This is not an accurate depiction of how people live, work or think, and it has loaded gendered connotations.[11] Emotions are dismissed as inherently feminine, and irrational. They are seen to undermine an ability to reason and reach sound judgement. Reason, devoid of emotion, has masculine implications, associated with the conduct of authoritative and pragmatic statesmen, above the vagaries of feeling. Yet such stereotypes do a disservice to both genders, and ignore the intrinsic symbiotic relationship between reason and emotion. In advocating for the inclusion of emotions in diplomatic theory and practice, this chapter contends that sound reason is informed by emotional intelligence and an awareness of the logics and power of emotion to connect people, shape ideas and motivate action. Although the extremes of emotion may be associated with people turning to populism, or supporting initiatives that go against their own self-interest, the extremes of reason, devoid of humanity, can be equally harmful. As neuroscientist Antonio Damasio has demonstrated, patients lacking emotional capacities display impaired judgement.[12] The affective turn, emphasizing the power of emotions in international relations, seeks to redress the balance.

Emotions pervade diplomatic interactions at all levels. Barbara Keys shows how Henry Kissinger, the main proponent of Realpolitik, was guided by his emotions and ego throughout his career.[13] Historian Frank Costigliola's work supports this, revealing how emotions are inescapable even for some of the most prominent and revered statesmen and practitioners. George Kennan's feelings for the Soviet Union, and love of Russia, were intertwined with his politics and shaped his thinking towards the region.[14] Indeed, Keys and Yorke articulate the unavoidable tensions that exist between a diplomat's personal emotions and ego, and their public perceptions and interpretations of official emotional signals and cues.[15] Emotions shape how diplomats communicate, how messages and policies are received, and give life to state and group identities and the meanings the attribute to their sense of self.

A human-centric and emotional approach thus moves the focus from the state level, to the conduct, experiences and feelings of the people acting on the state's behalf. This requires a closer look at its role on interpersonal relations, communications and signalling, and diplomatic practices.

Interpersonal relations

Negotiation and the importance of effective communications are central to diplomacy. Yet when two diplomats, or leaders, meet, their connection is based not only on the potential compatibility of the interests they represent, but also on their ability to read and understand the other and build a personal relationship.

Integral to this are the personalities and dispositions of the actors involved. Diplomats are often conceptualized as aloof, dispassionate and detached.[16] They are meant to represent their state and gather information and insights on other countries and peoples. Yet Keys and Yorke have explored the persistent tension between the individual and the national representative.[17] Indeed, diplomats are often empathetic by disposition.[18] Oral histories from the US State Department frequently feature statements of affinity with another country, or a fascination and curiosity with understanding the lives of others around the world. The ability to build connections is both part of the job, and often a product of a shared and unique experience. R. B. Mowat speaks of 'the "collegiality" of the diplomatic profession: the common outlook that binds diplomatists working together in foreign cities, in isolation from their country and in close communion with other foreign diplomatists'.[19] This helps forge emotional ties through a common identity.

Empathy in interpersonal relations can be both felt and constructed. It is closely aligned with ideas of rapport and the sense of 'synergy'[20] that exists between people or 'interpersonal attraction'.[21] Marcus Holmes argues this is due to the role of mirror neurons in building innate connection.[22] Nonetheless, it may result from a sense of mutual connection: that instantaneous chemistry and familiarity that exists between two people. Or it may be an emergent element that is the product of conscious study and practise designed to forge a constructive relationship. One of the surprising outcomes from the Northern Ireland Peace Process, for example, was the rapport, and genuine friendship, that evolved between former adversaries the Loyalist politician Iain Paisley and the Sinn Fein leader Martin McGuiness. Through the process of the peace negotiations they became close and formed a political partnership to lead Northern Ireland after the ratification of the St Andrews Agreement in 2007.[23] Such an arrangement, however, was short-lived due to ill-health and the lack of trust between their different parties, illustrating both the power, and limitations, of interpersonal relations to carry change.

On the international stage, the nuclear negotiations between the P5+1 and Iran were aided by the rapport and sense of connection experienced by US Secretary John Kerry and Iranian Mohamad Javad Zarif. Secretary Kerry made a point of speaking to the concerns of the Iranian side, recognizing Iranian pride in their country and history, and sought to build trust with his counterparts.[24] A commitment to engage with the other side as equals, and to listen to, and respond to, their concerns and interests helps the negotiation process. Similarly, during the US opening to the People's Republic of China in 1972, President Richard Nixon and Henry Kissinger understood the utility of rapport and personal connection with their Chinese counterparts.[25] Although not the typical candidates for discussions of empathy, they proactively sought to foster personal connections. This was aided by a series of meetings between Henry Kissinger and Chou Enlai, and by conscious measures from both Nixon and Kissinger to prove their credibility and trustworthiness, including sharing secret intelligence and information about Soviet Union's operations on the broader of the PRC. At a more personal level, Nixon sent Chou Enlai moon rock as an expression of their shared commitment to advancing humankind.[26]

These interpersonal relations help to foster trust, an asset in international diplomacy. As Nicholas Wheeler argues, it was the face-to-face relationship between General Secretary Gorbachev and President Reagan that facilitated the transformation of US-USSR relations, and helped build trust and a sense of commitment to a new relationship between the two powers.[27] Trust and trustworthiness are critical to diplomacy as the credibility of the information a diplomat communicates about their own country's interests and needs is dependent on whether others view them as reliable messengers. For diplomats there is therefore a careful balance between understanding their foreign counterpart's allegiances to their state and its interests, and cultivating a professional form of trust to help the relationship.

In many respects, such dynamics vary according to the level of seniority and the position of the figures involves. As diplomat Walt Rostow remarked, heads of state interact in very different ways to two senior government officials or diplomats.[28] The weight of responsibilities and decision-making power, as well as the vision of leadership and relations between the two countries, changes the dynamics of the relationship.

Beyond the personal relationship and development of trust that occurs between people on greater acquaintance, such knowledge helps leaders and diplomats to infer and interpret meaning. Speaking from Guam in 1969, President Nixon acknowledged how interpersonal relations gave him valuable insights into his foreign policy initiatives. He kept in regular contact with other leaders, and those in positions of influence that he had met during his travels:

> Now, insofar as the individuals are concerned, having met all of these leaders previously, I suppose the question could be raised, and with good reason, that once you know a leader then contact with ambassadors would be sufficient. However, I have found it in my previous travels in Asia, and in Europe as well, that as these situations change it is vitally important to have a renewed contact with the leader in each of the countries involved, a renewed contact because his attitudes may change. And in that way, when I read, as I do read day after day, the cables that come in from all over the world, I can have a much better understanding of what those cables mean, the nuances, if I have more recently had a direct contact, face-to-face, with the individual involved, the individual leader involved.[29]

Interpersonal relations and better understanding of another, however, do not always yield more propitious outcomes. Indeed, closer acquaintance may diminish respect and reduce any willingness to cooperate. When President Kennedy met with Premier Nikita Khrushchev in Vienna in 1961, for example, they failed to connect at a personal level. Their exchanges over several days were considered detrimental to American diplomacy, as Khrushchev was unimpressed by the young leader and sparred with the President.[30]

Moreover, too great a sense of empathy can be problematic. If a diplomat is seen to be too understanding or accommodating of a foreign country, as Wight explains, such sentiments and sympathies can be considered suspect or counter to the national interests.[31] The accusation that you have 'gone native' is damaging to a diplomat's domestic reputation and credibility.

Diplomats operate in a relatively unique position both as agents of the state, representing the interests of their country of origin, and as translators and interpreters between their home state and that of their host country. However, what goes on behind closed doors has implications in public spaces. Empathy is very often political. It can be difficult to publicly convey empathy towards a former adversary if the political climate is not amenable to it.

Therefore, although empathy can be an asset in forging productive personal relationships with counterparts, the concept needs to be situated in a broader context, encompassing its role in public spaces, communications and other diplomatic practices.

Communication

Empathy is a communicative, performative and iterative act. It is an expression of recognition, and understanding, exhibited and articulated through language, discourses, signs and images that demonstrate awareness of the considerations of another and their anticipated interpretations. It is further connected to an ability to read the public mood, and understand the nuances of an audience to find ways to connect with them. It is an asset in strategic communications.[32]

The belief that empathy and emotions are critical to diplomacy rests on an ontological assumption that states are motivated by a desire for recognition, and a wish to be seen and acknowledged on the world stage. A state's self-image and how it sees it reflected by others matter.[33] It speaks to the wider importance of identity in international relations, and how identities are expressed and legitimized. As Charles Taylor argues, recognition, or misrecognition, are part of the process of identity formation. It can be harmful if states feel that others do not view them as valid, or hold negative views that are not aligned with their own sense of self.[34] Such an assumption is further reflected in ideas of ontological security that look beyond the material interests and requirements of a state.³⁵ Constance Duncombe, for example, has argued that US-Iranian antagonism is rooted in mutual desires for respect and recognition, as well as historical grievances.³⁶

In the private space, empathy is visible in how diplomats engage with one another as part of negotiations or relationship building. Diplomats by their nature are known to be adept at communication. As Hedley Bull states:

> Diplomatists are specialists in precise and accurate communication. They are more than mere couriers or heralds; they are experts in detecting and conveying nuances of international dialogue, and are equipped not merely to deliver a message but to judge the language in which it should be couched, the audience to whom and that occasion at which it should be presented.³⁷

This skill connects with the efforts of diplomats to build relations and establish rapport and trust. As Neta Crawford articulates, 'Narratives of historical enmity, harm and aggression will rehearse and reinforce the fearful relationship. On the other hand, the development of a positive emotional relationship may help diminish or render irrelevant the structural reasons states' leaders have to distrust and fear each other.'³⁸

However, it can equally be a form of diplomatic signalling. Keren Yarhi-Milo and Marcus Holmes speak of the importance of empathy's 'relational quality' and what it signifies to participants in peace negotiations.³⁹ Empathetic language signals that the needs and interests of others have been heard and acknowledged. It addresses the need for states to feel proud, equal or legitimized in a space. Empathy can help build more cooperative and conciliatory outcomes between parties, helping them find common ground.

A challenge in diplomatic signalling, as well as interpersonal interactions, is the character and credibility of the communicator. As Seanon Wong has argued, if someone has a reputation of angering quickly their outbursts can appear less credible. Whereas if anger is seen as a last resort for someone known for a more measured temperament, it can hold far greater power.⁴⁰

Beyond overt signals, the reading of the mood and emotional cues can be critical to determining the seriousness and respect with which diplomatic representatives or their parties are viewed. In judging the evolution of the relationship with China, Kissinger paid attention to the atmospherics and the tone of the visits. Commenting he said:

> The mood of our Chinese hosts throughout the visit was extraordinarily warm and friendly – especially considering the circumstances. It was very apparent that the Chinese were determined not to let the Vietnam situation stand in the

way of an improvement in US-PRC relations; it was obvious that the rapport established during the past year was intact and that they wanted to build it.[41]

However, it equally has a public dimension as an expression of a state's perception of another, and a means by which to communicate with other audiences. In support of the nuclear negotiations with Iran, for example, President Obama did videos for the Iranian people to wish them Happy Nowruz, and reflect on the historic contributions, and rich civilization of Iran. Such moves are intentionally designed to help both states, and especially their people, move towards a new policy.

Such communication is not straightforward, however. In the public eye, political leaders and diplomats face scrutiny for their words and actions. As alluded to above, empathy is intrinsically political and incurs costs.[42] Positive interpersonal relations between leaders or diplomats have to be translated into policy outcomes and political benefits for a wider audience. The public may not be ready for such overtures, especially if there is a history of negative images or animosity.

Alternatively, public expressions of empathetic understanding and emotion displays of compassion, or pride, can have normative connotations that reflect attributes a state wishes to exhibit.[43] The emotions can be performative, rather than sincere, to convey meaning not only as a form of response to another, but as part of a state's public image.

Social media adds a new dimension to this dynamic. It democratizes diplomacy, reducing the private space that traditionally existed and giving access for leaders to have more direct contact with their populations. Platforms such as Twitter and Facebook can be used to galvanize action and mobilize people to support certain initiatives or to discredit diplomatic efforts before they reach fruition. As Duncombe explains, Twitter can be used by governments to exacerbate divides and to stoke popular public sentiments against another country.[44] Yet it also makes it far easier for political leaders to engage with foreign audiences to build support for changes in relations between states.

Looking beyond communications, there is a final dimension to consider: that of diplomatic practice and how empathy and emotions are intertwined with the everyday workings of the profession.

Practice

Reflecting on his experiences as Secretary of Defense between 1961 and 1968, Robert McNamara proffered his first lesson: empathize with the enemy.[45]

Empathy was seen as an asset in the practice of states to better divine the minds of their adversaries and inform decision-making. His ideas were informed, in part, by the work of political psychologist and United States Information Agency (USIA) employee Ralph K. White. Working in government during the 1960s, White spoke of the importance of 'tough-minded empathy' in US relations with the Soviet Union.[46] It was empathy with a realistic edge, designed to overcome the misperceptions and cognitive biases within government. More recently, Zachary Shore has reflected similar thinking, encouraging people to think like the enemy as part of a more calculated and strategic source of empathetic practice.[47]

In some ways, as Martin Wight contends, many diplomats have a natural predisposition to 'thinking the best of people, and trying to share their point of view, understand their interests' to reconcile differences and find common ground.[48] However, this form of empathy is not only a personal disposition, but also, to variable degrees, a professional competence and practice.

Emmanuel Adler and Vincent Pouliot describe diplomatic practices as 'socially meaningful patterns of action which, in being performed more or less competently, simultaneously embody, act out, and possibly reify background knowledge and discourse in and on the material world'.[49] In describing the daily roles of diplomats, Pouliot contends they act from a 'logic of practicality', and build their understanding on pre-existing and background knowledge, or 'metis'.[50] Drawing on Bourdesian sociology, Pouliot's accounts of practice reveal the everyday ways in which state actors interact and through their practices can influence and shape policy.[51] In his work with Adler-Nissen on the international negotiations on the intervention in Libya in 2011 they examine the relationship between practices and power, and how the 'endogenous skills' of diplomats can transform situations, yield influence and have a direct effect on the outcome of events.[52]

Such an approach offers a useful entry point to understand diplomatic practice, but it does not go far enough. It overlooks the integral role that empathy and emotions play in the quotidian work of diplomats. Yet diplomatic cables from the State Department between the period of 1967 and 1973, for example, reveal not only the routine and competent performances and practices that informed the State Department's approach to China as it evolved, but also the way in which the knowledge and understanding was infused with awareness of emotions and affect. It was through the reading of feelings and moods and personal judgements that meaning and significance were given to certain acts and pieces of information. Although limited attention has been given to these affective dimensions, they are implicit in this space. Beyond reason and interests, judgement, intuition and the reading of how people feel and why inform diplomatic practices. Emotions guide diplomats in what information to treat seriously, what to value and what to dismiss. A personal sense of connection with a foreign source, for example, can shape the priority accorded to the knowledge gained through their interaction. A sense of fear or anxiety around a certain actor can enhance the language of threat used to depict them, thus prompting a sequence of policy consequences. As Hannah Gurman and Pablo de Orellana have examined, how identities are constituted in diplomatic texts has significance.[53] Such discourse production is institutionalized through shared forms of meaning between practitioners, and through professional training.

Nevertheless, in organizational terms there are a number of challenges in incorporating empathy more explicitly into diplomatic practice. Critically, diplomats have to be able to self-reflect and seek to understand how their own country might be viewed, and why past actions or policies may have been problematic or harmful, irrespective of their intention. As Ralph K. White has counselled, for empathy to be useful, decision-makers have to be able to overcome the distortive impact of righteous self-images, their sense of moral superiority or perceptions of military strength.[54] This speaks to a central part of any definition of effective empathy: the role of self-reflection in order to grasp the impact one's own words and actions have on others, both in the present and historically.

In the 1950s, a pervasive fear of Communism, encapsulated in McCarthyism, led to suspicion of those in the US government and wider society who sought to understand the interests, ideas, perceptions and experiences of those in Communist States. In the State Department, twenty out of twenty-two foreign service officers working on China lost their jobs or were moved to other desks.[55] Many of these officers had reported on life within China during the 1940s, and reflected on the reasons behind the rise and popularity of Mao and context of his support. Senator Joseph McCarthy and his supporters did not view this as valuable insights into the lives of others, but considered it to give credibility and legitimacy to Communist ideas.

As a result of a purge of experts, there was a change in how diplomatic reporting was practiced. Margaret MacMillan speaks of how 'seasoned and knowledgeable experts were driven out or resigned in disgust. Those who survived were kept away from anything to do with Asia … The department as a whole was shell-shocked and became increasingly timid in offering unpalatable advice to its political masters'.[56] Within this bureaucratic culture, understanding the point of view of an adversary was considered politically dangerous and against the national interest, limiting attempts to articulate more nuanced insights into the dynamics of the PRC.

The politics of empathy are visible more recently. When senior foreign policy professionals have encouraged empathy with terrorists, for example, they have been criticized for willingness to countenance, and, by implication, legitimize views that are at odds with one's sense of self.[57] It reveals there is a lot more to be done to make empathy and emotions more central, and acceptable features of diplomatic theory and practice.

Conclusion

Acknowledging the importance of emotions to diplomacy does not deny the centrality of power or calculations of interests and security. These core tenets of international relations still hold. Nevertheless, a greater focus on the intrinsic role that empathy and emotions play within diplomacy, and how these dynamics shape relations between actors, and give meaning to diplomatic communications and signalling, can enrich not only the study of diplomacy but also its practice.

This chapter has concentrated on just three dimensions of diplomacy, yet it should be considered part of a bigger picture. While its essence remains, the environment of diplomacy has been transformed by new technologies and means of communication. Traditional distances of space and time have been bridged. Paradoxically, this change makes connection between diplomatic and public actors both more immediate and instantaneous, and yet more remote. Social media facilitates the dissemination of messages and politics to a global audience, and democratizes the process. Presidents can, and do, engage with members of the public, or convey their every thought in 280 characters. The ease of such platforms belies the power they still hold in conveying messages, meanings and emotions.

Diplomacy is no longer the preserve of diplomats. Non-governmental actors, protest groups and global causes have significant power to harness emotional forces, mobilize populations and shape the agendas of states and international organizations. The Climate Change initiatives, with prominent figureheads such as Greta Thunberg, galvanize anger for change and help shape international norms and expectations for the conduct and politics of officials.

Looking to the future, the global pandemic in 2020 poses new challenges for diplomacy and new prospects to study the role of emotions in this space. In the short term, imposed measures of social-distancing make it harder for diplomats to connect and build rapport in-person with their counterparts. Access to countries and their people will be limited, and many nations will turn inwards to address their own domestic situations. The universal experience of the COVID-19 crisis, and the economic and social implications that accompany it, also reveal how emotions play diverse roles in a crisis. Compassion and empathy for others in a shared experience have led some leaders to develop international cooperation and transnational relations based on aid, support or finding common solutions. Conversely, other leaders have used the fear and anxiety of the crisis to heighten tensions, with political and public figures resorting to negative images and stereotypes of those perceived to be part of an 'out-group', with consequences for foreign policy and diplomatic relations. The long-term impact on international relations and the conduct of diplomacy remains to be seen.

By expanding the aperture of how we approach diplomacy, and seeing it in its human richness, it not only challenges traditional and outdated concepts of power and security, but also renders it more nuanced, more citizen-centric and more able to adapt to whatever the future holds.

Notes

1 The National Archives UK (TNA), FO 1093/247, Peter Loxley for Alexander Cadogan to Lord Halifax, 29 August 1942.
2 For additional contemporary accounts of this trip, see those by Alexander Cadogan, Permanent Under-Secretary of the Foreign Office (1938–45): *The Diaries of Sir Alexander Cadogan, O.M., 1938–1945*, ed. David Dilks (New York: G.P. Putnam's Sons, 1971), 469–74, and by Sir Charles Wilson, Churchill's personal physician: Lord Moran (Sir Charles Wilson), *Churchill at War 1940–1945* (London: Constable & Robinson, 2002), 64–78.
3 A thank you is due to Dr H. Matthew Hefler for his kind assistance with the archival files.
4 'Negotiation' was the term used until 'diplomacy' was coined by Edmund Burke. See, for example, Geoff Berridge, Harold Maurice Alvan Keens-Soper, and Thomas G. Otte, *Diplomatic Theory from Machiavelli to Kissinger* (Basingstoke, UK: Palgrave Macmillan, 2001).
5 See, for example, Emma Hutchison and Roland Bleiker, 'Theorizing Emotions in World Politics', *International Theory* 6, no. 3 (2014). Jonathan Mercer, 'Feeling Like a State: Social Emotion and Identity', *International Theory* 6, no. 3 (2014); 'Human Nature and the First Image: Emotion in International Politics', *Journal*

of International Relations and Development 9, no. 3 (2006); 'Rationality and Psychology in International Politics', *International Organization* 59, no. 1 (2005). Neta C. Crawford, 'Institutionalizing Passion in World Politics: Fear and Empathy', *International Theory* 6, no. 3 (2014); 'The Passion of World Politics: Propositions on Emotion and Emotional Relationships', *International Security* 24, no. 4 (2000). Todd H. Hall, *Emotional Diplomacy: Official Emotion on the International Stage* (Cornell University Press, 2015); Todd Hall, 'Sympathetic States: Explaining the Russian and Chinese Responses to? September 11', *Political Science Quarterly* 127, no. 3 (2012).

6   The four principles in the Groatian tradition are seen to be honesty (or credibility), balance and moderation, courtesy, and respect. Martin Wight, Gabriele Wright, and Brian Porter, *International Theory: The Three Traditions* (London Leicester University Press, for the Royal Institute of International Affairs, 1996), 186–8.
7   Maurice Keens-Soper, 'Abraham De Wicquefort and Diplomatic Theory', *Diplomacy and Statecraft* 8, no. 2 (1997): 18.
8   See, for example, Nicholas J. Wheeler, 'Investigating Diplomatic Transformations', *International Affairs* 89, no. 2 (2013); Ken Booth and Nicholas Wheeler, *The Security Dilemma: Fear, Cooperation, and Trust in World Politics* (Palgrave: Macmillan, 2008). Naomi Head, 'Transforming Conflict Trust, Empathy, and Dialogue', *International Journal of Peace Studies* 17, no. 2 (2012). Carolyn Pedwell, *Affective Relations: The Transnational Politics of Empathy* (Palgrave: Macmillan, 2014). James G. Blight, and Lang, J. M., *The Fog of War: Lessons from the Life of Robert S. Mcnamara* (Maryland, USA: Rowman & Littlefield Publishers, Inc, 2005).
9   Hillary R. Clinton, 'Hillary Rodham Clinton Speaks on Security, Inclusive Leadership', Georgetown University, 3 December 2014, http://www.ustream.tv/recorded/56079087 (accessed 5 January 2017).
10 Pedwell, *Affective Relations: The Transnational Politics of Empathy*, 183.
11 See, for example, Wollstonecraft, Mary, *Wollstonecraft: A Vindication of the Rights of Men and a Vindication of the Rights of Woman and Hints* (Cambridge University Press, 1995).
12 Antonio R. Damasio, *Descartes' Error* (London: Random House, 2006).
13 Barbara Keys, 'Henry Kissinger: The Emotional Statesman', *Diplomatic History* 35, no. 4 (2011): 587–609.
14 Frank Costigliola, '"Unceasing Pressure for Penetration": Gender, Pathology, and Emotion in George Kennan's Formation of the Cold War', *The Journal of American History* 83, no. 4 (1997): 1309–39.
15 Barbara Keys and Claire Yorke, 'Personal and Political Emotions in the Mind of the Diplomat', *Political Psychology* 40, no. 6 (2019): 1235–49.
16 Sasson Sofer, 'The Diplomat as a Stranger' *Diplomacy and Statecraft* 8, no. 3 (1997): 179–86.

17 Barbara Keys and Claire Yorke. 'Personal and Political Emotions in the Mind of the Diplomat', *Political Psychology* 40, no. 6 (2019): 1235–49.
18 Wight, Wright, and Porter, *International Theory: The Three Traditions*, 186–8.
19 Quoted in Hedley Bull, *The Anarchical Society: A Study of Order in World Politics* (Columbia University Press, 2002), 176.
20 Ilan Bronstein et al., 'Rapport in Negotiation: The Contribution of the Verbal Channel', *Journal of Conflict Resolution* 56, no. 6 (2012): 1091.
21 Nancy J. Adler and John L. Graham, 'Cross-Cultural Interaction: The International Comparison Fallacy?', *Journal of International Business Studies* 20, no. 3 (1989).
22 Marcus Holmes, 'The Force of Face-to-face Diplomacy: Mirror Neurons and the Problem of Intentions', *International Organization* 67, no. 4 (2013): 829–61.
23 For a brief but interesting account of this, see David A Graham, 'The Strange Friendship of Martin McGuinness and Ian Paisley', 21 March 2017, The Atlantic, https://www.theatlantic.com/international/archive/2017/03/martin-mcguinness-ian-paisley/520257/.
24 See more on this in Constance Duncombe, *Representation, Recognition and Respect in World Politics: The Case of Iran–US Relations* (Manchester University Press, 2019).
25 Yafeng Xia, *Negotiating with the Enemy: Us-China Talks during the Cold War, 1949–1972* (Bloomington: Indiana University Press, 2006) 224.
26 Both letters are in this file. Letters from President Nixon to Chou Enlai, May 1973, EX CO 34-2 4/1/73-5/31/73, CFSU CO Box 20, Nixon Library.
27 Nicholas Wheeler, 'Investigating Diplomatic Transformations.'
28 See Walt Rostow, Diplomatic Oral History, transcript of an oral history conducted by Paige E. Mulhollan on 21 March 1969, ADST Foreign Affairs Oral History Project, http://www.adst.org/OH%20TOCs/Rostow,%20Walt.toc.pdf 26
29 Richard Nixon, 'Informal Remarks in Guam With Newsmen', 25 July 1969. Online by Gerhard Peters and John T. Woolley, *The American Presidency Project*, http://www.presidency.ucsb.edu/ws/?pid=2140.
30 Nathan Thrall and Jesse James Wilkins, 'Kennedy Talked, Kruschev Triumphed', *New York Times*, 22 May 2008. http://www.nytimes.com/2008/05/22/opinion/22thrall.html (accessed 25 August 2017).
31 Martin Wight, Systems of States, 56, quoted in Keith Hamilton and Richard Langhorne, *The Practice of Diplomacy: Its Evolution, Theory, and Administration* (Taylor & Francis, 2011), 11–12.
32 Claire Yorke, 'The Significance and Limitations of Empathy in Strategic Communications', *Defence Strategic Communications* 2, no. 2 (2017): 137–60.
33 Richard Ned Lebow articulates the importance of standing, prestige, self-esteem and honour in his 'Cultural Theory of International Politics'. Richard Ned Lebow, *A Cultural Theory of International Relations* (Cambridge University Press, 2008).

34 See, for example, Axel Honneth, *The Struggle for Recognition: The Moral Grammar of Social Conflicts* (MIT Press, 1996); Charles Taylor, 'The Politics of Recognition', *New contexts of Canadian Criticism* 98 (1997).
35 Jennifer Mitzen, 'Ontological Security in World Politics: State Identity and the Security Dilemma', *European Journal of International Relations* 12, no. 3 (2006).
36 Duncombe, *Representation, Recognition and Respect in World Politics: The Case of Iran–US Relations.*
37 Bull, *The Anarchical Society: A Study of Order in World Politics*, 173.
38 Crawford, 'Institutionalizing Passion in World Politics: Fear and Empathy', 548.
39 Marcus Holmes and Keren Yarhi-Milo, 'The Psychological Logic of Peace Summits: How Empathy Shapes Outcomes of Diplomatic Negotiations', *International Studies Quarterly* 61, no. 1 (2016): 107–22, 108.
40 Seanon S. Wong, 'Stoics and Hotheads: Leaders' Temperament, Anger, and the Expression of Resolve in Face-to-face Diplomacy', *Journal of Global Security Studies* 4, no. 2 (2019): 190–208.
41 Memorandum from Henry Kissinger to President Nixon, 'Atmospherics of My Visit to Peking', 27 June 1972, Lord Files – China Trip – Memcons HAK Visit – 19 – 23 June 1972, Box 851, Nixon Library.
42 Naomi Head, 'Costly Encounters of the Empathic Kind: A Typology', *International Theory* 18, no. 1 (2016).
43 Hall, 'Sympathetic States: Explaining the Russian and Chinese Responses September 11', 2012.
44 Constance Duncombe, 'Twitter and the Challenges of Digital Diplomacy', *SAIS Review of International Affairs* 38, no. 2 (2018): 91–100.
45 James G. Blight, and J. M Lang, *The Fog of War: Lessons from the Life of Robert S. Mcnamara* (Maryland, USA: Rowman & Littlefield Publishers, Inc, 2005).
46 Emma Harrison, 'Psychologist Asserts U.S. and the Soviet Union Share Similar Illusions about Each Other', *New York Times (1923-Current file)*, 6. 1961, September 05 6.
47 Zachary Shore, *A Sense of the Enemy: The High Stakes History of Reading Your Rival's Mind* (Oxford University Press, 2014).
48 Wight, Wright, and Porter, *International Theory: The Three Traditions*, 186–8.
49 Emanuel Adler and Vincent Pouliot, 'International Practices', *International Theory* 3, no. 1 (2011).
50 Vincent Pouliot, 'The Logic of Practicality: A Theory of Practice of Security Communities', *International Organization* 62, no. 2 (2008): 258. This is also covered in Pouliot, *International Security in Practice: The Politics of Nato-Russia Diplomacy*, Vol. 38 (Cambridge University Press, 2010).
51 Vincent Pouliot, *International Security in Practice: The Politics of Nato-Russia Diplomacy.*

52 Rebecca Adler-Nissen and Vincent Pouliot, 'Power in Practice: Negotiating the International Intervention in Libya', *European Journal of International Relations* (2014).
53 Hannah Gurman, '"Learn to Write Well": The China Hands and the Communist-Ification of Diplomatic Reporting', *Journal of Contemporary History* 45, no. 2 (2010); Pablo de Orellana, 'Struggles over Identity in Diplomacy: "Commie Terrorists" Contra "Imperialists" in Western Sahara', *International Relations* (2015).
54 Ralph K. White, 'Misperception and the Vietnam War', *Journal of Social Issues* 22, no. 3 (1966).
55 Gurman, '"Learn to Write Well": The China Hands and the Communist-Ification of Diplomatic Reporting', 430.
56 Margaret MacMillan, *Nixon and Mao: The Week That Changed the World* (Random House, 2007), 108.
57 Hillary R. Clinton, 'Hillary Rodham Clinton Speaks on Security, Inclusive Leadership', Georgetown University, 3 December 2014, http://www.ustream.tv/recorded/56079087 (accessed 5 January 2017).

# Counter-diplomacy: The many ways to say no

Dr Gerrit Kurtz

Diplomacy as the professional practice of representing institutional interests, usually on behalf of states through negotiation and communication, builds on a rich corpus of conventions, rules and norms. Over the past three decades or so, international society has seen an increasing legalization and institutionalization of world politics, including in the field of peace and security.[1] Human rights and human protection norms have gained considerable traction,[2] even though their evolution is not linear, and their implementation is far from consistent. Faced with such depth of international interventionism, some states deploy what we can call *counter-diplomacy*. According to Barston, 'The purpose of "counterdiplomacy" is the use of diplomacy to evade or frustrate political solutions or international rules.'[3] What are the main features of counter-diplomacy, its origins, practices and consequences for the conduct of principled diplomacy? That is the focus of this chapter.

Aside from brief references to the phenomenon, researchers have paid scant attention to counter-diplomacy so far. In an international order where nationalism and authoritarian politics are on the rise again, including in countries previously championing liberal rights and interventionism, counter-diplomacy is increasingly relevant. It is the conceptual equivalent to human rights diplomacy, that is, the use of diplomatic means to promote and protect human rights standards.[4] We can observe it in multilateral forums such as the UN Human Rights Council as well as in bilateral negotiations, for example, between the United States and the Democratic People's Republic of Korea (DPRK) on nuclear disarmament. Counter-diplomacy is the hallmark of authoritarian governments, but nationalist, isolationist or illiberal regimes also resort to versions of it to pursue their interests.

This chapter makes three contributions to the study of counter-diplomacy. Firstly, it further defines counter-diplomacy as a set of diplomatic practices and puts forward a framework to understand how they can operate. This includes three levels – bilateral, multilateral and systemic – and two dimensions – active and passive. Secondly, on a more theoretical level, I present some ideas about the origins of counter-diplomacy, locating it in authoritarian decision-making structures and the normative structure of the international system. Thirdly, there is an empirical contribution. I illustrate how counter-diplomatic practices work based on signets that draw on original research into international diplomacy in post-independence South Sudan, post-war Sri Lanka and secondary literature on multilateral diplomacy involving Iran, the DPRK and China.

The empirical data draws on in-depth research into international diplomatic engagement in post-war Sri Lanka and in post-independence South Sudan, based on more than 160 semi-structured interviews conducted between 2016 and 2019 during several research trips to the countries, but also with diplomats and experts in London, Berlin, New York, Copenhagen, Addis Ababa and Washington, DC.[5]

This chapter adopts a practice-theoretical perspective. Students of diplomacy have turned to practice theory frameworks, which combine a close attention to empirics with analytical concepts derived from the lived reality of practitioners.[6] According to Adler and Pouliot, practices are 'socially meaningful patterns of action, which, in being performed more or less competently, simultaneously embody, act out, and possibly reify background knowledge and discourse in and on the material world'.[7] Practices operate on different scales such as international order, bilateral relations or individual engagement. At the same time, all scales are considered artefacts of social science, as practitioners do not necessarily divide their work into clearly scalable categories.[8] For the purposes of this text, practice theory provides a convenient conceptual language with which to investigate counter-diplomacy.

After this introduction, the argument proceeds in three sections. The second section provides a conceptual discussion of counter-diplomacy by locating it in the state of the art of diplomacy research. In doing so, I develop a conceptual framework of counter-diplomatic practices. The third section includes a discussion of two possible sources of counter-diplomacy, a changing world order and authoritarian decision-making environments. In the fourth section, I illustrate the conceptual discussion with sample practices of bilateral, multilateral and system-level counter-diplomacy. The conclusion briefly discusses questions for further research and implications for policymakers.

Defining counter-diplomacy

Counter-diplomacy as a concept has its roots in the literature on human rights diplomacy. That alone is telling: the promotion and protection of human rights by the means of diplomacy has a strong normative emphasis. As such, counter-diplomacy is also an expression of the resistance to an expanding scope for international attention to domestic processes and the enduring tension between national sovereignty and international norms. Nonetheless, researchers have only defined counter-diplomacy in passing. O'Flaherty et al. describe three functions of counter-diplomacy:

> first, engaging in diplomatic action with the intention to undermine established human rights standards; second, the use of diplomatic means by states to minimise and refute criticism of their human rights record; and third, the instrumentalisation of human rights by some actors to achieve foreign policy goals not related to the promotion and protection of human rights.[9]

These three points are already everything the authors say about counter-diplomacy, as they only mention it to define their subject of human rights diplomacy. We can take two important aspects from this approach: counter-diplomacy can target established rules, norms and conventions such as human rights standards, and it may target the application of those rules in specific circumstances or with regard to a given country. O'Flaherty et al.'s last point can be understood as a specific case of the first aspect, as inconsistency or hypocrisy as a result of the instrumentalist use of normative standards may also serve to undermine their validity.

Barston places counter-diplomacy in the wider context of modern diplomacy, by noting that 'for some, the purpose of "counter-diplomacy" is the use of diplomacy to evade or frustrate political solutions or international rules. Counter-diplomacy seeks the continuation or extension of a conflict and facilitation of parallel violence'.[10] His definition of counter-diplomacy as evading or frustrating political solutions or international rules can be applied to a broad range of diplomatic interactions. For our conceptual discussion, we can distil the distinction between active and passive strategies from Barston's approach. Active strategies concern attempts to undermine international unity, defer action, divert attention and dissemble persuasive efforts, passive ones the ability of interlocutors to withstand external pressure and to ignore diplomatic arguments. There is no strict separation between the two in practice, as resistance may, for example, involve deliberate stubbornness to wear the negotiating partner out, splitting diplomatic groupings in the process.

Barston's conception clarifies that counter-diplomacy is more than mere non-cooperative behaviour. By its nature, it is an instrument directed against a stronger partner, a majority or dominant norms, making it commonly but not exclusively used by weak governments. Actors using counter-diplomacy are frequently involved in the violations of major international norms, for example, in active hostilities or repression. In contrast, we should separate such behaviour from anti-system forces that protest inequality in the international system itself, if they do so constructively. For example, the Non-Aligned Movement strongly argued in favour of decolonization in the 1950s and 1960s, but did so through established procedures and with references to established standards such as national self-determination promised in the UN Charter.[11]

Manipulation as part of counter-diplomacy still involves intergovernmental relations conducted by official agents, not clandestine practices of intelligence agencies such as 'active measures', for example, trying to influence foreign elites or publics through overt or covert means.[12] The Russian influence campaign during the US elections in 2016, for example, was not conducted by diplomats, but by the military intelligence service.[13] Conversely, denial and obfuscation at the diplomatic level form integral parts of foreign disinformation campaigns or so-called hybrid warfare as practiced by Russia in Eastern Ukraine and in Crimea.[14]

We may distinguish between three levels of counter-diplomacy: bilateral, multilateral and systemic (Table 1). The bilateral or direct engagement includes practices that concern the interaction between individual diplomats and policymakers. These aim at undermining the trust and integrity of diplomatic negotiations at an individual level, for example, denial and obfuscation. Multilateral practices of counter-diplomacy concern group dynamics. They may try to undermine collective cohesiveness to foster rifts and splits within a diplomatic community, making concerted pressure more difficult to apply. Lastly, systemic practices of counter-diplomacy target the rules, norms and conventions that undergird diplomacy more directly. Such practices may include weakening the application or interpretation of rules and diluting their scope.

All three levels inform each other. Repeated occasions of lies, denials and obfuscations in bilateral interactions add up to undermine the diplomatic conduct on a more systemic level. Furthermore, official statements are not always easy to check for countries with relatively small diplomatic capacity, access to first-hand information or with a strong support for national sovereignty. Calling out unclear, vague or outright wrong statements not only impacts the interactions between the individuals involved, but also group dynamics.

Table 1 Levels and practices of counter-diplomacy

Level of interaction	Practices of counter-diplomacy (examples)	
	Active	Passive
Bilateral	Denunciation	Denial
	Obfuscation	
Multilateral	Deferring the implementation of commitments	Wearing others out
	Simulated compliance	
	Shifting the international narrative	
	Forum shopping	
Systemic	Diluting international norms or their application	Refusing to take part in international institutions
	Weakening international accountability mechanisms	

Counter-diplomacy undermines the very fabric out of which diplomacy is made: the 'thin culture'[15] of norms, conventions and practices that enables relatively frictionless interactions. In contrast to conventional negotiation practices that are directed towards cooperation, even if interests diverge, counter-diplomacy has only a negative agenda. Practices of counter-diplomacy call attention to the many discursive instruments in the toolbox of non-compliant governments to successfully resist international pressure for a considerable period of time.

Origins in international order and regime type

Where does counter-diplomacy come from? We can hypothesize two broad areas that shape the conditions for counter-diplomacy: a changing international order and the decision-making environment resulting from the regime type of a government.

Counter-diplomacy is likely to have grown in line with the rise of principled diplomacy on human rights and peace.[16] On the one hand, counter-diplomacy is not a new phenomenon. Soviet diplomats sought to undermine human rights norms at the United Nations, South Africa resisted international pressure during Apartheid and Nazi Germany successfully played for time during negotiations in Munich in 1938. More broadly, deception, lies and obfuscation have been a feature of diplomacy just as they are of any social conduct. On the other hand, the spread of international norms and deepening of international cooperation in the past thirty years have created a more pronounced counter-reaction. At least formally, there is a greater expectation at the global level to adhere to democratic standards and abide by international human rights norms. International interventionism in political, economic and normative terms has intensified considerably.

The norms of international cooperation have thickened.[17] This includes regional integration in Europe, West Africa and South America, for example. International criminal justice and transitional justice mechanisms have not brought an end to impunity for atrocity crimes, but they have at least opened discussions that were largely absent during the Cold War. In specific settings such as the former Yugoslavia and Rwanda, international trials brought perpetrators of heinous crimes to justice.[18] The UN Security Council, despite its contested deliberations, remains much more active than it was during 1945 to 1990, including by managing peace operations that bring around a hundred thousand troops, police and civilian staff to conflict areas.[19] In the UN Human Rights Council, created in 2006, the Universal Periodic Review brings regular international attention to the human rights record of all member states, creating a measure of accountability at the intergovernmental level.

The result of these developments has been that governments face greater international scrutiny for their actions. Even if international norm evolution has not been consistent or linear, there is a discursive pressure to justify non-compliant behaviour or to portray government policy to be in line with global conceptions of democracy and human rights. Even in settings which are designed as purely intergovernmental such as the UN Security Council, justifications are often made in terms of international law.[20] Given the surge in nationalism in many countries around the world in the past few years, including in the United States and Europe, it is possible that these discursive pressures may recede again.[21]

This brings us to the second set of factors that may account for counter-diplomacy: authoritarian or nationalist decision-making environments. Foreign policy analysts have long identified the regime type of a state as a critical influence on its foreign policy behaviour, going back to the democratic peace theory and Immanuel Kant's perpetual peace.[22] Hudson argues that studying leadership in foreign policy is likely to be more important in a highly personalized system as compared to an institutionalized parliamentary democracy with its checks and balances, even though even in long-established democracies, the executive is usually much more independent of parliamentary oversight in foreign policy than in domestic affairs.[23] The regime type socializes diplomats and national leaders into specific decision-making environments that position them to adopt certain diplomatic practices.

We can assume two fundamental causal mechanisms in this area. One assumes an electoral or legitimacy benefit of a government domestically; the other is a more straightforward translation of domestic features of the decision-making environment to international diplomacy, which we may call 'mirror' mechanism.

The legitimacy mechanism includes instances where nationalist governments may benefit from presenting their policies as directed against foreign influence. In peace and conflict studies, this is known as 'diversionary theory of war', that is, the idea that leaders start military actions to divert domestic attention from internal failures and produce what is known as a 'rally around the flag effect' of additional support for the leadership.[24] Diplomats, in turn, may follow the same logic by attacking foreign governments or international organizations as a way of diverting attention from domestic governance shortcomings, even though this denial is not always successful in raising domestic legitimacy effectively.[25]

The domestic origins of counter-diplomacy track the initial phases of the 'spiral model' of human rights compliance. Starting with a 'denial phase' of governments not compliant with international norms, the model assumes that combined international and domestic pressure can move governments to make 'tactical concessions', thus entrapping them in a discourse on human rights compliance.[26] The 'rhetorical entrapment' does not always work though, as governments may only want to appear to be compliant with international demands to avoid further scrutiny in practice. One common example is the ratification of international human rights treaties without fully implementing them domestically.[27] Lack of compliance with international commitments may also be a result of fragmented governments, with one part sponsoring a commitment and another part of a government – for example, key line ministries, coalition partners or a head of state – frustrating implementation. Sri Lanka's commitment to transitional justice in the UN Human Rights Council between 2015 and 2019 illustrates this dynamic, with the prime minister and president pulling in different relations, despite being formally allied in a unity government.[28]

The 'mirror' mechanism of the domestic origins of counter-diplomacy assumes that the conditions of domestic decision-making environments influence diplomatic behaviour directly, without necessarily a domestic feedback effect. Autocratic rule is based on the close control of information vis-à-vis the public, and distrust among elites.[29] Rulers constantly fear that rising members of the elite could dispose them, or that small groups could mobilize popular grievances to run an insurgency.[30]

In personalized authoritarian regimes, members of the elite engage in constant positioning based on the signal they want to send to the leader. For East African countries such as Sudan and South Sudan, de Waal writes about a 'political marketplace' on which loyalties are traded, often against monetary or military means.[31] Other authors have described the 'neo-patrimonialism' in many African regimes, where personal relationships sustained by favours, gifts, bribes or other signals of commitment dominate formal institutional processes.[32] One of their distinctive features is the uncertainty that governs all decision-making processes, as citizens and members of the elite do not know whether formal bureaucratic or personal clientelist structures will apply in a situation.[33] Where dissent is treated as treason, the quality of decision-making inevitably suffers, leading to 'group think' and isolationism.[34] Leaders encircle themselves with trusted advisors that confirm, rather than challenge, their opinions, and become increasingly difficult to reach from outside the inner circle of power. The more beleaguered a leader, the more he or she often withdraws from reality. 'You run against a wall,' said an international interviewee about the Rajapaksa government in 2014. 'Such regimes are emotional. They don't think about the population, but take everything personally.'[35]

There are pernicious effects of authoritarian control and manipulation of information. Objectivity and authenticity gradually erode. When nothing can be relied upon to be true anymore, everything can be said without consequences. As a result, diplomats have a hard time holding their counterparts to account. Duplicity, lies and obfuscation in the domestic realm lead diplomats and leaders to question the sincerity of international interactions, gradually eroding the grounds on which diplomacy functions.

Counter-diplomacy in practice

Bilateral level: Denunciation, denial and obfuscation

Interactions with authoritarian governments offer countless examples of counter-diplomacy. Usually, governments use more subtle methods than those offered by the likes of the Democratic People's Republic of Korea. Given its international isolation, its representatives do not shy away from open *denunciation* of the United States, Japan or other states. Chairman Kim Jong Un and US President

Trump exchanged a series of public insults, with Trump calling Kim 'little rocket man' at his speech at the UN General Debate in 2017, and Kim calling Trump 'dotard', using a derogatory term for a senile person.[36] While these were very personal comments, both sides have used belligerent rhetoric frequently in the past.[37] The rhetoric signals to their respective domestic audiences their resolve in dealing with the perceived enemy. Denunciation is a sign that relations have deteriorated to a very low state indeed.

A more common form of counter-diplomacy is *denial*. In situations of repression and conflict, denial is a frequent practice in dealing with allegations of violations of international norms. The absence of international witnesses and documentary evidence facilitates denial, for example, because governments have expelled journalists and other international observers from remote conflict areas. With an increasing presence of smartphones, mobile internet, commercially available satellite pictures and other open-source data, however, at least large-scale violations are becoming more difficult to hide. For example, the Russian government still denies responsibility for providing the weapon that was used to shoot down flight MH17 over Eastern Ukraine on 17 July 2014. The private investigative organization Bellingcat used openly available information to trace the origin of the Buk missile back to Russia.[38] The Iranian government may have had this experience in mind when they admitted in January 2020 that a unit of the Iranian Revolutionary Guard Corps had erroneously shut down another passenger plane (flight PS759), after having denied previous reports and having talked about an accident immediately after the downing on 8 January 2020.[39] In short, being able to deny allegations credibly depends on the other's access to specific information and evidence.

Outright denials are difficult to sustain in the long run. *Obfuscation* aims to obscure facts, victim and perpetrator, or responsibility generally. In May 2017, for example, the South Sudanese government declared a unilateral ceasefire.[40] A UN official complained in an interview about the political intentions of that statement:

> It makes the government look good, because you put it in all the communiqués that the government has declared a ceasefire. So it is also being used politically. [With] a negotiated ceasefire, the government won't have any argument anymore that it is being attacked.[41]

According to other interviewees, the South Sudanese government frequently justified its military operations as 'self-defence'. 'They have been particularly good in the last year in doing offensives which were not completely full scale, so more difficult to see,' an EU diplomat said referring to the South Sudanese government.⁴² With little access to the field, and international monitors only being able to reach sites of reported fighting after days, if at all, diplomats struggled to raise apparent violations in meetings with the government or opposition effectively.

Multilateral level: Dividing and diverting international attention

Counter-diplomatic practices at the multilateral level concern the dynamics of diplomatic groups. The chief aim of those practices is to divide international actors, making it more difficult for them to exert pressure. *Deferring international commitments* is one such way to avoid having to say no openly. For example, the South Sudanese government accepted a so-called regional protection force (RPF) as a more robust force within the existing UN Mission in South Sudan (UNMISS) during a visit by the UN Security Council led by the United States in September 2016. Actual deployment took a long time afterwards, as a diplomat explained: 'Then they dragged it. They get everything into a process. They would never say no, we won't do this. They would say yes, but then you would have these endless processes of […] the clearing of the equipment or visas for the troops, all of this, it drags on and on.'⁴³ This way, South Sudanese diplomats could refer to an ongoing process of cooperation, which some member states were ready to accept.

Sometimes governments do not even pretend to be willing to comply with international demands and just try to resist international pressure by *wearing others out*. In 2015, for example, President Salva Kiir announced the creation of twenty-eight states mere weeks after signing the Agreement for the Resolution of Conflict in the Republic of South Sudan (ARCSS). As the agreement's power-sharing formula was based on the original ten states, Kiir's move was in clear violation of the agreement. He knew that international and regional attention would substantially decrease after the high-level signing ceremony, that Western countries would (at least initially) defer to the region and that the region would take time to set up the body charged with monitoring the agreement's implementation. Given the relatively muted response beyond a few statements, Kiir went ahead with announcing the nomination of the governors of the new states on Christmas Eve, appointing them on New Year's Eve. 'They knew perfectly well that all the capitals would be on leave during that time because it was Christmas, so the reaction would not happen,' an EU diplomat said in an interview. 'They are extremely smart, not in governing the country, but in playing with the international community including the region, they are excellent.'⁴⁴

Simulated compliance is a flavour of multilateral counter-diplomacy that goes a step further. Instead of deferring implementation of a commitment, governments establish institutions, procedures and policies that seem to comply with international demands, norms and commitments. At a closer look, they can be designed to shift attention by acting disingenuously. The national dialogue was one such example in South Sudan that occupied and divided the diplomatic community in Juba for at least a few months in early 2017. The basic concept of the national dialogue, as communicated by the government, was to engage in open consultations on a grassroots level, with the idea that all problems facing local communities would be discussed at the lowest possible level.[45] Diplomats in Juba were split on what to make of it. Even the strongest critics of the process acknowledged that the civil society drivers of the national dialogue, the Sudd Institute and the Ebony Centre, genuinely believed in its merits. But they had serious doubts about the government's intentions. 'I think that the national dialogue was launched mainly as a smokescreen to delay sanctions in the Security Council and to buy time from the international community,' said a Troika diplomat.[46] For Germany and Japan, the dialogue provided an opportunity to move away from the model of transactional power-sharing that many saw as having failed.

To the extent that the launch of the national dialogue helped to convey a story of a local peace-making initiative away from the glitzy hotel rooms of high-level negotiations in Addis Ababa, it was an exercise in *shifting international narratives*. The Iranian nuclear programme exemplifies this discursive battle well. The Iranian government would portray it as a response to their energy needs, in line with the nuclear Non-Proliferation Treaty. It would also allege the United States to be highly hypocritical, as not fulfilling its own obligations to substantially reduce its nuclear arsenal. The US government and its partners, on the other hand, put the programme in the context of regional and international security, taking Iran's aggressive rhetoric towards Israel and enmity with its Arab neighbours as a cue.[47] If successful, shifting narratives serve as claims to international legitimacy of policies and practices.[48]

Domestic actors try to carve out a political space for themselves when they are under pressure. Manipulating the positions of international actors is a convenient way of doing so. In the multilateral sphere, *forum shopping* is a common (counter) diplomatic practice that researchers have described with regard to negotiations.[49] It also occurred in the peace mediation that IGAD and its international partners pursued to end South Sudan's civil war. In 2014, Tanzania, supported (in some cases later) by Kenya, Uganda, South Africa and

Egypt, introduced a dialogue process that ran separate to the peace negotiations in Addis Ababa under the aegis of IGAD and dominated by Ethiopia, the then-chair of IGAD. The Arusha process, as it came to be known, aimed to reconcile the fragmented governing party, the Sudan People's Liberation Movement/Army (SPLM/A). The problem was that nearly the same groups and sets of people participated in the two tracks. With the Arusha process taking a softer approach, it became harder for mediators to sign the parties up for an agreement for a comprehensive peace settlement in Addis Ababa. 'We need to be extremely careful not to be manipulated or played against each other. Because they are very good at that,' a Troika diplomat said in an interview.[50]

Systemic level: Diluting norms, weakening accountability

The international order is governed by norms, rules and conventions, which allow diplomacy to function. Counter-diplomacy at the systemic level seeks to *dilute* those *norms*, or at least their application, and the mechanisms by which actors may be held accountable for their infringements. Major powers are in a privileged position to influence these dynamics through their policies and practices. China, for example, has consistently argued that international human rights norms need to adjust to 'national circumstances'. Analysing Chinese statements on human rights in the UN between 2000 and 2010, Kinzelbach found that 'Beijing accepts, by and large, the normative frame provided by international human rights, but it rejects many of its implications'.[51] Kent agrees with the analysis, warning that 'China is gradually undermining the universal principles underlying international institutions and the perceived legitimacy of the international rules'.[52] In July 2019, China demonstrated how this could look like. In a reaction to a letter to the United Nations by twenty-two states criticizing its mass detention of Uighurs in the province of Xinjiang, it organized a group of thirty-seven countries lauding its human rights practices.[53]

Despite their other efforts to advance international norms, the United States has been even more aggressive than China in certain instances in their counter-diplomacy to *weaken accountability mechanisms*. Under President George W. Bush, the US government not only rejected the Rome Statute of the International Criminal Court, it also asked states to sign 'bilateral immunity agreements' guaranteeing that they will not transfer US citizens or contractors to the court. The US Congress passed the American Service-Members' Protection Act, linking US military assistance to the signing of an immunity agreement.[54] More than 100 states signed the agreements; 56 of the State Parties to the Rome Statute refused.⁵⁵ Early US resistance to the court made it easier for other governments, in particular in Africa, to question the court later on, for example, regarding the accountability of sitting heads of state. The US exemption and efforts to secure them worldwide substantiated the view by many African governments and observers of a 'partisan notion of justice'.⁵⁶

A passive dimension of systemic counter-diplomacy is for major powers to reject international institutions by simply *not joining or withdrawing* from them. The United Nations draws significant strength from its near-universal membership and the representation of (many of) the most powerful countries on the Security Council. This is in marked contrast to the League of Nations, which the United States helped give birth to but then refrained from joining. In June 2018, the US government withdrew from the UN Human Rights Council, aborting its elected membership. With the election of President Trump, the US government also ceased inviting UN special rapporteurs, an important instrument of the Human Rights Council. While the United States justified its move as a protest against what it perceived as bias against Israel and a membership that included countries with problematic human rights records, its withdrawal left it without a vote on the issues that are discussed at the Council. Jamil Dakwar, director of the American Civil Liberties Union's human rights program, pointed to the pernicious effect of the US withdrawal: It was a 'very dangerous message to other countries: that if you don't cooperate with UN experts they will just go away.'⁵⁷ That message is a subversive consequence of counter-diplomacy.

Conclusion: Maintaining resilience vis-á-vis counter-diplomacy

This chapter outlined a first detailed treatment of counter-diplomacy. It argued that counter-diplomacy goes beyond mere resistance and denial, involving a broad spectrum of practices and mechanisms at the bilateral, multilateral and systemic levels. Common to them all is the destructive nature of counter-diplomacy, which undermines trust, unity and the validity of international norms and processes. If we accept that diplomacy is based on a 'thin culture' of professional norms, rules and conventions,⁵⁸ counter-diplomacy is a thorn in the thickening of such a culture. It is important to distinguish counter-diplomacy from mere antagonism and confrontation. Counter-diplomacy does not mean simply opposing peace, human rights, democracy or what are perceived as foreign ideas and values. It is about undermining the practices, processes and mechanisms that diplomacy has developed to negotiate these difficult and complex issues.

Understanding the multifaced nature of counter-diplomacy is essential not just for diplomatic and human rights studies, but for policymakers as well. A significant amount of diplomatic studies focuses on the practices and perspectives of liberal democratic states or great powers. Counter-diplomacy frequently targets the weaknesses and guiding tenets of their diplomacy, including through exploiting state-centric, formal and other biases of diplomatic practices. Deconstructing some of the practices of counter-diplomacy can help understand the conditions under which principled diplomacy can flourish. Trust, consistency, unity and upholding international norms are, conversely, crucial characteristics of such principled engagement.[59]

Further research on all aspects of counter-diplomacy is needed. This chapter suggests that a thickening normative international order as well as authoritarian and nationalist decision-making environments may explain the origins and emergence of counter-diplomatic practices. At the same time, there is a lot of variation in the diplomatic conduct of authoritarian and nationalist governments: when do they see conventional diplomatic practices in their interest, and when do they resort to subvert them? It is also possible that historical comparisons that study the diplomacy of the Soviet Union as major power or small isolated regimes like Enver Hoxha's Albania can bring further factors to light.

At the other end of the causal chain, the effects and consequences of counter-diplomatic practices should be further explored. Case studies and process tracing can be helpful in specifying the causal mechanisms under which some counter-diplomatic practices undermine conventional diplomacy – and under which conditions they are less effective. The discussion and examples focused on state-based diplomacy, in a rather narrow and conventional definition of diplomacy. How do non-state actors use counter-diplomacy, for example, rebel movements or jihadist groups? Possibly, effective counter-diplomacy depends on a minimal legitimacy and integration in the international system: if no one trusts an armed group, they cannot destroy relationships that do not exist internationally.

Counter-diplomacy is a set of practices to be reckoned with. At a time when the international normative order is changing and closed regimes are on the rise around the world, it is likely that counter-diplomacy is going to be more prevalent in the future. Developing resilience will require more systematic attention to the phenomenon and ongoing reflection by academics and diplomats alike.

Notes

1. Kenneth W. Abbott, Robert O. Keohane, Andrew Moravcsik, Anne-Marie Slaughter and Duncan Snidal, 'The Concept of Legalization', *International Organization* 3, no. 54 (2000): 401–19.
2. Alex J. Bellamy, 'The Humanisation of Security? Towards an International Human Protection Regime', *European Journal of International Security* 1, no. 1 (2016): 112–33; Gerrit Kurtz and Philipp Rotmann, 'The Evolution of Norms of Protection: Major Powers Debate the Responsibility to Protect', *Global Society* 1, no. 30 (2016): 3–20.
3. Ronald Peter Barston, *Modern Diplomacy*, 4th edition (New York: Routledge, 2013), 5.
4. Katrin Kinzelbach and Julian Lehmann, *Can Shaming Promote Human Rights? Publicity in Human Rights Foreign Policy. A Review and Discussion Paper*, 2015, European Liberal Forum, Berlin; Michael O'Flaherty, Zdzisław Kędzia, Amrei Müller and George Ulrich, 'Introduction. Human Rights Diplomacy Contemporary Perspectives', in *Human Rights Diplomacy: Contemporary Perspectives*, ed. Michael O'Flaherty, Zdzisław Kędzia, Amrei Müller and George Ulrich (Leiden: Brill Nijhoff, 2011), 1–18.
5. Interviews with international diplomats focused on their analysis of the situation, interaction practices with local stakeholders, and coordination mechanisms. I also talked to South Sudanese and Sri Lankan policymakers. Most interviews took place on a confidential basis, as most interlocutors requested anonymity to speak freely. References to interviews are numbered and include a place and date.
6. Vincent Pouliot, 'The Logic of Practicality: A Theory of Practice of Security Communities', *International Organization* 2, no. 62 (2008): 257–88, Neumann, Iver B., *At Home with the Diplomats: Inside a European Foreign Ministry* (New York: Cornell University Press, 2012), Ole Jacob Sending, Vincent Pouliot and Iver B. Neumann, eds., *Diplomacy and the Making of World Politics* (New York and Cambridge: Cambridge University Press, 2015), Jeremie Cornut, 'Diplomacy, Agency, and the Logic of Improvisation and Virtuosity in Practice', *European Journal of International Relations* 3, no. 24 (2018): 712–36.
7. Emanuel Adler and Vincent Pouliot, 'International Practices: Introduction and Framework', in *International Practices*, ed. Emmanuel Adler and Vincent Pouliot (Cambridge: Cambridge University Press, 2011), 3–35, 4.
8. Christian Bueger and Frank Gadinger, *International Practice Theory*, 2nd edition (Cham: Palgrave Macmillan, 2018), 107.
9. O'Flaherty et al., *Introduction. Human Rights Diplomacy Contemporary Perspectives*, 2.
10. Barston, *Modern Diplomacy*, 5.

11 Chris Alden and Marco Antonio Vieira, 'The New Diplomacy of the South: South Africa, Brazil, India and Trilateralism', *Third World Quarterly* 7, no. 26 (2005): 1077–95.
12 Len Scott, 'Secret Intelligence, Covert Action and Clandestine Diplomacy', *Intelligence & National Security* 2, no. 19 (2004): 322–41, 323.
13 Robert S. Mueller, *Report on the Investigation into Russian Interference in the 2016 Presidential Election* (Washington, DC: US Department of Justice, 2019).
14 Cf. Alexander Lanoszka, 'Russian Hybrid Warfare and Extended Deterrence in Eastern Europe', *International Affairs* 1, no. 92 (2016): 175–95.
15 Ole Jacob Sending, 'United by Difference: Diplomacy as a Thin Culture', *International Journal* 3, no. 66 (2011): 643–59.
16 Paul J. Zwier, *Principled Negotiation and Mediation in the International Arena: Talking with Evil* (Cambridge: Cambridge University Press, 2013), Morten B. Pedersen and David Kinley, eds., *Principled Engagement: Negotiating Human Rights in Repressive States* (Ashgate: Farnham, Surrey, England; Burlington, VT, 2013).
17 Alec Stone Sweet, 'A Cosmopolitan Legal Order: Constitutional Pluralism and Rights Adjudication in Europe', *Global Constitutionalism* 1, no. 1 (2012): 53–90.
18 Mark Kersten, *Justice in Conflict: The Effects of the International Criminal Court's Interventions on Ending War and Building Peace* (Oxford: Oxford University Press, 2016).
19 Sebastian von Einsiedel, David M. Malone and Bruno Stagno Ugarte, eds., *The UN Security Council in the Twenty-first Century* (Boulder, Colorado: Lynne Rienner Publishers, 2016).
20 Ian Johnstone, 'Security Council Deliberations: The Power of the Better Argument', *European Journal of International Law* 3, no. 14 (2003): 437–80, Ian Johnstone, *The Power of Deliberation. International Law, Politics and Organizations* (Oxford: Oxford University Press, 2011).
21 Sarah Margon, 'Giving up the High Ground: America's Retreat on Human Rights Letting Go', *Foreign Affairs*, no. 97 (2018): 39–47, Philip Alston, 'The Populist Challenge to Human Rights', *Journal of Human Rights Practice* 1, no. 9 (2017): 1–15.
22 Nils Petter Gleditsch, 'Democracy and Peace', *Journal of Peace Research* 4, no. 29 (1992): 369–76, James Lee Ray, 'Wars between Democracies: Rare, or Nonexistent?' *International Interactions* 3, no. 18 (1993): 251–76.
23 Valerie M. Hudson (2007), *Foreign Policy Analysis. Classic and Contemporary Theory* (Plymouth: Rowman and Littlefield), 38.
24 Jack S. Levy and William R. Thompson, *Causes of War* (Oxford: Wiley and Sons, 2010), 99–104.
25 For a discussion of the case of Russia after the annexation of Crimea, see Elias Gotz, 'Putin, the State, and War: The Causes of Russia's Near Abroad Assertion Revisited', *International Studies Review* 2, no. 19 (2016): 228–53.

26 Thomas Risse, Stephen C. Ropp and Kathryn Sikkink, eds., *The Persistent Power of Human Rights: From Commitment to Compliance* (Cambridge: Cambridge University Press, 2013).
27 Ibid.
28 International Crisis Group, *Sri Lanka's Transition to Nowhere* (Brussels: International Crisis Group, 2017).
29 Ronald Wintrobe, *The Political Economy of Dictatorship* (Cambridge: Cambridge University Press, 1998), 24–5.
30 Milan W. Svolik, *The Politics of Authoritarian Rule* (Cambridge: Cambridge University Press, 2012), Philip Roessler, *Ethnic Politics and State Power in Africa. The Logic of the Coup-civil War Trap* (Cambridge: Cambridge University Press, 2016).
31 Alex De Waal, *The Real Politics of the Horn of Africa. Money, War and the Business of Power* (Cambridge: Polity Press, 2015).
32 Pierre Englebert, 'Pre-Colonial Institutions, Post-Colonial States, and Economic Development in Tropical Africa', *Political Research Quarterly* 1, no. 53 (2000): 7–36.
33 Paul Williams, *War and Conflict in Africa*, 2nd edition (Cambridge: Polity, 2016), 68.
34 Irving L. Janis, *Victims of Groupthink; a Psychological Study of Foreign-policy Decisions and Fiascoes* (Boston: Houghton, 1972).
35 Interview #7, location withheld, 21 October 2016.
36 Austin Ramzy, 'Kim Jong-Un Called Trump a "Dotard." What Does That Even Mean?' *New York Times*, 22 September 2017, https://www.nytimes.com/2017/09/22/world/asia/trump-north-korea-dotard.html (accessed 31 August 2020).
37 Linus Hagström and Magnus Lundström, 'Overcoming US-North Korean Enmity: Lessons from an Eclectic IR Approach', *The International Spectator* 4, no. 54 (2019): 94–108.
38 Bellingcat, 'JIT Indictments and Reactions: Analyzing New Evidence Linking Separatists and Russian Officials to MH17', 2019, https://www.bellingcat.com/news/uk-and-europe/2019/07/17/jit-indictments-and-reactions-analyzing-new-evidence-linking-separatists-and-russian-officials-to-mh17/ (accessed 16 January 2020).
39 *BBC News*, 'Iran Plane Crash: What We Know about Flight PS752', *BBC*, 2020, https://www.bbc.com/news/world-middle-east-51047006 (accessed 16 January 2020).
40 Reuters, 'South Sudan's Kiir Declares Unilateral Ceasefire, Prisoner Release', 2017, https://www.reuters.com/article/us-southsudan-violence/south-sudans-kiir-declares-unilateral-ceasefire-prisoner-release-idUSKBN18I1KY (accessed 16 January 2020).
41 Interview #111, UN official, Juba, 3 October 2017.

42 Interview #121, EU diplomat, by phone, 13 November 2017.
43 Interview #122, European diplomat, by phone, 14 November 2017.
44 Interview #121, EU diplomat, by phone, 13 November 2017.
45 UNDP, *Guide on the National Dialogue Process in South Sudan*, 2017, Juba.
46 Interview #92, Troika diplomat, by phone, 12 September 2017. The Troika on Sudan and South Sudan consists of Norway, the United Kingdom and the United States.
47 Constance Duncombe, 'Representation, Recognition and Foreign Policy in the Iran–US Relationship', *European Journal of International Relations* 3, no. 22 (2016): 622–45.
48 Barbara Warnick and Valerie Manusov, 'The Organization of Justificatory Discourse in Interaction: A Comparison within and across Cultures', *Argumentation* 4, no. 14 (2000): 381–404.
49 Marc L. Busch, 'Overlapping Institutions, Forum Shopping, and Dispute Settlement in International Trade', *International Organization* 4, no. 61 (2007): 735–61, Katharina P. Coleman, 'Locating Norm Diplomacy: Venue Change in International Norm Negotiations', *European Journal of International Relations* 1, no. 19 (2013): 163–86.
50 Interview #92, Troika diplomat, by phone, 12 September 2017.
51 Katrin Kinzelbach, 'Will China's Rise Lead to a New Normative Order? An Analysis of China's Statements on Human Rights at the United Nations (2000–2010)', *Netherlands Quarterly of Human Rights* 3, no. 30 (2012): 299–332, 331.
52 Ann Kent, 'China and the International Multilateral Human Rights System', in *Handbook on Human Rights in China,* ed. Sarah Biddulh and Joshua Rosenzweig (Cheltenham: Edwar Elgar, 2019), 61–83, 72.
53 Nick Cumming-Bruce, 'China's Retort over Its Mass Detentions: Praise from Russia and Saudi Arabia', *New York Times*, 12 July 2019, https://www.nytimes.com/2019/07/12/world/asia/china-human-rights-united-nations.html (accessed 31 August 2020).
54 Robert C. Johansen, 'The Impact of US Policy toward the International Criminal Court on the Prevention of Genocide, War Crimes, and Crimes against Humanity', *Human Rights Quarterly* 2, no. 28 (2006): 301–31.
55 International Coalition for the International Criminal Court, 'Status of US Bilateral Immunity Agreements (BIAs)', 2006, http://www.iccnow.org/documents/CICCFS_BIAstatus_current.pdf (accessed 31 August 2020).
56 Mahmood Mamdani, 'Responsibility to Protect or Right to Punish?' *Journal of Intervention and Statebuilding* 1, no. 4 (2010): 53–67.
57 Ed Pilkington, 'US Halts Cooperation with UN on Potential Human Rights Violations', *The Guardian*, 4 January 2019, https://www.theguardian.com/law/2019/

jan/04/trump-administration-un-human-rights-violations (accessed 31 August 2020).
58 Sending, *United by Difference: Diplomacy as a Thin Culture*.
59 Pedersen and Kinley, *Principled Engagement: Negotiating Human Rights in Repressive States*.

8

Small state security and diplomacy in the not-so-new Europe: Comparing experiences from the Balkans to the Baltic in the twenty-first century

Professor James Gow

Vulnerability has long been seen as a defining feature of the small state.[1] As Tony Payne noted, this is the 'most striking' sign of 'the consequences of smallness in global politics'.[2] Assessments of vulnerability are predicated on material capabilities – small states lack physical resources, most notably military and economic wherewithal.[3] This vulnerability has been historically signalled in Thucydides' account of the Melian conference, which ended with 'great' power Athens' crushing 'small' Melos, killing all the men and taking women and children as slaves.[4] This fate of the small state, which preferred not to ally with Athens, and the famous phrase – the strong do what they want and the weak suffer what they must – epitomizes the condition of the small state, conventionally. In reality, the plethora of small states in the world confirms that not all smaller states suffer Melos' destiny – and, indeed, vulnerability is more complex. Nonetheless, it remains the key challenge however small, or large, a state might be objectively.

Diplomacy has been the chief means historically for tackling this challenge. The main way in which states traditionally address this vulnerability is alignment – forming friendships, partnerships and alliances with others, or establishing forms of neutrality, or non-participation, as appropriate.[5] Addressing vulnerability is a key challenge for all small states and the theory and practice of their security and diplomacy suggests that the way to tackle this susceptibility is to work with others to foster a stable environment.

This is an inherently normative perspective. However, the seemingly positive assumption in the theory is brought into question by the twenty-first-century experiences of small, formerly communist, states in a front stretching from the Balkans to the Baltic. Faced with Russian resurgence, the positive value associated with working with others might be brought into question, depending on the relative closeness of relations to different partners, notably a more threatening Russia vis-à-vis the EU, NATO and the United States. What happens if those prepared to establish closer relations with a small state are more malign and exploitative? What happens if those with whom relationships could, or should, be more positive are distracted, or, generally, not interested, or available? What happens if there is no alternative to cooperation, but that cooperation is not normatively beneficial? To what extent is the positive normative aspect of small state diplomacy theory challenged by the experiences of small states confronting Russian assertiveness, on one side, and frailties in the EU and NATO, on the other?

Following a discussion of 'smallness' and small state diplomacy theory, this chapter compares these experiences in relation to three categories of state: those outside the EU and NATO; those inside one or both of these organizations and directly threatened by Russia; and those inside one or both of these organizations and ostensibly not directly threatened by Russia. As I show, Russian manoeuvring and disruption in the EU and NATO mean that some countries that looked to the latter two for a secure future were left increasingly exposed to the former. This shows not only that the normative aspect of the theory can be questionable, but also that, in the real world of European security, EU and NATO member states needed to be more conscious of the importance of providing security for Central and South East European small states.

Small states and security

There are two main threads in the study of small states in international life. The first is the question: 'what is small?' The other is the need to work with others diplomatically and economically to ensure a secure and stable environment in which to prosper. First, the issue of 'smallness' and why a flexible and contextual approach to it is advisable is explored. The reason for this flexible approach to definition is evident from consideration of security needs and small state security theory, which places emphasis on diplomacy to foster alignment and stable international environments, albeit that this largely normative theory may not be as positive as the theory appears to assume. Nor is practice of the diplomatic theory entirely a matter of a small state's will.

'What is small?' is a question often – probably wisely – answered without precision. Zlatko Šabić eschews a firm definition as too limiting,[6] while Jeanne A. K. Hey points to the advantages of a more flexible definition based on the psychological disposition of either those states feeling themselves to be small, or the perception that a state is 'small' by other states. There are difficulties in seeking objective criteria – to which, she maintains, there would always be exceptions.[7] In a similar vein, Matthias Mass argues for plural, or flexible, definitions in the interest of accommodating research needs and the diversity of small states.[8] In effect, Mosser does the same, suggesting that 'power' is the objective measure of a state's size. However, there is no way to avoid a need to be 'fungible' in definition and categorization. It is hard to avoid concluding that agreement on a single definition is impossible.[9]

The problems with definition quickly become clear with a brief survey of possible criteria. In some cases, as noted above, capabilities,[10] meaning the absence of material resources – physical, economic, military – were the starting point for defining smallness. In Hans J. Morgenthau's representation of power and 'great powers', small states 'have always owed their independence' to great ones.[11] In this sense, certain states are 'big' and others are defined as 'small' in relation to them. Indeed, this reasoning is why Geoffrey Baldachinno prefers to use the term 'smaller' states, emphasizing the relative aspect.[12] His reasoning includes good discussion of why a small state might be hard to define, including how American domination, in particular, of international studies literature appears to treat 'big' as normal and to dismiss, or ignore most smaller states – although he recognizes this probably began with the Treaty of Vienna, in 1815. He points out that, if population is used as a measure, then (at his time of writing), from 237 territories (not all formally 'recognized' as having independent international personality), eleven states had a population over 100 million, and a further twenty-three had over 50 million inhabitants, while 158 had populations under 10 million – with 41 of those having fewer than 100,000. This, he suggests, would make being 'smaller' the normal condition, yet, the main focus remains on larger, if not 'big', states.

The issues are also evident in Vital's attempt to use population in combination with economic development, resulting in a definition of small that is duplex. He regarded 'economically advanced' countries with a population of 10–15 million and 'underdeveloped countries' of 20–30 million as small.[13] Clearly the duality here confirms the challenge of precision. That challenge is little better addressed if the definition adopted by the Commonwealth is considered. The Commonwealth's official definition of a small state is based on the very precise and limited objective criterion (assuming sovereignty and independent international personality) of having a population smaller than 1.5 million people.[14] This definition is shared by the World Bank, which adds some flexibility by using the term 'small population' and adding limited human capital and confined land area to the mix. This makes for a reasonable and flexible understanding.

At the same time, many states that might generally be regarded as small – such as Slovenia, with a population of almost two million – would not be classified as such. This is a point made strongly by Ali Naseer Mohamed, who indicates that adopting the 1.5-million boundary wipes out the category of micro-states, while excluding states with populations of 3–5 million, such as Uruguay and Paraguay, that cannot be considered 'middle' powers, given how much smaller they are than states that might be considered 'middle',[15] if population is the sole criterion. Moreover, although Paul Sutton sees merit in definitions based on vulnerability used by the Commonwealth, he gives a general nod to the utility of having no fixed definition, acknowledging the lack of a single definition and how this is a product of both accident and design.[16] Perhaps this suggests that support for the Commonwealth definition is misguided. Certainly it confirms the problem of a tightly drawn and would-be objective definition.

This problem is noted by Tom Crowards, who somewhat problematically points to the difficulties of attempts to define small states based on what he regards as arbitrary points of delineation, while, at the same time, arguing for a definition that incorporates countries with low income levels. He generates a selection of seventy-nine states that differ from many others.[17] This view serves to underline his starting point, however, that there is no generally accepted definition of a small state. Going beyond the difficulties of precise definition, it is hard not to agree with Payne, who not only notes that there is 'no agreed definition' and 'no sharp dichotomy between a small state and a large state', but also suggests that 'no firm category of analysis will ever be carved out' and this might be preferable. He suggests there might be more benefit simply to 'recognize the multiple natures of the small state phenomenon and focus on their variations in practice'.[18] Thus, attempts at purely objective and empirical definition are not only problematic, but also inadvisable.

The problems of objective criteria and the benefits of flexibility in definition can be seen clearly by reference to the Netherlands. Seeing the country as a wealthy member of the European Union and Nation and with a population of 17 million, it does not seem small. Yet, the Dutch self-perception is that of a small state, which needs to work with other states and, in particular, to shadow the United States as a major power in NATO, while working with Allies in the

European context. Without doubt, on some measures, the Netherlands could be seen as far from small. Economically, for example, a study of the 100 largest economies, as measured by revenue (including 69 corporations), placed the Netherlands at number 13.[19] It was 18th in two other surveys,[20] and 17th in another,[21] all seeking to rank economies by GDP. With a population of 17 million, in 2017,[22] over ten times greater than the World Bank and Commonwealth thresholds for being 'small', and in a world where 130 of the 193 recognized states in the world had populations under 10 million and were regarded as 'small',[23] the Low Lands hardly constituted a good case. Yet, in terms of territory, the Netherlands is small: its area of 41,543 sq km is less than the 45,228 sq km of Estonia, a country mostly regarded as being small.[24] The Netherlands illustrates the problems of seeking objective empirical criteria by which to define a small state, while also pointing to the need for a flexible approach, based largely on the cathectic – whether states feel themselves to be small, which might, itself, be contextual.

Some states that might view themselves as small, by some empirical measures, might not be judged as such. Another reason is that states of quite different sizes, including clearly middle-sized and big states could face the same challenges in an age of internationalization and globalization.[25] While sovereign and independent, paraphrasing John Donne, no state is an island – in the sense that, just as no person can be an island because of necessary human connections – no individual state can exist in isolation (although many small states – and a few larger ones, are islands, or collections of them). All might be vulnerable to international trends and exposed to dynamics in their environment. Thus, any attempt by a state to isolate itself would negatively impact on its political and economic position, and add to its vulnerability. All states are 'system dependent', but the smaller the state, the greater its dependence.[26] The key challenge for all states, mutatis mutandis, is to mitigate and minimize vulnerability, irrespective of a state's objective size.

The traditional ways for states to address this vulnerability are: to form friendships, partnerships and alliances with others; to emphasize the importance of rules and maintaining them internationally; and, last, to be 'open' economically, boosting the state in ways that will preserve its exercise of the sovereign rights that qualify it as a state with independent international personality, even if this involves decisions to exercise sovereign rights in ways that require a relative loss of independence. There is an imperative to work cooperatively and to trade with other states to create a stable and secure environment, in which to prosper. This requires flexibility and a capacity to adapt and make good judgements.[27]

While there are other aspects of diplomacy that small states might deploy, such as pursuing 'niche' positions (as Liechtenstein pursued the questions of self-determination and international criminal justice, in particular, the crime of aggression[28]), the key parts of theory governing small state security intertwine a commitment to a rule-based environment with aligning relationships with others, whether 'big' friends, or collectives, including alliances, or agreeing neutral or non-aligned status, of some kind with different powers.[29] During the Cold War, for example, while many states were allied to the United States or the Soviet Union, numerous others had relations with both sides. Finland, Austria and Yugoslavia, in Europe, all faced both ways, in different senses; in the twenty-first century, as another example, Djibouti leased military bases to both China and the United States, ensuring the state's protection. While Gärtner suggests that a small state's interest in alliance might be debatable and subject to its particular situation,[30] and Hey questions the importance of security in small state foreign policy,[31] there is no doubt that vulnerability and insecurity are core considerations for small states and they are destined to find partners, friends, allies and multilateral and organizational frameworks. Moreover, if they do so, they benefit and vulnerability will be reduced.

However, the need for involvement with other states is not as straightforward as this theory appears to assume. There is a dark underside. To return to the questions posed in the introduction: what happens if those pushing for deeper involvement with a small state are more malign and exploitative than not, while those with whom the small state would seek to work are distracted? The core susceptibility can become greater and can turn to danger, when small states find that those with whom they wish to cooperate are otherwise preoccupied and the frameworks on which they depend are absent. In such a situation, others, especially historically predatory, big states, might exploit weakness. The logic in the theory of small state security remains the need to cooperate with others. But, what if the beneficial normative aspect is largely removed? What if it only exists on the mafia principle of offers being made that cannot be refused? These questions can be explored, and the main theory of small state diplomacy somewhat challenged, in practice, by reference to the current experiences of former communist Central and Eastern Europe. The positive normative aspect of the theory is brought into question, if account is taken of Russian resurgence on one side, and frailties in the EU and NATO, on the other, which left the small states in a region from the Balkans to the Baltic in a fragile position. The remainder of this analysis reviews the situation of different small states across the region, in the face of an assertive Russia and a lack of focus in the EU and NATO.

Russia resurgent, the EU and NATO distracted

In the course of 2016, building on previous years' groundwork and its misdeeds in Ukraine, Russia cast a worrying shadow across Central and South Eastern Europe. Several events had an ominous character: massive military exercises, close to the Baltic states of Estonia, Latvia and Lithuania; a major campaign of subversion and information manipulation, in those countries; and an inexplicable increase in staffing at the Russian Embassy, in Helsinki, to 450 – from a normal level of around 80 – according to US sources. At the same time, Russia actively sought to penetrate everywhere in the Western Balkans, making offers small and weak countries could not afford to reject, which could leave the countries of the region dependent and unable to diversify. Russia gained a highly influential – though far from absolute – hold on much of the region. This was the result of an active policy 'to weaken the bonds between Europe and the United States and among EU members, undermine NATO's solidarity, and strengthen Russia's strategic position in its immediate neighborhood [original] and beyond'.[32]

Russia's resurgence was possible because of various weaknesses surrounding the region's small states. The Western Balkans, in particular, was fragile with armed conflict, or major political violence, an increasing risk. The area was a fabric of domestic crises, fractured political community, tensions within borders and across them, and growing pressures concerning transnational (especially Islamist) terrorism. These growing challenges were augmented by the geopolitical involvement of extra-regional actors – the EU and some of its Member States, NATO, the United States, Turkey, Middle Eastern countries and transnational groups, and, most notably, Russia. The Baltic States, while embedded in the EU and NATO, were not free from frailty in their demographic fabric, with large Russian-speaking populations and Russia's backing for these kin-populations strong, making those communities potential kindle for conflagration.

All of this was compounded by a downward spiral of endemic corruption and economic decline, and the overwhelming impact of the migration crisis, affecting many countries, and also the EU. Most significantly of all, the faltering position of the EU, in the wake of the migration crisis and Brexit, changed the strategic dynamic in the region. These two major crises effectively crippled the EU, removing enlargement from the immediate agenda, a key factor in security and stabilization, and impeding Russian influence. The UK was one of the most ardent supporters of further enlargement as a strategy to enhance regional stability. Without this impetus, the EU was set to be more influenced by strong voices against enlargement in the foreseeable future. Moreover, whatever the preferences of remaining member states, the UK's unexpected vote to leave the Union put the EU's future into question and made member states turn towards negotiating diminution, rather than enlargement.

It is this distraction that opened the way for wider Russian activity, as the EU and the Alliance, and their individual member states, lost sight of the ball. It left the region and its small states worse off and in their most vulnerable condition for a decade, or more. Several small, former communist states – Slovenia and the Baltics, notably – had often aligned themselves with the UK in the Union. The effective absence of the UK and its prospective departure left small states that shadowed London, and also gained backing and support from it, more vulnerable and needing reorientation.

When the phenomenon of the US presidency of Donald Trump was added to the equation, albeit only with reference to NATO, then the predicament of the countries of the region became worse. The perceived weakness of his predecessor, President Barack Obama, especially regarding Russia, was already a concern in Central and South Eastern Europe. However, Donald Trump's succeeding him was a matter for alarm. Trump had publicly asked, 'Wouldn't it be nice if we got along with Russia?' and stated that he did not see why the United States should come to the defence of Central and East European countries. In addition, the persistent and growing evidence-based allegations that Trump, or at least his team, received campaign funding and other assistance from Russia left those in the region concerned. While there might be hope that the US system would, eventually, get Washington to do the right thing, the absence of certainty encouraged Moscow and left the small states needing to work with other states, in the growing hold of Vladimir Putin's Russia.

Insiders, not ostensibly threatened

In the present section, two countries that joined both the EU and NATO, albeit at different stages, will be considered: Slovenia and Croatia. The former was one of the most advanced former communist countries. It made strong and fast early progress in transition, albeit suffering significant economic dislocation in the combined processes of overcoming transition from communism, gaining a full independent international personality, and recovering from a brief war of independence. The latter only acceded to the European security organizations later, taking longer to make the transition, in particular because of its involvement in war for a longer period. As will be shown, this left Croatia more open to manipulation than Slovenia.

Slovenia was fortunate to accede to both the Union and the Alliance in 2004 (having missed the first wave of NATO enlargement, in 1999). The country could establish itself, while these Western organizations were still predisposed to enlargement and widening security in the region. Slovenia's accession to both NATO and the EU, and its performance since joining those organizations, was shaped by a conscious approach to bilateral relationships.[33] The pattern of bilateral relations gave Ljubljana a relatively secure position vis-à-vis Russia.

One critical example in this regard was Italy's provision of air defence, under the rubric of a collective NATO initiative. With no fixed wing fighter capability and little in the way of ground-based air defence systems, Slovenia could not effectively control its own air space. The arrangement with the Alliance essentially meant Italy offered Slovenia protection. At the same time, it also signalled a degree of flexibility, cooperation and role specialization, shaping the Alliance, as a whole.

The relationship with Italy within NATO was not the only example of Slovenia's military cooperation with its new Allies. In the run-up to accession, Slovenia engaged in building a defence relationship with France. While cooperation with Italy offered clear substantive benefit, cooperation with France had more to do with diplomacy, as Ljubljana sought to balance its security policy position within the Alliance and the EU. Defence cooperation with France offset closer relationships with countries such as the UK and the United States. This was a canny move to ensure the country was not seen to be entirely in one camp.

The relationship with the UK was clearly calculated. Ljubljana had made the judgement at an early stage that its vision of the EU and the core of defence issues in NATO meant a general approach that shadowed London's policy.[34] At the heart of Ljubljana's assessment was a vision shared with the UK, in which state sovereignty remained important in defining the nature of the EU. The EU agenda should not be marked by centralization and federalization. Shared views could be seen once Slovenia joined the Union, for example, in terms of the overall EU Budget for the 2007–13 period.[35]

Comparable with both its emerging relationship with Italy, based on physical proximity, and its political proximity to the UK, Ljubljana developed good links with Austria in the European context. The relationship with Vienna predated Slovenia's independence, as Austrian diplomats sought to create a zone of influence corresponding to the former Habsburg Empire, just at the moment the Socialist Federative Republic was falling apart and Slovenia was picking up speed towards independence. The Ljubljana–Vienna relationship continued on broadly good terms. This was despite frictions in the context of cultural politics. These included the rights of ethnic Slovenes in Austria and claims in some Austrian quarters that Slovenia had a minority of its people of German origin. They also involved suggestions that Ljubljana might owe compensation to ethnic Germans who lost their properties in the 1945 expulsion of ethnic Germans from communist-controlled Yugoslavia, and sensitivities over the Slovenian 20-cent coin, which bore an engraving of Lipizzaner horses, reminding their Austrian neighbours that these famous horses originated from the Karst region of Slovenia. Nonetheless, the generally positive tenor of bilateral relations predominated, balanced with other relationships, leading to a positive role being played in the security context.

Alongside these important links, Slovenia fostered its relationship with the United States, in particular. It used its position not only to gain influence in, and friendship with, Washington, but also to serve as a bridge to Russia. The Slovenian government tried to promote itself as a conduit for the United States, offering itself as a 'bridge' between Eastern and Western nations. Ljubljana sought to play its dual position, well established in the Western sphere and aligned with its Italian and Austrian neighbours, on one side, but with Slavic culture and a communist past, on the other.

The country maintained good relations with the United States and Russia, and Slovenia, secure in its membership of the EU and NATO, looked for increased economic cooperation with Russia. At times, there was domestic criticism of deeper involvement with Russia, and there were specific moves to re-balance by working closely with Washington – a specific initiative when Marjan Šarec became Prime Minister, in 2018. But, he, too, walked the line between the United States and Russia, developing business projects through a bilateral body, the Slovenia–Russia commission, and visiting Russia to inaugurate a monument to the Slovenes who died on Russian territory during the First and Second World Wars, reinforcing cultural links.

Slovenes were well aware of the risks for a small state engaging with a power, such as Russia. Their neighbours to the south and east, in the Western Balkans, offered evidence of problems that could emerge. Some of these will be discussed in the following section, which addresses countries outside the EU and NATO realms.[36] It could also be seen, for example, in EU and NATO member Croatia, Slovenia's immediate southern neighbour, as much as in the non-EU states in the region.

Croatia had joined both the Union and the Alliance several years after Slovenia, in 2013 and 2009, respectively. This was because it had been weaker, and continued to be in a more vulnerable position. Yet, it had acceded to the Union, just before the EU lost its appetite for enlargement, so, while the passage of time left it less well positioned than Ljubljana, time was on Zagreb's side. Nonetheless, in 2016, Croatia's economy was shaken, as a consequence of businesses' accepting Russian loans – inevitably state-backed – that seemed too good to refuse. That also made them too good to be true.

This was the case with Croatian agricultural conglomerate Agrokor – worth over one sixth of the country's economy, which experienced major troubles that had devastating impact in Bosnia and Herzegovina, where Agrokor had a major presence. Agrokor's crisis threatened Croatia's economic standing and stability. As Agrokor tottered towards collapse, owing around €6 billion, around six times its capital, it threatened to devastate the country's economy. With a 25 per cent unemployment rate, among the highest in Europe, the impact of losing one of its biggest employers (with over 40,000 employees) was dangerous enough for social stability. However, the company's €6.5 billion revenues represented 16 per cent of Croatia's GDP.

The scale of the collapse meant that the Croatian state was completely hamstrung, as any bailout was beyond the state's means. This lack of capacity was enough to keep the government on the sidelines; however, evidence of irregularities and corruption – rife throughout the region – meant that intervention would be a poisoned chalice. This led to Prime Minister Andrej Plenković's sacking Finance Minister Zdravko Marić, at the end of April 2016,[37] as Marić had been a senior executive at Agrokor.[38] Thus, the government was confronted with a massive economic and security challenge, but unable to intervene, aside from encouraging buyers and investors to take on parts of the business, or seeking to encourage arrangements with the company's mainly Russian creditors.

The Agrokor catastrophe was, in part, a problem of Russian making. Agrokor, as with much of the regional economy, had become dependent on Russia. Russian loans, at unrealistically favourable rates, linked to energy sales by Gazprom, left companies like Agrokor and countries like Croatia indebted to Russia. When Russia called in loans, the crisis was generated, opening the way for Russia to generate even greater dependency, and leaving Croatia (and others) without significant alternatives. This made businesses and countries dependent in ways that raised security concerns and threatened greater instability. Agrokor revealed Russia's increasing presence in the region, seemingly attempting to control it through a mixture of destabilization, security infiltration and domination, and economic and financial control. There appeared to be a link between membership and the degree of integration, as Slovenia's longer-term and more embedded status put it in a stronger position, even if vulnerable, still.

Outsiders, ambiguously positioned

If Russia could cause problems with countries inside the EU and NATO, especially if membership was less long-standing, its scope for leverage was greater with countries outside the EU or NATO embrace. Serbia and, prior to its accession to NATO, Montenegro illustrate this. The scope of Russia's infiltration and the challenges faced were evident, as were the degree to which closeness to the EU, or NATO, served to impede Moscow's manipulation.

Serbia stalled on the path towards the EU because of the EU's own crisis. That crisis left Serbia and others in the region drifting. With momentum towards the EU's secure embrace lost, Serbia was vulnerable to the Russian bear's hug. There were strong prospects of Serbia's following Croatia into the EU, until 2015. Serbia was on a fast track to an accession agreement, but Brexit in 2016 was enough to put any prospect of Serbia's joining the EU on hold, despite a strong strategic logic to do this swiftly, in the interests of the region. What is more, the migration crisis stemmed the pace and prospects of Serbia's accession – as well as any prospect of positive improvement in relations between the EU and all the countries across the region. Indeed, the reaction by the EU and the majority of its member states to the enormous influx of people was, in effect, to put pressure on the already vulnerable countries of South Eastern Europe, using them as a barrier to control the human flow. It created a 'frontier' region to impede migrants where the Austro-Hungarian Empire had historically created a 'military frontier' to block the advance of the Turkish Empire.

Serbian President Aleksandar Vučić, re-elected in 2017, continued a fine balancing act between the West and Russia. Vučić was oriented to the EU, despite a nationalist past, and recognized that the best future for Serbia and the region lay in Belgrade's acceding to the Union. However, his position became constrained by Russian penetration of Serbian politics. It was likely that he did not trust and could not rely on his security and intelligence service chiefs with many of them friendly to Moscow. At the same time, a cadre of Western-trained and oriented military officers was largely squeezed aside.

Meanwhile Moscow's economic hand gave Serbia limited freedom to manoeuvre. In December 2016, Vučić was obliged to accept Russian military aircraft and other pieces of military equipment that Serbia did not need for operational purposes.[39] Moscow revelled in gifting six MiG-29 high-level (though last generation) fighter aircraft, 30 T-72 tanks (similar to the M-84 model once produced in the region and familiar to the Serbian military) and 30 combat reconnaissance vehicles. Welcomed by many in the Serbian security sector, these gifts that could not be refused were costly. The modernization costs had to be paid (which Vučić put at €180-230 million for the aircraft alone, an amount Belgrade could not afford), as well as the on-costs that would, inevitably, be paid to Moscow. But, beyond these financial costs, it engendered military and security dependency on Moscow, even if Vučić, while accepting the gifts, insisted that Serbia remained neutral.[40]

Russia's hold on Serbia translated into Belgrade's being obliged to offer diplomatic support at the UN General Assembly.[41] Previously, Serbia had made efforts to mediate as a go-between, to provide goodwill services and enhance conflict monitoring in Ukraine, while it held the Chair in Office of the OSCE, in 2015. However, in December 2016, Serbia joined Russia (and 24 other states) in voting against a resolution in the UN General Assembly, proposed by Kiev, calling for an international monitoring force in Crimea. While the non-binding resolution was adopted, the Serbian vote against it was a product of Russia's heavy influence and a sign that Belgrade was ever more indebted to Russia. Vučić walked a narrow line between Russia and the West, albeit, in practice, significantly weakened and undermined by Russian penetration of his country's security apparatus. The EU's stalling left Serbia, attempting to balance Moscow and the West, all the more under the sway of the former, indicating that there was an inverse correlation between proximity to the European security organizations and a small state's vulnerability to Russia's grasp.

Moscow's attempts to control countries in the region were, however, not completely successful. Indeed, Russia suffered a setback in miniscule Montenegro, which became the 29th member of NATO, in May 2017. This outcome might have been very difficult, had an attempted coup, organized by Russian security operatives, on election day, in October 2016, succeeded.[42] The plot was to stir up trouble, with demonstrators attacking the parliament building; agents provocateurs, disguised as policemen, would then fire into the crowds; and, in the resulting disarray, the plan was to assassinate Prime Minister Milo Djukanović. Those involved in the plot were Serbian nationals, whose mission was organized by members of the Russian military intelligence service, the GRU, via Belgrade and the Serbian security apparatus, all under Moscow's influence. Although Moscow, reportedly, apologised to Belgrade that the two GRU officers were 'rogue', this was deeply implausible.[43]

While the official version was that one of the participants in the plot had been an insider-informant who had told a Montenegrin policeman about the scheme, it is probable that some NATO member states played a role in uncovering the coup attempt, engaging in close diplomacy with Podgorica, building on close ties established with the UK and the United States since the 1990s. Those two and others were quick to act in offering support and ensuring that the country's accession to the Alliance would not be deterred. With this, Russia's influence on Montenegro reduced. In part, this was a self-inflicted consequence of a 'retaliatory' ban imposed by Moscow on Montenegrin goods after the failed coup and the clear commitment to joining NATO. This saw the proportion of Russian visitors (mainly tourists) fall from 19.2 per cent in March 2016 to 7.3 per cent a year later. Russia's diminished position did not mean that it could not foster destabilisation in the future, given strong political divisions in Montenegro. But, membership in NATO went a long way towards providing a more stable and secure future.

Indeed, the prospect of imminent NATO membership was a crucial factor in blocking the Moscow-backed assassination and coup. While impeding Serbia's path to EU accession was a factor in its greater openness, or vulnerability, to Russia, Montenegro's experience provided a clear contrast. The impending and credible prospect of friends, partners and allies in the Alliance appears to have been effective in stopping Russia.

Insiders, threatened

In contrast to the various South East European countries, Estonia, Latvia and, perhaps to a lesser extent, Lithuania faced a threat of Russian subversion, or, even, direct action. All three gained membership of both the EU and NATO. These were great assets for a small state. The prospect of membership – and eventual membership itself – was important in creating a context in which Estonia could limit Russia's scope for action. While the same points applied equally to all three Baltic neighbours, the focus in the present section is on Estonia, both as an example and as the most threatened of the three.

Large-scale – and sometimes unannounced – military exercises close to the borders of Estonia, Latvia and Lithuania, including a major exercise, Zapad, in September 2017, created an atmosphere of uncertainty.[44] So did the major campaign of subversion and information manipulation in those countries that had been under way for several years, as well as pioneering cyber-attacks launched from Russia (albeit with no absolute certainty that they could be attributed to the state itself).[45] This unnerving environment entailed questions surrounding the inflation in staff levels at the Russian Embassy in Helsinki during 2016. The most likely scenarios appeared to be preparations for action in Estonia (or perhaps Latvia, or both), or intimidation, based on the possibility that such action might occur. This situation made all too clear what vulnerability could really mean for a small state with a prospectively highly hostile and certainly large neighbour.

Engagement by NATO member states, as well as activity in the framework of the CSCE (and later, the OSCE), in the 1990s, secured the Baltic States. When Russian Foreign Minister Yevgeny Primakov announced what sounded, rhetorically, like a harsh Moscow policy position regarding the Baltic States, in February 1997, this was testimony that the sovereign independence of those states had now been won. Eight years of no policy and ambiguity, with former Soviet military and security personnel living in Estonia and Latvia, and prepared with weapons under their beds, had become something clear and unambiguous. The space that had been left open to subvert and join the Baltic States to Russia again (using the Serbian model applied in Croatia and Bosnia and Herzegovina, during the 1990s armed conflict) was closed. And key to preventing annexation was the role played by the EU and NATO, and some of their member states. In particular, NATO's rolling programme of peacekeeping training exercises, helping to develop the nascent BALTBAT – an integrated unit from the three former Soviet Baltic States. The engagement through rolling exercises, and the prospect and achievement of membership in both organizations, deterred Moscow sufficiently.

However, the relative security achieved in that period diminished. Russian hostility never went away, even if its more intrusive and bullying manifestations relented. After 2008, and Russia's military incursion into Georgia, this changed. The Putin regime showed an old-fashioned taste for power assertion,[46] disregarding both the sovereignty of small neighbours and international law. At the same time, subversion in Estonia and its neighbours increased. This psychological, digital and information-driven intimidation became all the more menacing with the conduct of armed forces exercises. In large part, this was because the Russian intervention in Georgia was preceded by an exercise named Kavkaz 2008, which was the cover for the invasion of South Ossetia in Georgia. Exercises called Zapad (West), in 2013 and 2017, carried the message that Estonia and its small neighbours were not safe. Indeed, the sense of alarm was greater because, in contravention of the Conventional Forces in Europe Agreement (CFE), overseen by the OSCE, Russia increasingly conducted unannounced, snap exercises, without informing the OSCE. This went against the CFE, under the terms of which, as an act of transparency and confidence-building, Moscow should have both given notice and invited observers. Failing to do so created the uncertainty and tension the CFE was supposed to remove.

Estonia's small population and armed forces, with no defence in depth, made the country open to Russian power. However, with EU and NATO membership and engagement, Moscow could be impeded. Nonetheless, risks and threat remained, because of frailties in the EU and NATO. There were internal weaknesses in the EU, because of Brexit and the migration crisis; and in NATO, because of the seeming unreliability of Trump's United States and its sometimes half-hearted commitments to the Alliance. With an army of only 5,500 soldiers spread thinly across the country and its 180-mile border with Russia and the latter's military of over 700,000, Estonia had to be on high alert and ensure the involvement and commitment of others. In this context, at Tapa, the largest military base in the country, a combined British-French-Danish Battle Group (800 from the UK, as leader; 300 from France; and a Danish mechanised unit, from 2018) was based and constantly engaged in exercises. Tapa was on the strategically vital direct route from Russia to Tallin, the capital. The base, with its NATO guests, was an obstacle to the quickest way to overrun the country. While the Battle Group was led by the UK, it was under the command of the Estonian armed services, working with Estonians at all levels.

This presence – repeated with different contributors in Latvia, Lithuania and Poland – would meet a Russian invasion head-on, though, in itself, it would be unlikely to block a Russian attack, without further commitment from NATO, in particular (but, strategy was in place to do that, should it occur). However, after a history of invasion and occupation, Estonia was prepared to fight for its independence. As former Defence Minister Margus Tsahkna told the armed forces, 'We now know that not fighting was not the safer option ... We will not repeat the mistakes of the past, we will never go quietly again.'[47] As a colonel in the Estonian military expressed it, this was why most Estonians regarded joining NATO as 'the greatest thing ever' and a positive factor in the country's security situation[48] – and understandably so.

Yet, before any Russian invasion, there would be destabilization, beyond that which happened in the years after Estonia gained its independence as the Soviet Union disintegrated. That destabilization would almost certainly involve insurgents who would move in and out of Russian-speaking populations. Some of those readied for such action were known, including their general age, their build, their clothing – and that they bore scars, an indication that they might well have already seen combat. Based among the quarter of Estonia's 1.3 million population who spoke only, or mainly, Russian it was said that no Estonian was spoken in Nava, in the border area. Whatever the clear security benefits of the NATO Battlegroup and NATO membership, a tiny state with a large and hostile neighbour manipulating a disaffected kin-population remained insecure. That population was subject only to Russian information including divisive messaging, as occurred in Ukraine before the occupation there. However, threatening the Russian military might be, the greatest threat to Estonia's security was manipulation of events by its large neighbour and inter-communal disruption.

In this context, aside from the rolling military exercises with the NATO Battle Group, Estonia's most important security need was solidarity in the EU and NATO. In general terms, the migration crisis and Brexit largely stalled the EU, leaving it divided and incoherent. Brexit brought an additional range of questions for Estonia (and others) that looked to the UK for a sensible position to be shadowed and a sound partner to be worked with closely. Whatever assurances were offered, what would the British commitment be, if and when Brexit proceeded? and how focused could the UK be on Estonia, as it managed its own major security and diplomatic challenges? Most of all, given the importance of NATO and of the United States within NATO, how far could the seemingly erratic and certainly less-than-whole-heartedly-and-unquestioningly alliance-committed presidency of Donald Trump be relied on? These were questions that, despite Estonia's and its neighbours' successes in acting in line with small state theory and enhancing their position, revealed how vulnerable the Baltic States remained.

Conclusion

Small states need larger frameworks to preserve and reinforce sovereignty. They need them to overcome the predicament of vulnerability that a lack of material capacities – military, economic and physical – that being smaller than some other states creates. Of course, vulnerability based on differences in material capacity does not mean that every small state finds itself constantly in the position of Melos. Nonetheless, whatever their prevalence, because small states are – or feel themselves to be – small, they will be – or feel – more vulnerable. In a sense, the feeling of smallness can be linked to a feeling of insecurity. This is the defining aspect of a small state. Yet, the growth in the number of small states in the world indicates that there is more to their story than size and threat. Indeed, it confirms that the majority of states are small and that smallness is both relative and founded in feeling. As with security, it is ultimately not a matter of objective conditions, but a cathectic phenomenon.

This is why, seeking precise, objective definition of 'small' in relation to states may be unnecessary and, even, unhelpful. Despite vulnerability, small states show resilience and develop this in a variety of ways: innovation and ingenuity; single issue focus, whether the issue is normative and political, economic and commercial, or cultural; embedding in a rules-based international environment; and, crucially, active diplomacy focused on maintaining the state's independent international personality and ensuring relations with other states that would preserve and protect its identity and sovereignty. The diplomacy of alignment is a vital requirement to enhance security – situating the state in a web of relations that protect it and enhance security.

Webs and networks of partnerships and alliances are essential, as are multilateral relationships with major states. Across Europe, from the Netherlands to Slovenia to Estonia, this broad approach to foreign and security policy was, indeed, theory adopted in practice, for decades. Yet, the types of framework that theories of small state diplomacy suggest can sometimes both challenge sovereignty and be fragile. Russia's clear turn towards disruptive manoeuvring across Europe proved the theory of small state security and diplomacy, in one sense: those small states needed partnership and alliance with others to fend of Moscow's moves. Yet, at the same time, that same Russian action clearly challenged the theory and brought its full value into question.

As shown in this study, the simple and valuable idea of finding friends and partners, and embedding in larger frameworks, depended on the character of those friends, partners and frameworks. These needed to be strong, robust and, so far as possible, timely and proximate. Where positive associations were problematic, small states might have little choice but to succumb, to a greater or lesser extent, to getting into bed with those whom they might prefer otherwise to avoid. With the EU and NATO distracted, small states that looked to them for greater security and, as a matter of identity and belonging, were left vulnerable and more exposed than they would wish to be. The normative aspect of the theory is clearly challenged. But, so too, in the real world, was European security challenged. Security would depend on clear and stronger awareness among those EU and NATO member states in less vulnerable situations of the need for them to act in ways that would reduce the vulnerability of their friends and allies and enhance the security of small states in Central and South East European.

The theoretical and practical challenges were evident in the comparative analysis of states in three different situations – first, completely outside the EU and NATO; secondly, inside one or both of them, but not obviously directly threatened by Russia; and, last, those inside one or both of these organizations and feeling a direct threat from Russia. The comparative review showed proximity and timing to be factors, alongside membership (or not) and the degree to which prospective partners maintained focus. This points to a link between membership and degree of integration. A small state in Central and Eastern Europe outside the EU and NATO was all the more vulnerable to Russian advances – and obliged to align itself with Moscow, in some degree. However, the importance of membership and close integration is clearest in the case of Estonia and the other Baltic States, where the credibility and presence of partners and allies appear to have been effective in ensuring Russia being rebuffed.

The foregoing analysis confirms that the normative aspect of small state theory might be questioned and more complex and variegated than supposed. Without doubt, the importance of diplomacy has been the principal way to tackle the challenges of vulnerability and can only remain so. In the same vein, alignment is vital – having friends, partners and allies with others, or ensuring forms of neutrality, or non-participation, as might be appropriate. Addressing vulnerability is critical for a small state and working with others to enhance security and maintain a stable environment is imperative, as small state diplomatic theory suggests and the practice and theory of small state security confirms. Yet, as I have shown, the positive, normative sense in which theory and practice might be recommended is more problematic, in reality, as the twenty-first-century experiences of the small, former communist countries studied in this piece reveal, from the Balkans to the Baltic. Yet, however problematic it is to turn theory into practice, it is clear that such theory retains value and that diplomatically driven, relative closeness to different partners and allies is essential to small state resilience and security.

Notes

1 This chapter is based on a longer paper originally presented at the ASEEES Convention in 2019, in Boston. I am very grateful to those who commented on

the paper, especially Chuck Bukowski, who first suggested the topic and offered generous comment, and Carole Rogel.

2   Anthony Payne, 'Small States in the Global Politics of Development', *Round Table* 93 (2004): 634.

3   David Vital, *The Inequality of States: A Study of Small Powers in International Relations* (Oxford: Oxford University Press, 1967); Iver B. Neumann and Sieglinde Gstöhl, 'Introduction', in *Small States in International Relations*, ed. Christine Ingebretsen, Iver Neumann and Sieglinde Gstöhl (Seattle: University of Washington Press, 2006), 17ff.

4   Thucydides, *The History of the Peloponnesian War*, trans. Richard Crawley, Project Gutenberg [EBook #7142] 2009, Updated: 7 February 2013, Ch. XVII, https://www.gutenberg.org/files/7142/7142-h/7142-h.htm (accessed 7 May 2020).

5   Zlatko Šabić and Charles Bukowski, 'Introduction', in Zlatko Šabić, 'Small States Aspiring for NATO Membership: Some Factors Influencing the Accession Process' in *Small States in the Post-Cold-War World: Slovenia and NATO Enlargement*, ed. Zlatko Šabić and Charles Bukowski (Westport: Praeger, 2002), xvi; Sverrir Steinsson and Baldur Thorhallsson, 'The Small-State Survival Guide to Foreign Policy Success', *The National Interest*, 28 September 2017; Dan Reiter, 'Learning, Realism and Alliances; The Weight of the Shadow of the Past' in Ingebretsen, Neumann and Gstöhl, *Small States in International Relations*, 235.

6   Zlatko Šabić, 'Small States Aspiring for NATO Membership: Some Factors Influencing the Accession Process' in Šabić and *Small States*, ed. Šabić and Bukowski, Chapter 1.

7   Jeanne A. K. Hey, 'Introducing Small State Foreign Policy', in *Small States in World Politics; Explaining Foreign Policy Behaviour*, ed. Jeanne A. K. Hey (Boulder: Lynne Rienner, 2003), 3.

8   Matthias Maas, 'The Elusive Definition of the Small State', *International Politics* 46, no. 1 (2009): 65–83.

9   Michael W. Mosser, 'Engineering Influence: The Subtle Power of Small States in the CSCE/OSCE', in *Small States and Alliances*, ed. Erich Reiter and Heinz Gärtner (Berlin: Springer-Verlag, 2001), 65.

10 Neumann and Gstöhl, 'Introduction' in Ingebretsen, Neumann and Gstöhl *Small States in International Relations*, 17ff; Vital, *The Inequality of States*, 8.

11 Hans J. Morgenthau, *Politics Among Nations: The Struggle for Power and Peace* (New York: Knopf, 1948), 196.

12 Geoffrey Baldachinno, 'Thucydides or Kissinger? A Critical Review of Smaller State Diplomacy', in *The Diplomacies of Small States between Vulnerability and Resilience*, ed. Andrew F. Cooper and Timothy M. Shaw (London: Palgrave-Macmillan, 2009), 23.

13 Vital, *The Inequalities of States*, 8.

14 See http://thecommonwealth.org/small-states (accessed 5 November).
15 Ali Naseer Mohamed, *The Diplomacy of Micro-States*, Discussion Papers in International Diplomacy, no. 78 (The Hague: The Netherlands Institute of International Relations, Clingendael, 2002), 1.
16 Paul Sutton, 'The Concept of Small States in the International Political Economy', *The Round Table: The Commonwealth Journal of International Affairs* 100, no. 413 (2011): 141–53.
17 Tom Crowards, 'Defining the Category of Small States', *Journal of International Development* 14, no. 2 (2002): 143–79.
18 Anthony Payne, 'Afterword: Vulnerability as a Condition, Resilience as a Strategy', in *The Diplomacies of Small Powers*, ed. Cooper and Shaw, 279.
19 Duncan Green, 'The World's Top 100 Economies: 31 States, 69 Companies', https://blogs.worldbank.org/publicsphere/world-s-top-100-economies-31-countries-69-corporations (accessed 5 November 2017).
20 World Development Indicators. World Bank, 1 July 2017; 'World Economic Outlook Database', International Monetary Fund, 24 October 2017.
21 'GDP Breakdown at Current Prices in USD', United Nations Statistics Division, National Accounts Main Aggregates Database, https://unstats.un.org/unsd/snaama/dnlList.asp (accessed 5 November 2017).
22 *The CIA World Factbook*, http://www.worldbank.org/en/country/smallstates (accessed 5 November 2017).
23 George W. Grayson, 'Foreword' in Šabić and Bukowski, *Small States*, xi.
24 *The CIA World Factbook*.
25 See James Gow, *Defending the West* (Cambridge: Polity, 2005), and Philip C. Bobbitt, *The Shield of Achilles: War, Peace and the Course of History* (London: Penguin, 2003).
26 George W. Grayson, 'Foreword' in Šabić and Bukowski, *Small States*, xi.
27 Šabić and Bukowski, 'Introduction', xvi.
28 See https://asp.icc-cpi.int/en_menus/asp/crime%20of%20aggression/Pages/History-CoA.aspx (accessed 5 November 2017).
29 Alan K. Henrikson, 'TEN TYPES OF SMALL STATE DIPLOMACY – What different kinds of diplomacy have been used by small states? Which have been the most successful, and in what circumstances?' Unpublished Paper, The Fletcher School of Law and Diplomacy, Tufts University, n.d., https://is.muni.cz/el/1423/podzim2008/MVZ157/um/TEN_TYPES_OF_SMALL_STATE_DIPLOMACY.pdf (accessed 5 November 2017); see also Alan K. Henrikson, *Diplomacy and Small States in Today's World*. Dr. Eric Williams Memorial Lecture Series, Port of Spain: Central Bank of Trinidad and Tobago, 1998.
30 Heinz Gärtner, 'Introduction', in *Small States and Alliances*, ed. Erich Reiter and Heinz Gärtner (Berlin: Springer-Verlag, 2001), 2.

31 Hey, 'Introducing Small State Foreign Policy', 10.
32 Ivo Daalder, 'Responding to Russia's Resurgence: Not Quiet on the Eastern Front', *Foreign Affairs* 96, no. 6 (November/December 2017): 30.
33 James Gow and Cathie Carmichael, *Slovenia and the Slovenes: A Small State in the New Europe*, 2nd edition (London: Hurst and Co., 2010), chapter 7.
34 This view was clearly expressed to the author by those responsible initially for building relationships with the UK, following Slovenia's independence. Foreign Ministry officials confirmed this in the run-up to NATO and EU accession in discussion with the author.
35 STA 23 June 2004.
36 Montenegro is a partial exception here, as will be explained below.
37 *Balkan Insight*, 27 April 2017, https://balkaninsight.com/2017/04/27/croatian-govt-shakes-as-3-minister-sacked-04-27-2017/ (accessed 30 July 2017).
38 Documents revealed later also confirmed that Marić had not only had a leading position in Agrokor, but he had also been fully aware of the problems. *Nacional*, 11 July 2017.
39 *B92*, 21 December 2016, https://www.b92.net/eng/news/politics.php?yyyy=2016&mm (accessed 22 December 2016).
40 As Branislav Radeljić observes, actions to 'assist' Belgrade were always only really concerned with Moscow's 'own standing', which understood 'involvement as an opportunity, geoeconomic or geopolitical'. Branislav Radeljic [original] 'Russia's Involvement in the Kosovo Case: Defending Serbian Interests or Securing Its Own Influence in Europe?' *Regional Studies of Russia, Eastern Europe, and Central Asia* 6, no. 2 (2017): 300.
41 *B92*, 20 December 2016, https://www.b92.net/eng/news/world.php?yyyy=2016&mm= (accessed 22 December 2016).
42 *The Associated Press*, 16 October 2016, https://accesswdun.com/article/2016/10/458522 (accessed 22 December 2016).
43 *The Guardian*, 11 November 2016, https://www.theguardian.com/world/2016/nov/11/serbia-depor (accessed 22 December 2016).
44 See Dave Johnson, 'ZAPAD 2017 and Euro-Atlantic security' *NATO Review*, 14 December 2017, https://www.nato.int/docu/review/articles/2017/12/14/zapad-2017-and-euro-atlantic-security/index.html (accessed 13 May 2020).
45 Oscar Jonsson, 'Russian Information Warfare and Its Challenges to International Law', in *Routledge Handbook of War, Law and Technology*, ed. James Gow, Ernst Dijxhoorn, Rachel Kerr and Guglielmo Verdirame (New York: Routledge, 2019), 346.
46 James Gow 'UK Strategic Defence and Russia: A Brief History of Unrequited Wooing', in *Security Narratives in Europe: A Wide Range of Views*, Democracy,

Security and Peace Series No. 221, ed. Wolfgang Zellner (Baden Baden: Nomos for the Institute of Peace and Security Policy Research, University of Hamburg, 2017), 157–70.
47 *Army: Behind the New Frontlines,* Episode 2 'The New Cold War', *BBC2*, 26 October 2017.
48 *Army,* Episode 2.

9

South Africa's diplomacy of conflict resolution in the post-apartheid era: The case of the DRC

Dr Flavia Gasbarri

The end of the Cold War marked an important phase in the history of conflict resolution in Africa. The vanishing of the rivalry between the two superpowers for influence and resources removed a significant element of external interference from many conflicts in the continent. In the early 1990s, several countries afflicted by long-lasting wars, such as Angola, Ethiopia and Mozambique, opened the doors to negotiations and peace processes, which saw the significant involvement of international mediators.

In contrast, when in 1990 South Africa moved towards the resolution of the internal conflict between the apartheid regime and the anti-apartheid movements, it became the only case of a completely self-managed negotiation. The four-year process leading to the first free elections in April 1994 is still considered one of the few successful examples of a peaceful democratic transition in Africa. After the end of the apartheid, despite the enormous challenges of dealing with the legacy of the previous regime, South Africa consolidated its role as regional hegemon. With the inclusion in the BRICS in 2010, the country confirmed its status as an emerging economy.

This chapter explores how the rehabilitation of South Africa as respected member of the international community translated into its increasing involvement as mediator in several conflicts across Africa. The chapter consists of three sections. In the first part, it investigates how during the 1990s the success of South Africa's own experience, as well as the international prestige of Nelson Mandela, played a fundamental role in the beginning of South Africa's mediation role. In the second section the chapter analyses South Africa's intervention in the negotiation to end the war in the Democratic Republic of Congo, one of the most important interventions of the South African diplomacy in conflict resolution. The analysis of this case eventually leads, in the third part of the chapter, to an assessment of the strengths and limits of South Africa's mediation strategies. The main argument is that in its diplomacy of conflict resolution in Africa, Pretoria must balance the powerful legacy of its own experience with a pragmatic approach to the challenges and realities of the continent. This can be done through regional coordination (particularly within the Southern African region) and a conscious use of military force. On a broader level, the chapter presents a reflection on the increasingly common view that the expectations raised in the mid-1990s that South Africa could become a prosperous democracy and play a positive role the continent have progressively vanished. Over the last decade the country has faced important domestic difficulties; however, the story of Pretoria's diplomatic involvement in the DRC shows that South Africa can still play a leading role in enhancing the African capabilities in conflict resolution in the continent.

1994: Back to the world stage

The first national, non-racial, one-person-one-vote election in the history of South Africa took place on 27th April 1994, and marked a watershed in the history of the African continent. The so-called 'Rainbow Nation', which had been for many years on the edge of a civil war, was eventually able to manage a peaceful transition to democracy. It was greeted internationally with enthusiasm as a very rare case of successful conflict resolution in Africa.

Right after the 1994 elections and the establishment of the Government of National Unity led by Nelson Mandela, South Africa was ready to be welcomed again by the international community. Between May and August 1994 Pretoria was readmitted to the United Nations[1] and it joined the Organization of African Unity (OAU) and the South African Development Community (SADC). Thanks to the strength of its economy and military power,[2] South Africa was bound to become a crucial actor in the continent and to play the influential role that had been denied in the past due to the apartheid regime.

The pillars of the post-apartheid South African foreign policy, outlined by Mandela and the African National Congress, included an important emphasis on the promotion of human rights, democracy and peace. They also stressed the inescapable 'African destiny' of South Africa, namely the importance that the whole continent and particularly the Southern African region had for Pretoria's future.[3] Mandela also stressed the rejection of militaristic approaches to security and cooperation: 'peace is the goal for which all nations should strive, and where this breaks down, internationally agreed and nonviolent mechanisms (...) must be employed.'[4] This approach rapidly opened the doors to the start of South Africa's intervention as mediator for conflict resolution across the continent. Besides being the most powerful state in the region, Pretoria could also count on its own experience of peaceful negotiations and on the international prestige of its president, which became one of the most defining characteristic of the very early stage of South Africa's mediation role.

This last aspect was particularly evident in Angola, which in 1994 was still entangled in a decades-old civil war between the Movimento Popular de Libertação de Angola (MPLA), led by the President José Eduardo dos Santos, and the opposition movement União Nacional para a Independência Total de Angola (UNITA), led by Jonas Savimbi. At that time, the UN and the 'troika' composed of the United States, Russia and Portugal were attempting to negotiate a second accord between the parties, after the failure of the Bicesse Agreement in 1992.[5] Frustrated by the setback of the negotiations, in June 1994 the United States decided to play the 'South African card'.[6] As stated by the US Special Representative for the Angolan peace process, Paul Hare, 'We concluded that the best option would be to engage Nelson Mandela. With his unquestionable political and moral stature on the international scene, the South African president just might be able to persuade Savimbi to accept the mediation proposals'.[7] After initial concerns due to the past involvement of the apartheid regime in the Angolan conflict,[8] the Angolan leaders from both parties seemed to show high esteem for Mandela and his Deputy President Thabo Mbeki, as well as admiration for the success of South Africa's own democratic transition.[9]

While South Africa's role and practical achievements in the negotiations in Angola eventually remained limited,[10] the episode shows the dramatic shift in the stance of the South African diplomacy. In just a few years, Pretoria moved from being a belligerent in the Angolan war to being involved as mediator in its solution. In 1994, the South African Embassy in Angola commented, 'The involvement of South Africa at this stage in the Angolan peace process may well prove to be a test for South African diplomacy, considering that the promotion of regional stability is a corner stone of our foreign policy'.[11]

Despite the positive effects of the end of Pretoria's diplomatic isolation, however, the return of South Africa into the continental chessboard was also perceived with concerns by other African countries, who were worried about the possible South Africa's hegemony. The first important clash happened with Nigeria. In November 1995, Mandela reacted strongly to the execution of the

Nigerian human rights activist Ken Saro-Wiwa by the military dictatorship of General Sani Abacha. During the Commonwealth Heads of Government Meeting, held in New Zealand on 10–13 November 1995, Mandela was the driving force behind the assembly's decision to suspend Nigeria from the Commonwealth.[12] In an interview to the Johannesburg's *Sunday Independent*, he stated that 'Abacha is sitting on a volcano. And I am going to explode it underneath him'.[13] However, when the South African president attempted to explode the volcano by calling for the imposition of oil sanctions on Nigeria he received little support from the Western countries. The OAU and many African countries also criticized Mandela, as they saw in his action an attempt to break African unity and solidarity.[14] The SADC declined to call a meeting of SADC heads of state to develop a regional Southern African strategy on Nigeria, maintaining that the question of Nigeria had no direct correlation with SADC as a corporate regional body.[15] Interestingly, Mandela was also criticized for his previous soft policy of 'appeasement' towards Abacha, which led to a failure to prevent the execution of the activist and to a sudden South African reverse of approach.[16] The South Africa–Nigeria rupture resulted in the Nigerian boycott of the South African–hosted Africa Cup of Nations in 1996.[17]

This failure offered an important lesson for South African diplomacy, one that influenced the future direction of Pretoria's mediation policy. In the following years South Africa was involved in many attempts of conflict resolution across the continent: Burundi, Ivory Coast, Democratic Republic of Congo (DRC), Zimbabwe, Libya. Among these cases, DRC was one of the most challenging situations, not only for the nature of the conflict that affected this country, but also for its geographical proximity and its role in the region of Southern Africa, which directly affected Pretoria's interests.

South Africa and the wars in the DRC

The war in the DRC began in autumn 1996, when the rebel movement Alliance des Forces Démocratiques pour la Libération du Congo-Zaïre (AFDL), led by Laurent-Desiré Kabila, started a military advance from the Kivu region, in the eastern part of the DRC (then Zaire), towards the capital city Kinshasa. The main aim of the rebellion was the removal of the Zairian dictator Joseph Mobutu, in power since 1965. The AFDL's military action was sponsored and supported by Zaire's neighbouring countries: Uganda, Burundi and most notably Rwanda. The government in Kigali, in fact, led by the largely Tutsi Rwandan Patriotic

Front (RPF), wanted to solve the security threat posed to its western border by the Zairian-based refugee camps. These camps were controlled by the Hutu extremists, who were responsible for the 1994 Rwandan genocide and who had escaped Rwanda after the RPF's seize of power. With the support of his foreign sponsors, who in early 1997 also included Angola, Kabila was able to arrive close to Kinshasa by the end of April 1997. At the time, Mobutu was terminally ill and his kleptocratic regime was completely discredited, having lost all international support after the end of the Cold War. As a result, questions about the future of the biggest and mineral-richest country of central Africa became particularly pressing.

The international attempts to mediate between Zaire, Rwanda and Uganda[18] and to establish a direct dialogue between Mobutu and Kabila saw the intervention of President Mandela. South Africa was quite a natural and 'inevitable' actor to be involved as peacemaker in the DRC, due to the consequences that a possible destabilization in central Africa could have on Pretoria's interests. As mentioned by the Deputy Minister of Foreign Affairs, Aziz Pahad, in 1996, 'There is no "Great Wall" between us and the Great Lakes Region. The consequences of what happens there will have serious and disastrous consequences for all of us.'[19] Chris Landsberg also observed that 'Any assessment of the rationales behind South Africa's policy toward the conflict in the DRC should focus not so much on exclusive, bilateral relations but on Pretoria's broader georegional policy and strategies. For South Africa the conflicts in central and southern Africa are inextricably intertwined, forming as they do an "arc of conflict".'[20]

After a series of contacts between Mandela and both the parties of the conflict,[21] on 18 April 1997 Pahad announced that the president had invited Mobutu and Kabila to South Africa and that the two leaders had agreed in principle to start direct peace talks.[22] Thanks to the support of the US ambassador to the UN, Bill Richardson, the meeting was eventually set for 2 May on a South African warship, called *Outeniqua*, in international waters off Pointe Noire in Congo-Brazzaville.[23]

On the day of the meeting Kabila, who was supposed to travel from Luanda to Porte Noire with Thabo Mbeki, decided not to go. The AFDL leader raised last-minute concerns about the security arrangements of the meeting and claimed that he had not enough information about the participants in the Mobutu's delegation. Mbeki warned Kabila about the dangers that his behaviour was causing to his reputation, and told the AFDL leader that he was letting down vital international friends, including Mandela himself, who was presumably 'waxing furious'.[24] Kabila replied that he was still prepared to attend the meeting with

Mobutu, provided that his concerns about security were answered.[25] At the end of the meeting, Mbeki eventually left to join Mandela, Mobutu and Richardson on the *Outeniqua*, while Kabila returned to his headquarter in Lubumbashi.

Mandela and Mbeki decided to have another try at arranging the talks for the following day. Mandela shared with Ambassador Richardson his suspicions about the role played by the Angolans in Kabila's refusal to show up.[26] Indeed, the Americans shared the view that Kabila was very 'susceptible' to pressure from his allies (Rwanda, Uganda and Angola), who had not pledged support to the South African efforts. They also suggested that, considering the AFDL's continuous military advance, Kabila was delaying the talks with Mobutu in order to first take Kinshasa.[27]

The Mobutu–Kabila talks eventually took place on the *Outeniqua* on 4 May 1997. Kabila presented a written proposal for an immediate transfer of power from Mobutu to the AFDL, which would become the Transitional Authority of the country and would call on board members of other political forces to participate. This process would not include Mobutists and Kabila himself would act as president with executive powers. Mobutu proposed instead to organize a transition to elections under his own authority. South Africa's aim was to mediate between these two plans and to push Kabila to accept an 'inclusive transitional arrangement which itself, rather than the Alliance, would assume executive authority from Mobutu',[28] who would be asked to leave office at the end of this process. According to Mbeki, this arrangement would also benefit Mobutu because it included forces to counter-balance Kabila and it allowed him not to surrender to the AFDL.[29] The parties then agreed to convene another meeting after ten days. Before that meeting could take place, it was necessary to gather the support of the regional countries for the South African plan. On 6 May Mbeki left for a tour that included Angola, Rwanda, Tanzania, Gabon and Congo-Brazzaville, to discuss the situation in Zaire with the leaders of those countries.[30]

The day before the scheduled second meeting, neither Kabila nor Mobutu had yet accepted the South African plan. In a meeting with the US ambassador to South Africa, James Joseph, Mbeki's chief of staff, Frank Chikane, declared that the South Africans would not go to the ship again unless there was a prior agreement from the parties on the modalities of the transition in Zaire. The mediation team did not want a repetition of the first round of talks.[31] On 14 May, the day of the second meeting, Kabila once again did not show up, causing the collapse of the negotiations. Two days later, Kinshasa fell to the hands of the AFDL, Mobutu fled Zaire and Kabila proclaimed himself president of the renamed Democratic Republic of Congo.

There was one main reason why the South African attempt to mediate between Mobutu and Kabila failed. When the direct talks were being arranged, the AFDL's troops were no more than two weeks from Kinshasa. Kabila had no real incentives to negotiate, considering that he still had the alternative of a military victory. After the first meeting with Mobutu on 4 May, he made it clear that while his proposed plan was being considered by Mobutu and the mediators, the AFDL's forces would continue to fight. The South Africans did not make any attempt to include the issue of the ceasefire in the negotiations.[32] So the aim of the talks was not to mediate between two parties but to ensure a 'soft landing' to the situation in Zaire, by allowing a smooth departure to Mobutu and avoiding a bloodbath over Kinshasa. While nobody said it overtly, everyone already considered Kabila the president-to-be.[33]

In this sense, the role of Kabila's regional allies was particularly important. Despite Mbeki's attempts to gather the regional support for the South African mediation effort, Kabila's sponsors, particularly Angola and Rwanda, all had an interest in seeing Mobutu leaving office very rapidly and in opposing any move that could prolong his, or his supporters, staying in power. These countries were following their own national agenda. The MPLA government in Luanda saw the situation in Zaire in connection to its war with UNITA, which had had in Mobutu one of its most important supporters for two decades. Therefore, the MPLA continued to provide substantial military equipment, logistics and advice for Kabila's forces. Furthermore, the need to secure the northern border from the destabilization in Zaire gave the MPLA the opportunity to extend its armed forces into the final provincial capital (Mbanza Congo) still in control of UNITA.[34]

Rwanda was appalled by the refugee crisis that had affected its western border since the end of the 1994 genocide and then–Vice President Paul Kagame had never made a secret of his will to solve the problem.[35] In a meeting with Ambassador Richardson, Kagame stated that Rwanda 'was one of the first beneficiaries of the new stability in Zaire, and so the Rwandans have felt free with advice on what must be done to continue moving in the right direction'.[36] As observed by Colin Waught, 'Clearly the military objectives of Paul Kagame in 1996 meshed closely with those of Laurent Kabila and indeed, for the early stages of the campaign at least, the defence of Rwanda was almost synonymous with the defeat of Mobutu and regime change in Zaire'.[37]

The relationship with the regional actors thus became one of the most important issues in the second phase of South African mediation in the DRC. Just over one year after the end of what was called the First Congo War, the

DRC precipitated again into war. Kabila's attempt to get rid of the Rwandan influence and interference in his new government caused Kigali to sponsor and support another rebel group, the Rassemblement Congolais pour la Democratie (DCR), which began a military campaign against Kabila from the Kivu region in August 1998. This was the beginning of the Second Congo War, and saw a split within the regional coalition that had supported Kabila during the previous conflict. While Uganda immediately joined Rwanda, Angola decided instead to support Kabila. The further intervention of Zimbabwe and Namibia on the side of Angola[38] caused an important fracture within the SADC.

South Africa found itself in the middle of this fracture and showed a quite contradictory attitude. In fact, in 1997 Pretoria pushed to include the DRC as new member in the SADC, but one year later it failed to condemn the Rwandan/Ugandan 'invasion' against the Kabila government.[39] It also admitted regret in its previous support for the DRC's membership, as this ended up 'unpleasantly' stretching the geographical boundaries of SADC, and exacerbating the internal divisions.[40] Indeed, the intervention of Zimbabwe in the DRC conflict, in particular, opened the doors to a profound political and personal rivalry between Mandela and the Zimbabwean President Robert Mugabe. In his capacity as Chair of the SADC Organ for Politics, Defence and Security – the institution in charge of supporting the achievement and maintenance of security and the rule of law in the SADC region – Mugabe presented the military intervention of Zimbabwe, Angola and Namibia in the DRC as an action endorsed by the SADC. Mandela, who held the Chairmanship of the SADC instead refused the military action and pushed in favour of a negotiated solution, in line with the non-violent approach to conflict resolution of the post-apartheid South African foreign policy. This opened an unresolved debate on whether the SADC had ever formally approved the deployment of the so-called 'SADC forces' (Zimbabwean, Namibian and Angolan troops) to the DRC and it sparked several discussions on the need to reform the Organ.[41] Furthermore, just a few months after the dispute over the DRC, South Africa intervened military in Lesotho, under the aegis of the SADC, to avoid a coup d'état.[42] This action raised the harsh criticisms of the pro-Kabila front within the SADC, which saw Pretoria's double standard as the evidence of South African support for the Rwanda–Uganda invasion.[43]

All these contradictions in Pretoria's course of action[44] between 1997 and 1998 paralysed a prominent diplomatic role for South Africa in the Second Congo War. In September 1998, the SADC appointed Zambian president Frederick Chiluba to lead the mediation efforts in the DRC, assisted by the Tanzanian and the Mozambican presidents.[45] The mediation team embarked on a complex process of negotiations, which first achieved success in July 1999. The parties, who were multiplying in the meantime,[46] signed the Lusaka Agreement, establishing a ceasefire in the war. The agreement further established the deployment of a UN mission (United Nations Organization Mission in the Democratic Republic of the Congo – MONUC)[47] to monitor the ceasefire and the beginning of the so-called Inter-Congolese Dialogue (ICD). This was supposed to be a process of negotiation among the Congolese parties of the conflict aimed at providing a 'new political dispensation for the DRC'.[48] Former president of Botswana Ketumile Masire was appointed facilitator of the ICD process in December 1999.[49]

However, 1999 saw the restart of the South African initiative thanks to some changes implemented by the new president Thabo Mbeki, who had replaced Mandela after the South African election in June 1999. Mbeki tried first and foremost to soothe the fracture with Zimbabwe which was one of the most important factors that had constrained South African action in the DRC. Its resolution had to wait until the end of Mandela's presidency, due to the personal dislike between Mandela and Mugabe.[50] Mbeki invited Mugabe as special guest to his inauguration ceremony in 1999 and adopted a less confrontational attitude towards Zimbabwe. As part of this new approach, Mbeki was also progressively involved in the crisis that affected Zimbabwe after 2000, when a new-formed organization, the Movement for Democratic Change (MDC), challenged Mugabe's hold of power for the first time since 1980. Mbeki started a long action of mediation between the two parties (in 2008 he was officially mandated by SADC) which culminated in a power-sharing agreement.[51] Mbeki's policy became famous as 'quiet diplomacy', for its 'soft' approach towards Mugabe, based on constructive dialogue and persuasion. Indeed, Pretoria opposed the proposal of suspending Zimbabwe from the Commonwealth, as well as the sanctions promoted by Western countries after the violence that marked the 2002 presidential elections.[52]

The quiet diplomacy in Zimbabwe did have the effect of favouring the re-involvement of South Africa in the last phase of the Lusaka process in the DRC, in support of the official mediator Chiluba. Together with Tanzania, Pretoria drove the effort to pressure the rebel groups and their allies, Rwanda and Uganda, to sign the ceasefire.[53] The improvement of relations with Mugabe allowed Mbeki to resume contacts with Kabila, whose association with, and dependency on, Zimbabwe were quite strong. The Zimbabwean Minister of Justice, Emerson Mnangagwa, declared that Zimbabwe wanted 'Kabila to open his heart to Mbeki' and that it was pushing the Congolese leader to distinguish

South Africa and Mbeki from Mandela 'whom Kabila never liked'.⁵⁴ Another important difference from the Mandela's years was Mbeki's greater willingness to employ South African military forces, particularly in peacekeeping missions. In October 1999, the South African Parliament adopted the 'White Paper on South African Participation in International Peace Missions', which committed the country to supporting UN and OAU peace initiatives. The paper stated that 'for obvious historic reasons',⁵⁵ South Africa had not yet provided troop contributions for peace support operations under the auspices of the UN or other international organizations. However, since 1995, the South African National Defence Force (SANDF) had gone through a process of restructuring and training for peace operations. When Mbeki became president this process had been largely completed, so deployment as part of multilateral peace missions started to become a key task of the SANDF.⁵⁶ As a consequence of these developments, Mbeki announced that Pretoria was ready to deploy peacekeeping troops for the MONUC mission.⁵⁷

Mbeki then became one of the leading actors in the ICD. Throughout the year 2000, this process had been quite difficult and it had experienced a series of setbacks despite Masire's efforts and shuttle diplomacy. Indeed, Kabila showed little enthusiasm for the ICD and he was hindering the deployment of the MONUC's troops.⁵⁸ He opposed the facilitator role of Masire who, at the same time, was not receiving much support from SADC.⁵⁹ According to South Africa's new Foreign Minister Nkosazana Dlamini-Zuma, the regional states were issuing carrots to Kabila without applying the stick. Acquiescence to his rejection of Masire and the ICD would allow him to partition the country and become a 'true dictator'. Mbeki's intention was to review the situation in the DRC and try to 'catalyze new energy in support of Lusaka'.⁶⁰

An important turning point in this sense occurred in January 2001 when Laurent Kabila was assassinated and replaced by his son Joseph Kabila.⁶¹ The new Congolese leader seemed to show a more moderate and cooperative approach.⁶² In a meeting held in Lusaka in February 2001, attended by the signatories of the Lusaka agreement (but with the significant absence of Rwanda and Uganda) the 'young' Kabila announced that he would eventually accept Masire as mediator and he was ready to endorse the ICD.⁶³

The ICD officially started in October 2001 but it immediately experienced a failed opening session in Addis Ababa. The meeting was seriously undermined by lack of funding, by the consequent absence of many delegates, as well as by mutual accusations between the rebels and the government of stalling the process.⁶⁴ According to the former Nigerian Foreign Minister Baba Ghana

Kingibe, who acted as informal peace process advisor at Addis Ababa, the failure of that meeting required a 'sustained diplomatic effort' in order to prevent the Congolese actors 'from tinkering too heavily with the balance of power on the ground. Every hour you force them to discuss peace is one less hour they can play at war'. In Kingibe's view, the power-oriented focus of the Congolese leaders could far outweigh Masire's ability to push the peace process by himself.[65] South Africa's diplomatic initiative at this juncture turned out to be crucial in solving the initial stalemate. After a series of meetings held between the main parties of the conflicts in New York and in Abuja, it was agreed that the ICD would be definitively moved to South Africa, in the Sun City resort near Pretoria.[66] The process resumed on 25 February and lasted until December 2002. Mbeki became the *de facto* and 'behind-the-scene' facilitator of the negotiations, and South Africa provided a significant financial and logistic contribution to the ICD.[67] The South African president, in cooperation with the UN Secretary-General's special envoy Moustapha Niasse, was particularly important in several aspects of the complex negotiations. First of all, he helped to overcome the deadlock created by the parties' divergent views of a power-sharing agreement, especially Kabila's intransigence in maintaining the presidency during the transition period.[68] Secondly, Mbeki made many efforts to maintain the dialogue all-inclusive and he rejected a partial agreement reached in April by Kabila and just one of the rebel groups, the Movement for the Liberation of the Congo (MLC).[69] Finally, Mbeki maintained a continuous diplomatic pressure on the parties in order to reach an agreement and not to end up in never-ending and inconclusive talks.

The negotiations eventually led to the signature of the Global and Inclusive Agreement on Transition in the Democratic Republic of Congo on 17 December 2002. The accord established a twenty-four-month period of transition, followed by democratic elections. During this period, a power-sharing formula ensured the participation of all the parties of the conflict to the government, whose president remained Joseph Kabila.[70] In February–March 2003, three additional documents were added to the original one. All the agreements were eventually signed during the final session of the ICD, held in Sun City on 1–2 April 2003.[71] The first elections since 1960 took place in the DRC on 30 September 2006.

Conclusion

The 2002 Agreement officially ended the Second Congo War and ensured elections, but unfortunately it did not bring peace to the DRC which has continued to experience rebellions and disorders, particularly in the Eastern region. However, there are still important conclusions and lessons learned from Pretoria's involvement in the DRC.

Chris Landsberg states that South African action in the DRC has been assessed positively at the international level, mostly in the West, but with mixed feelings at the regional level, where Pretoria looked as an 'ambivalent regional power that did not know how to wield influence'.[72] Other scholars have pointed out South Africa's responsibility in the flaws of the Global and Inclusive Agreement, which looked as an 'elite deals locking in place "low-intensity democracy" and neo-liberal economic regimes'[73] or as a 'de facto trusteeship' which 'imposed elections on a reluctant domestic political class'.[74] In this regard, Filip Reyntjens observes that during the ICD in Sun City, in some occasions Mbeki and Niasse confronted the parties with a *fait accompli*, for instance when they presented to them the draft of the final agreement and of the transitional constitution with a 'take it or leave it' approach, without much room for debate.[75] Emeric Rogier shares the same view and states that the result of this approach was that the parties signed the agreement not out of political will but mostly to avoid being marginalized and to have their share of power preserved.[76]

The agreement was certainly 'externally induced', and it included some sort of imposition on the Congolese parties. However, this approach also responded to the necessity, stressed by Kingibe after the failed opening session, to neutralize the power-oriented focus of the Congolese leaders and to prevent them from exploiting prolonged and inconclusive negotiations only to improve their position on the military ground. In other words, it was the way to avoid the same situation of 'talk and fight'[77] which had led to the failure of the Kabila–Mobutu talks in spring 1997. Reyntjens concludes that the externally induced nature of the transition was precisely its weakness, as it is unlikely that, due to the limited interest of the Congolese players in democracy, the ICD could produce an outcome without the strong pressure/imposition of South Africa.[78] In those circumstances, however, it can be concluded that this was also South Africa's main merit.

On a more general level, there are a few conclusions that can be drawn regarding Pretoria's intervention in mediation and conflict resolution from the end of the apartheid up to the Global and Inclusive Agreement. First of all, it is important to note the legacy of South Africa's own experience. After the 'miraculous', peaceful democratic transition in 1994, it seemed that the post-apartheid South Africa had some sort of moral duty in promoting the same approach in the African continent and in acting as a model and example to follow.

However, it became very soon evident that while South Africa's own democratic transition remains an undisputed positive example of conflict resolution, its model is hardly replicable elsewhere. The failed mediation attempt between Mobutu and Kabila proved that South Africa's fixation with its own approach based on power-sharing agreements and governments of national unity was not always appropriate to different regional and domestic contexts.[79] In this sense, the role of personalities is another particular important factor to consider. Nelson Mandela, the hero of the anti-apartheid struggle and the promoter of a reconciliation narrative in post-apartheid South Africa, seemed the perfect actor to be involved in conflict resolution around the continent. His moral status and his international prestige made him a respected and influential mediator, as the case of Angola demonstrates. However, at a closer analysis, it seems that precisely because of his celebrity and iconic status, Mandela was also a quite cumbersome figure and accidentally fuelled those concerns, raised among several African countries, about the future intentions and aspirations of the new South Africa. The peaceful rhetoric at the core of the South African model and the inspirational leadership of Mandela sometimes turned out, when it comes to diplomatic engagement in the continent, to be counterproductive. This aspect became evident in Mandela's clash with Nigeria and, even more important, with Zimbabwe.

The negative reactions of many African countries to Mandela's strong condemnation of Nigeria in the case of Saro-Wiwa showed that that rhetoric and leadership were not necessarily shared. As observed by James Hamill, many countries in the region resented 'the presumptuousness of a newly reconstituted state – particularly one led by a movement that had received extensive African assistance throughout its liberation struggle – believing that it had the right to lecture the continent's veteran leaders on their political behaviour'.[80]

As shown above, the fracture with Zimbabwe in 1997–9 caused a setback in South Africa's action in DRC and, broadly speaking, within the SADC. An important part of this fracture was due to a clash of roles between Mandela and Mugabe. As stressed by several authors, the end of South Africa's pariah status in 1994 and its return on the international stage threatened Zimbabwe role as regional leader in Southern Africa. The international acclamation that the charismatic Mandela received only served to cast shadow on the figure of Mugabe, whose autocratic power was experiencing a progressive decline.[81]

The less prominent figure of Thabo Mbeki and his softer approach towards Mugabe helped to heal the rupture. His 'quiet diplomacy', based on the rejection of sanctions and confrontation with Zimbabwe, significantly diverged from

Mandela's attitude towards Nigeria. Ironically, South African 'quiet diplomacy' had a lot in common with the 'constructive engagement' policy that the United States implemented towards the apartheid regime during the 1980s. Rather than promoting economic sanctions and political isolation, the Reagan administration at the time opted for a constructive dialogue with Pretoria, in order to progressively 'persuade' the apartheid regime to move towards democracy. As it happened for the US constructive engagement, the South African quiet diplomacy also became an object of criticisms, by those who saw in this approach an endorsement of Mugabe's undemocratic behaviour towards the opposition parties in Zimbabwe.[82] The criticisms had some foundations and arguably the 'quiet diplomacy' had not been the ideal solution for democracy in Zimbabwe. However at least one of the assumptions behind that policy was correct: contrasts with Harare were detrimental to South African diplomatic action in the region, particularly in the DRC. As shown before, the détente with Zimbabwe was instrumental to South Africa regaining momentum in the negotiations to end the Second Congo War.

This led to another important consideration, namely the importance of the coordination of the South African diplomacy within SADC. The case of the DRC clearly shows that Pretoria's diplomacy cannot afford clashes with the other regional powers or fractures within the SADC. A successful South African action in peacemaking goes through regional coordination.[83]

The DRC case also demonstrates that this regional coordination must include the military aspect. As mentioned, Pretoria adopted an anti-militaristic attitude in its post-apartheid foreign policy in order 'to compensate – and in some cases overcompensate – for its aggressive behavior in the apartheid era by explicitly avoiding the use of economic and military power to pressure African states into acceptance of its grand ideological designs'.[84] In the case of the DRC this approach had needed a review. South Africa's decision to participate to the MONUC mission arguably backed its diplomatic efforts. This change in approach was confirmed in 2013 when the UN approved the SADC-led Force Intervention Brigade (FIB) to be deployed in Eastern Congo, with the first-ever offensive mandate in UN history. The mandate included the task of carrying out targeted operations to neutralize and disarm groups considered a threat to state authority and civilian security.[85] South Africa was the leading troop contributor of the FIB, and the SANDF played a key role in the offensive operations.[86] As stressed by Thomas Mandrup, contrary to the 1994–2001 period, SANDF today is an integral part of South Africa's diplomacy.[87] However, particularly in the case of the DRC, the increased use of the military power was still profoundly linked to the Mandela-inspired belief in, and commitment to, the political and diplomatic solution.[88]

Over the last decade, several observers have raised concerns that South Africa has failed to deliver the promises of the mid-1990s: establishing a functioning democracy, becoming the 'natural leader' of the continent and exploiting the incredible soft power it had after the successful democratic transition. Economic difficulties, socio-economic legacies of apartheid and a crisis of leadership, among other factors, have contributed to this 'decline' of South Africa.[89]

These difficulties are certainly real. However, the case of the DRC is an important historical reminder suggesting that in the field of mediation and conflict resolution South Africa can still play an important role, thanks to a more prominent power projection within the framework of the regional institutions. This becomes particular important in view of another consideration. Since the end of the Cold War, subregional organizations in Africa, like the SADC, have progressively acquired a prominent role in the field of security and conflict management, especially after the several UN failures in the 1990s.[90] This trend is likely to continue in the twenty-first century, giving the Rainbow Nation the chance to prove its indispensable role in the peacemaking game in the continent.

Notes

1 South Africa was suspended in 1974.
2 In 1994 South Africa was 'the most advanced economy in the sub-region and in the African region as a whole'. See UN Economic Commission for Africa, 'The African Economy in 1994 – An overview', https://www.uneca.org/cfm1995/pages/i-african-economy-1994-overview
3 Foreign Policy Perspective in a Democratic South Africa, African National Congress, http://anc.org.za/content/foreign-policy-perspective-democratic-south-africa; White Paper on national Defence for the Republic of South Africa: Defence in a Democracy, 1996, SANDF, http://www.dod.mil.za/documents/whitepaperondef/whitepaper%20on%20defence1996.pdf; Nelson Mandela, 'South Africa's Future Foreign Policy', *Foreign Affairs* 72, no. 5 (1993).
4 Ibid.
5 Elizabeth Schmidt, *Foreign Intervention in Africa: from the Cold War to the War on Terror* (Cambridge: Cambridge University Press, 2013), 127–33.
6 Paul Hare, *Angola's Last Best Chance for Peace: an Insider's Account of the Peace Process* (Washington: United States Institute of Peace Press, 1998), 51.
7 Ibid., 51–2.

8   See Piero Gleijeses, *Visions of Freedom: Havana, Washington, Pretoria and the Struggle for Southern Africa, 1976–1991* (Chapel Hill: The University of North Carolina Press, 2013).
9   Te Makatu to R Vassen, 15 January 1997, Vol. 3, 1/22/1, South African Foreign Affairs Archives (SAFAA).
10 Hare, *Angola's Last Best Chance*, 133.
11 First Secretary to Dep Director General Africa, 30 June 1994, Vol. 2, 1/22/1 (SAFAA).
12 'Commonwealth Suspends Nigeria Over Executions', *New York Times*, 12 November 1995.
13 Robert Block, 'Mandela Guns for Nigerian Dictator', *Independent*, 27 November 1995.
14 John Siko, *Inside South Africa's Foreign Policy: Diplomacy in Africa from Smuts to Mbeki* (London: I.B. Tauris, 2014), 35; James Barber, 'Reaching for Values: the Commonwealth and Nigeria', *World Today* 53, no. 1 (1997): 21; James Barber, 'The New South Africa's Foreign Policy: Principles and Practice', *International Affairs (Royal Institute of International Affairs 1944–)* 81, no. 5 (2005): 1083–4.
15 US Embassy in Gaborone to Secretary of State, 11 December 1995 – Wikileaks, https://search.wikileaks.org/plusd/cables/95GABORONE6513_a.html
16 Robert Block, 'Mandela under Fire for Failing to Act', *Independent*, 13 November 1995; James Myburgh, 'Mandela and Abacha: How Not to Deal with Dictators', *PoliticsWeb*, 7 August 2008, http://www.politicsweb.co.za/news-and-analysis/mandela-and-abacha-how-not-to-deal-with-dictators
17 'AFRICA-SPORTS: Nigeria Versus South Africa in Political Football', *Inter Press Service*, 8 January 1996, http://www.ipsnews.net/1996/01/africa-sports-nigeria-versus-south-africa-in-political-football/
18 There were two conferences in Nairobi and other initiatives by the EU, the OAU, the United States and other African countries. See Filip Reyntjens, *The Great African War: Congo and Regional Geopolitics, 1996–2006* (Cambridge: Cambridge University Press, 2009), 118–31.
19 Quoted in Ian Taylor, Paul Williams, 'South African Foreign Policy and the Great Lakes Crisis: African Renaissance Meets Vagabondage Politique?' *African Affairs* 100, no. 399 (2001): 266.
20 Chris Landsberg, 'The Impossible Neutrality? South Africa's Policy in the Congo War', in *The African Stakes of the Congo War*, ed. John Clark (Basingstoke: Palgrave Macmillan, 2002): 169.
21 Judy Johnson to GEM, 7 April 1997, Zaire, March–April 1997 (3), OA/ID 1438, Ernst J. Wilson, African Affairs, National Security Council, Clinton Presidential Records, Box 7, William J. Clinton Presidential Library and Museum (CPL); Reyntjens, *The Great African War*, 118–31.

22 'Mobutu and Rebel Said to Agree to Talks', *New York Times*, 18 April 1997.
23 Richardson met separately with Mobutu and Kabila and cleared all the problems that both the parties raised about the location of the meeting. See US Embassy in Kinshasa to Secretary of State, 30 April 1997, US Department of State Freedom of Information Act (FOIA), https://foia.state.gov/searchapp/DOCUMENTS/FOIA_Sep2017/F-2008-02139E1-5/DOC_0C06215382/C06215382.pdf and Secretary of State to US Del Secretary, 30 April 1997, US Department of State FOIA, https://foia.state.gov/searchapp/DOCUMENTS/FOIA_Sep2017/F-2008-02139E1-5/DOC_0C06215375/C06215375.pdf
24 US Embassy in Luanda to US Embassy in Kinshasa, 2 May 1997, US Department of State FOIA, https://foia.state.gov/searchapp/DOCUMENTS/FOIA_Sep2017/F-2008-02139E1-5/DOC_0C06215403/C06215403.pdf
25 Ibid.
26 US Embassy in Libreville to Secretary of State, 3 May 1997, US Department of State FOIA, https://foia.state.gov/searchapp/DOCUMENTS/FOIA_Sep2017/F-2008-02139E1-5/DOC_0C06215413/C06215413.pdf
27 Ibid.; US Embassy in Kinshasa to Secretary of State, 3 May 1997, US Department of State FOIA, https://foia.state.gov/searchapp/DOCUMENTS/FOIA_Sep2017/F-2008-02139E1-5/DOC_0C06215411/C06215411.pdf
28 Secretary of State to US Del Secretary, 6 May 1997, US Department of State FOIA, https://foia.state.gov/searchapp/DOCUMENTS/FOIA_Sep2017/F-2008-02139E1-5/DOC_0C06215433/C06215433.pdf
29 Ibid.; Secretary of State to US Del Secretary, 5 May 1997, US Department of State FOIA, https://foia.state.gov/searchapp/DOCUMENTS/FOIA_Sep2017/F-2008-02139E1-5/DOC_0C06215420/C06215420.pdf
30 South Africa's Mbeki says fresh Zaire talks still on, 7 May 1997, Vol. 3, 1/22/1 (SAFAA); South Africa's Mbeki plans six-nation tour over Zaire, 6 May 1997, Vol. 3, 1/22/1 (SAFAA); Secretary of State to US Del Secretary, 6 May 1997, US Department of State FOIA, https://foia.state.gov/searchapp/DOCUMENTS/FOIA_Sep2017/F-2008-02139E1-5/DOC_0C06215433/C06215433.pdf
31 US Consulate Cape Town to Secretary of State, 13 May 1997, US Department of State FOIA, https://foia.state.gov/searchapp/DOCUMENTS/FOIA_Sep2017/F-2008-02139E1-5/DOC_0C06215447/C06215447.pdf
32 Rebels fight on in Zaire, 5 May 1997, Vol. 3, 1/22/1 (SAFAA); Judy Johnson to GEM, 7 April 1997, Zaire, March–April 1997 (3), OA/ID 1438, Ernst J. Wilson, African Affairs, National Security Council, Clinton Presidential Records, Box 7, CPL.
33 On 31 March 1997, a local Kinshasa paper, *La Cité Africaine*, had published a 'putative' listing of the future Kabila government. See US Embassy in Kinshasa to Secretary of State, 2 April 1997 – Wikileaks, https://search.wikileaks.org/plusd/cables/97KINSHASA2238_a.html

34 US Embassy in Luanda to US Embassy in Kinshasa, 30 April 1997, US Department of State FOIA, https://foia.state.gov/searchapp/DOCUMENTS/FOIA_Sep2017/F-2008-02139E15/DOC_0C06215384/C06215384.pdf; US Embassy in Luanda to US Embassy in Kinshasa, 30 April 1997, US Department of State FOIA, https://foia.state.gov/searchapp/DOCUMENTS/FOIA_Sep2017/F-2008-02139E1-5/DOC_0C06215389/C06215389.pdf

35 See Reyntjens, *The Great African War*, 45–57; Gerard Prunier, *From Genocide to Continental War: The Congolese Conflict and the Crisis of Contemporary Africa* (London: C. Hurst&Co, 2009), 1–72.

36 Secretary of State to US Consulate in Cape Town, 6 May 1997, US Department of State FOIA, https://foia.state.gov/searchapp/DOCUMENTS/FOIA_Sep2017/F-2008-02139E1-5/DOC_0C06215426/C06215426.pdf

37 Colin Waugh, *Paul Kagame and Rwanda: Power, Genocide and the Rwandan Patriotic Front* (London: McFarland, 2004), 125.

38 On the Second Congo War, see Filip Reyntjens, 'Briefing: The Second Congo War: More than a Remake', *African Affairs* 98, no. 391 (1999): 241–5; Prunier, *From Genocide to Continental War*, 181–223.

39 Landsberg, 'The Impossible Neutrality?' 173–4; Taylor, Williams, 'South African Foreign Policy', 281.

40 US Embassy in Pretoria to Secretary of State, 25 November 1998 – Wikileaks, https://search.wikileaks.org/plusd/cables/98PRETORIA15505_a.html

41 US Embassy in Gaborone to Secretary of State, 24 November 2000 – Wikileaks, https://wikileaks.org/plusd/cables/00GABORONE5265_a.html; US Embassy in Pretoria to Secretary of State, 25 November 1998. See also Stefaan Smis and Wamu Oyatambwe, 'Complex Political Emergencies, the International Community & the Congo Conflict', *Review of African Political Economy* 29, no. 93/94 (2002): 417; Reyntjens, *The Great African War*, 202.

42 Fako Johnson Likoti, 'The 1998 Military Intervention in Lesotho: SADC Peace Mission or Resource War?' *International Peacekeeping* 14, no. 2 (2007): 251–63.

43 Landsberg, 'The Impossible Neutrality?' 174; Taylor, Williams, 'South African Foreign Policy', 281.

44 Several authors argue that South Africa's controversial policy was linked to its commercial and economic interest, particularly those of the arms industry. Pretoria was attracted by the commercial opportunities in the mineral-rich DRC, and it was selling arms to almost all the parties of the conflict, particularly Uganda and Rwanda. See Paul Williams 'Pragmatic Multilateralism? South Africa and Peace Operations', in *The New Multilateralism in South African Diplomacy*, ed. Donna Lee, Ian Taylor, and Paul Williams (Basingstoke: Palgrave Macmillan, 2006), 193; Landsberg, 'The Impossible Neutrality?' 174; Taylor, Williams, 'South African Foreign Policy', 281.

45 'Background report on peace efforts', Nairobi IRIN, 22 June 1999.
46 Emizet Kisan, 'Conflict in the Democratic Republic of Congo: A Mosaic of Insurgent Groups', *International Journal on World Peace* 20, no. 3 (2003): 51–80.
47 UNSC, S/RES/1279, 30 November 1999.
48 'Briefing on the Lusaka peace process', Nairobi IRIN, 10 November 1999.
49 'Interview with Ketumile Masire, inter-Congolese dialogue facilitator', Gaborone IRIN, 24 August 2001.
50 US Embassy in Pretoria to Secretary of State, 25 November 1998 – Wikileaks, https://search.wikileaks.org/plusd/cables/98PRETORIA15505_a.html
51 See David Compagnon, ed., *A Predictable Tragedy: Robert Mugabe and the Collapse of Zimbabwe* (Philadelphia: University of Pennsylvania Press, 2011).
52 On the quiet diplomacy, see Martin Adelmann, 'Quiet Diplomacy: The Reasons behind Mbeki's Zimbabwe Policy', *Africa Spectrum* 39, no. 2 (2004): 249–76; Chris Landsberg, 'African Solutions for African Problems: Quiet Diplomacy and South Africa's Diplomatic Strategy Towards Zimbabwe', *Journal for Contemporary History* 41, no. 1 (2016): 126–48.
53 'South Africa's new drive to achieve progress in the DRC', Johannesburg IRIN, 30 July 1999; The Agreement on a cease-fire in the Democratic Republic of Congo; An analysis of the agreement and prospects for peace – *ReliefWeb*, 20 August 1999. See also Landsberg, 'The Impossible Neutrality?', 178.
54 US Embassy in Harare to USUN, 21 April 2000 – Wikileaks, https://wikileaks.org/plusd/cables/00HARARE2198_a.html
55 *White Paper on South African Participation in International Peace Missions*, 1999, https://www.gov.za/sites/default/files/gcis_document/201409/peacemissions1.pdf, 24.
56 Barber, 'The New South Africa's Foreign Policy', 1090; Thomas Mandrup, 'An Uncertain future: South Africa's National Defence Force Caught between Foreign-Policy Ambitions and Domestic Development', *Journal of Eastern African Studies* 12, no. 1 (2018): 140–1.
57 'SOUTH AFRICA: Troops for DRC', Bissau IRIN, 2 May 1999.
58 'Security Council meets on Situation in Democratic Republic of the Congo' – *ReliefWeb*, 15 June 2000; US Embassy in Harare to Secretary of State, 24 July 2000 – Wikileaks, https://search.wikileaks.org/plusd/cables/00HARARE4061_a.html
59 US Embassy in Harare to Secretary of State, 22 April 2000 – Wikileaks, https://search.wikileaks.org/plusd/cables/00HARARE2200_a.html; US Embassy in Harare to Secretary of State, 25 April 2000 – Wikileaks, https://search.wikileaks.org/plusd/cables/00HARARE2222_a.html
60 US Embassy in Harare to Secretary of State, 18 July 2000 – Wikileaks, https://search.wikileaks.org/plusd/cables/00HARARE3941_a.html
61 Reyntjens, *The Great African War*, 252–3.

62 Ibid., 252; 'Renewed Hopes for Peace in Congo under Young Kabila', Nairobi IRIN, 9 February 2001; US Embassy in Kinshasa to Secretary of State, 29 January 2001 – Wikileaks, https://search.wikileaks.org/plusd/cables/01KINSHASA478_a.html

63 'Glimmer of hope After Congo Summit', *BBCNews*, 15 February 2001; US Embassy in Harare to Secretary of State, 16 February 2001 – Wikileaks, https://search.wikileaks.org/plusd/cables/01HARARE762_a.html

64 'DRC: SADC Appeals for Funds for Inter-Congolese Dialogue', *ReliefWeb*, 11 December 2001; Reyntjens, *The Great African War*, 255; Prunier, *From Genocide to Continental War*, 269.

65 US Embassy in Abuja to Secretary of State, 24 November 2001 – Wikileaks, https://search.wikileaks.org/plusd/cables/01ABUJA2974_a.html

66 US Embassy in Abuja to Secretary of State, 28 January 2002 – Wikileaks, https://search.wikileaks.org/plusd/cables/02ABUJA242_a.html; The Inter-Congolese Dialogue – Department of International Relations and Cooperation, http://www.dirco.gov.za/foreign/Multilateral/profiles/icd.htm; Emeric Rogier, 'The Inter-Congolese Dialogue: A Critical Overview', in *Challenges of Peace Implementation. The UN Mission in the Democratic Republic of the Congo*, ed. Mark Malan and Joao Gomes Porto (Pretoria: ISS, 2004), 29.

67 Tjiurimo Hengari, 'South Africa's State Building Role in the DRC: Kicking the Can Down the Road', *Policy Insights* 39, December 2016, South African Institute of International Affairs, 4; Katabaro Miti, 'South Africa and Conflict Resolution in Africa: From Mandela to Zuma', *Southern Africa Peace and Security Studies* 1, no. 1 (2012): 32; Landsberg, 'The Impossible Neutrality?' 179–80.

68 Miti, 'South Africa and Conflict Resolution', 32; US Embassy in Kinshasa to Secretary of State, 2 March 2002 – Wikileaks, https://search.wikileaks.org/plusd/cables/02KINSHASA673_a.html

69 Reyntjens, *The Great African War*, 257–8; Rogier, 'The Inter-Congolese Dialogue', 31–2.

70 Global and Inclusive Agreement on Transition in the Democratic Republic of Congo, UN PeaceMaker, https://peacemaker.un.org/drc-agreementontransition2002

71 Rogier, 'The Inter-Congolese Dialogue', 37–8.

72 Landsberg, 'The Impossible Neutrality?' 180.

73 Patrick Bond, 'The ANC's "Left Turn" & South African Sub-Imperialism', *Review of African Political Economy* 31, no. 102 (2004): 605.

74 Reyntjens, *The Great African War*, 7.

75 Ibid., 260.

76 Rogier, 'The Inter-Congolese Dialogue', 35–6.

77 Reyntjens, *The Great African War*, 126.

78 Ibid., 7 and 284.

79 See Devon Curtis, 'South Africa's Peacemaking Efforts in Africa', in *Foreign Policy in Post-Apartheid South Africa: Security, Diplomacy and Trade*, ed. Adekeye Abebajo and Kudrat Virk (London: I.B. Tauris, 2018), 69–92; Daniela Kroslak, 'South Africa's Implementation of Its Own Peacekeeping Model in Africa: a Reality Check', in *Africa's Peacemaker? Lessons from South African Conflict Mediation*, ed. Kurt Shillinger (Pretoria: Fanele, 2009), 41–8.

80 James Hamill, *Africa's Lost Leader: South Africa's Continental Role since Apartheid* (Routledge, 2018), 2.

81 Adelmann, 'Quiet Diplomacy', 257; Barber, 'The New South Africa's Foreign Policy', 1086; Daniel Compagnon, 'The International Community and the Crisis in Zimbabwe', in *A Predictable Tragedy*, ed. Compagnon, 242–3; Chris Saunders, 'South Africa and Africa', *The Annals of the American Academy of Political and Social Science*, 652 (2014), 225.

82 US Embassy in Pretoria to Secretary of State, 29 March 2007 – Wikileaks, https://search.wikileaks.org/plusd/cables/07PRETORIA1110_a.html. See also Mediel Hove, Enock Ndawana, 'Regional Mediation Strategy: The Case of Zimbabwe', *African Security Review* 25, no. 1 (2016): 74; Compagnon, 'The International Community and the Crisis in Zimbabwe', 248–9.

83 On this point, see Saunders, 'South Africa and Africa', 232.

84 Hamill, *Africa's Lost Leader*, 42.

85 UNSC, S/RES/2098, 28 March 2013.

86 Curtis, 'South Africa's Peacemaking Efforts in Africa', 78; Mandrup, 'An Uncertain future', 147.

87 Ibid., 147.

88 Ibid., 144–5.

89 See, for instance, Hamill, *Africa's Lost Leader*; R. W. Johnson, *South Africa's Brave New World: the Beloved Country since the End of Apartheid* (London: Penguin Books, 2010); Robert Mattes, 'Forging Democrats', in *After Apartheid: Reinventing South Africa?*, ed. Ian Shapiro and Kahreen Tebeau (Charlottesville: University of Virginia Press, 2011); Susan Booysen, *Dominance and Decline: The ANC in the Time of Zuma* (Johannesburg: Wits University Press, 2015); John Daniel, Prishani Naidoo, Devan Pillay, and Roger Southall, ed., *New South African Review 3: The Second Phase – Tragedy or Farce?* (Johannesburg: Wits University Press, 2013).

90 See Abiodun Alao, 'The Role of African Regional and Sub-Regional Organisations in Conflict Prevention and Resolution', *UNHCR Working Paper*, no. 23, July 2000,

10

Life as a diplomat

Ambassador Nigel Thorpe

Diplomats enjoy a unique vantage point from which to observe global change. Both at home and abroad they are confronted with a constant range of issues affecting their country's interests. The nature of these issues is almost unlimited: from the environment to high politics, to commercial and economic problems, to issues affecting citizens. They might require urgent resolution, or they may be long-term issues, requiring international cooperation. The job of the diplomat is to advise on the response and suggest action, or take action that can affect the outcome in ways beneficial to his government.

When I joined Her Majesty's Diplomatic Service in January 1969, Britain was a global player. It was the height of the Cold War and, as Douglas Hurd later put it, the UK punched above its weight on the world stage. The UK was a Permanent Member of the Security Council, a leading member of the North Atlantic Treaty Organization (NATO) and the Commonwealth, but not yet a member of the European Economic Community. At that time, the Soviet Union, and the communist regimes of East and Central Europe, seemed immutable, and proxy wars between groups supported by the Russians and the West were in progress in many parts of the world. By the time of my final job, as ambassador in post-communist Hungary, we were dealing with the aftermath of the Soviet era, and the building (or so we hoped) of a new, liberal, free market democracy. Now Britain faces the consequences of its departure from the European Union.

During that period, political changes mirrored, or were prompted by, societal changes or technological advances that have altered the way we work, helped to improve the way we live, and enhanced the terms and conditions of service. Here, I offer recollections from a life in the diplomatic service and what it reveals about diplomatic practice. I reflect on some of the key global shifts that changed the themes and priorities of diplomacy during a career spanning over thirty years, detail the daily life and challenge of a diplomat, and consider how the service itself has changed and adapted to keep pace with the world around it.

At the heart of events

I began my career in 1969 as a junior desk officer in the then East European and Soviet Department. I sat in a large room which I shared with two other officers, responsible for our relations with the Soviet Union. Earlier that year a British academic, Gerald Brooke, had been arrested in the Soviet Union and sentenced to five years' imprisonment for allegedly distributing anti-Soviet leaflets. Unbeknownst to me, as a new entrant, my senior colleague, the head of our department and our Embassy in Moscow were in negotiations with the Soviet authorities that led in July to the exchange of Brooke for two Soviet spies, who had lived in Britain under a false identity (the Krogers) and been arrested in 1961 for their involvement with a Soviet spy ring targeting the Royal Navy's Underwater Research Establishment at Portland.

This early exposure made clear how much of my life would be dominated by our engagement with the communist world, particularly Eastern and Central Europe. This would be the theme of my service, and much of my subsequent career was dominated by the Cold War, and then by its unexpected, and sudden end with the collapse of the Soviet Union. Given the nature of diplomatic service, however, the journey was eclectic. I gained knowledge and a repertoire of skills through additional experiences on Southern Africa, and postings in Bangladesh and Canada before I became ambassador to Hungary.

My first overseas posting was in Warsaw in 1970. At that time, Poland sat behind the Iron Curtain, a member of the Warsaw Pact, a close ally of the Soviet Union and a hostile place for a British diplomat. It was a difficult place live in, with a tiny Western community, and a shortage economy. Constant scrutiny by the Polish security service made living and working difficult. But it was challenging and very interesting as we observed the struggle between the communist government and the Polish people, many of whom resented it. It was my first overseas experience and I watched two outbreaks of protest, a change of leader (always a big moment in a communist system) and the attempts by the new leadership to calm the country and restore order. I saw that the problems of Polish society were so deep-seated that there was no easy solution. I did not realize that I had watched the beginnings of a movement that would lead to the creation of the Solidarity trade union in 1980 and ultimately the fall of the communist regime in 1989. For me this was a period when I was learning the crafts of the trade. I was lucky to have good teachers in the Embassy and to meet Poles who also, perhaps unwittingly, instructed me.

Curiously one of my last tasks in Warsaw was to take part in the negotiations with the Poles over Britain's entry into the European Economic Community, which would affect many Polish exports to Britain. During this time, of course, Europe had been a constant and prominent feature of British diplomacy. Joining the European Economic Community on January 1973 was a huge step change in Britain's relationship with Europe, indeed in its place in the world. Membership of the EEC, and later the European Union, buttressed our international position and gave us greater influence. It also changed the Foreign and Commonwealth Office (FCO) and the Diplomatic Service. A European cadre of people who specialized in the arcana of the European treaties and the way the EEC worked quickly developed as the FCO took the lead on many EEC issues in Whitehall, and there was the big Brussels Embassy to staff and head up. One detrimental impact was the loss of functions to EEC officials, especially trade policy and the General Agreement on Tariffs and Trade (the GATT, now the World Trade Organization). That expertise became redundant. When I went to Ottawa as First Secretary Economic in 1979 I found that many of the interesting parts of my job were by then dealt with by the EEC representative and his staff, on behalf of all the member states. Later, with the development of Political Cooperation, we worked ever more closely with our European partners. By the time I became head of my own post the monthly EU Heads of Mission meeting (EUHOMS) was a byword.

I spent 1988 in Warsaw, watching – though not fully appreciating – the unravelling of the communist world. It was my second time in communist Poland and I was struck by the changes I saw, a more rebellious society and the steady loss of authority of the regime. Our contacts were talking of change but we were not sure how far this would go. We did not (nor did the Embassy in Moscow) know of the decision already taken by Gorbachev that the Soviet Union would not prop up the Central European regimes by military force.

In November 1988 Prime Minister Margaret Thatcher came to talk to the Polish regime and, at her strong insistence, met the leader of the Solidarity movement, Lech Wałęsa. He had just been invited to take part as a member of the lay Catholic team in Round Table talks on the future government of Poland. The talks were designed to neutralize the opposition and enable the communist regime to continue in spite of the strong and articulate opposition to it. Wałęsa had one question for Mrs Thatcher: should he accept the invitation? She said yes. He accepted, and the Round Table talks took place and led to a compromise election, in which Solidarity demonstrated its strong popular support. Less than a year after Thatcher's visit one of Wałęsa's advisors, Tadeusz Mazowiecki, a lay Catholic intellectual and a prominent opposition figure, was appointed Prime Minister. It was just two months before the fall of the Berlin Wall. Communism was ending.

Change was sudden, and significant. Three years after this meeting, I was Head of the FCO's Central European Department, responsible for policy towards most of the former Soviet satellites. Having observed the end of the Communist period in Europe, I now had to advise on our approach to the post-communist world. In this role, I inherited a policy of supporting the creation of liberal, free market democracies. But it was not all plain sailing. Czechoslovakia, which had been at the heart of the revolution in 1989, split into two countries in 1993. One, Slovakia, had a distinctly unattractive leadership. In Poland and Hungary, the right-wing parties which had led the reform movements, lost power, succeeded by Socialist or left-leaning parties, partly formed out of the remnants of the old communist parties who had run these countries. In Hungary's case, the party was led by a man whose role in the suppression of the 1956 revolution was dubious. There was debate about how to react. I argued successfully that these changes were the result of democratic process and should be respected, and that we should continue our approach of supporting the construction of liberal, free market democracies and cautiously integrating our new friends into Western institutions. By 2005, several of them had joined NATO and the European Union.

The international agenda changed again in the late 1990s, with the rise of terrorism and the growing importance of climate change. Today, for example, we face new problems such as appalling air pollution in cities like Beijing, Shanghai or New Delhi, and very hot or humid climates can be very trying. Yet, there have always been dangers. The British Embassy in Beijing was attacked and set on fire by Red Guards during the Chinese Communists' Maoist Cultural Revolution. Staff were lucky to escape with their lives. In 1979 Iranian students occupied the US Embassy in Tehran and 52 US diplomats were held prisoner for over 400 days before their release. The rise in terrorism has brought new risks to embassies, and new priorities. American and British diplomats have been the target of terrorist attacks, with the US embassies in Nairobi and Dar es Salaam targeted by car bombs. My colleague and friend Roger Short was murdered by Al Qaeda in Istanbul in 2003, one of several British diplomats killed in terrorist attacks. The family of another colleague, Michael Atkinson, ambassador to Romania, sheltered in the basement of his Residence while government forces fought from the Residence balcony during the Romanian revolution of 1989. The risks are real and have not diminished, merely changed.

Amidst all this, technology has revolutionized the way diplomats work. In the Embassy in Warsaw in 1970, when I was on my first posting, our communications with the Office in London were a confidential diplomatic bag, carried by a Queen's Messenger on the BEA flight once a week, and a wireless link. This was operated by an ex-navy wireless operator who tapped out our messages to London in Morse code. They had already been encrypted by hand, using a machine rather like a typewriter. The process was laborious and time consuming. If you wanted to send a message out of office hours then you had to call in the wireless operator and possibly a registry clerk to encrypt your message. The arrival of the computer and the internet has changed all this. At first even word processors were regarded by the Service with caution because of the security risks, but once these were overcome computers were embraced with enthusiasm. On top of this, in Poland at this time the British Embassy, like those in other communist countries, was very isolated, with little access to people, and no worthwhile media to study. It was a challenge to know what the government was doing or what the populace thought. Fortunately, the internet and social media have changed this. It is hard for countries like China to run a closed society.

In the British High Commission in Bangladesh in 1973, our daily contact with the rest of the world was through the BBC World Service, and even then, it was often hard to pick up. There was no local television and it was before the arrival of easily accessed satellite TV. British newspapers arrived once a week and were circulated in groups, according to seniority. If, like me, you were third or fourth on the list you might not get the papers for a couple of weeks. It meant we were all very cut off. The only issues we were up to date with were local and regional, as the Foreign and Commonwealth Office's reporting systems kept us in the picture. It was a challenge for many British diplomats at that time, especially those in the communist or developing worlds. The arrival of satellite television, and then the internet and the mobile phone of course, changed all that. Our sources of information also multiplied, as did our ways of communicating our policies. Embassies now have home pages, Facebook accounts, blogs and so on. At an extreme, the US president conducts foreign policy by Twitter.

The qualities and roles of a diplomat

I was surprised when I was accepted into the Diplomatic Service. I had hardly ever been abroad, spoke no foreign languages and knew nothing of the life I was embarking on. The other new entrants all seemed much better qualified. Yet there are common qualities and competencies that diplomats share. An interest in the outside world and some knowledge of international affairs and foreign countries is a start. But a good brain, an inquisitive mind and a strong ability to communicate are essential. An aptitude for languages helps, though the lack of this is not a barrier. Above all good judgement is vital, as is the ability to assess a situation or problem and offer sensible ways forward, towards a resolution. Judgement develops over time and with experience. When I think of the things I got wrong as well as the things I got right I can see that my judgement improved as I acquired new experiences and encountered different problems. Add to that integrity of character and an ability to work with others and to mix easily with people you have never met in order to establish relationships is valuable.

For a diplomat, the emphasis will always be on people rather than paper. Your ability to function as a member of an Embassy team requires you first and foremost to deal with the local population. This requires a network of contacts who are well placed and can answer your questions with knowledge and insight. You need to reach people who are influential and can help you to deliver whatever it is that you are expected to achieve.

As an ambassador in Hungary during the controversial Iraq war of 2003 I was instructed to recruit the Hungarian government to the political and military coalition of Britain and the United States. It was a difficult task, but a typical challenge. I succeeded in large part due to my close relationship with the Hungarian prime minister's private secretary. I had built a relationship with her when her party was in opposition, and that paid dividends once they were in office. I knew that whenever I needed access or insights I could call her and she would help me.

As a result, a diplomat abroad usually spends a lot of time outside of their office: making new contacts, establishing themselves as a valuable and interesting interlocutor. They should be travelling and getting to know what life is like beyond the capital, meeting local politicians, businessmen, journalists and academics. Travel is essential. Not only does it get you out of the office, and away from the main city, but it enables you to see so much of the lives of ordinary people. To go up country in Bangladesh and see how the average Bengali lived was a revelation, to see the rice being winnowed on the roads, people bathing in the tanks of water by their huts, water buffalo in the many rivers. Or to travel in order to see the extent of flooding during the monsoon with all the hardship that caused. You cannot get this by sitting in the office.

On top of that is the public face, and performance of diplomacy. Entertainment was a core component of diplomatic outreach and engagement, especially overseas. All professions entertain their contacts, and diplomats are no exception. However, the reality does not resemble the myths of diplomatic receptions with mountains of Ferrero Rocher. If used effectively, it can help develop relationships with key players, widen your circle of acquaintances, help you build rapport and gain insights, as well as providing an opportunity to make friends and enjoy yourself. Personally, I was never a great fan of the cocktail party, but in Warsaw in the late 1980s I attended them religiously as I was sure to meet senior figures from the Solidarity movement there, with whom I could have good conversations and learn useful information. As ambassador in Budapest I hosted lots of parties for senior visitors to meet key players on the Hungarian scene, but I also liked to hold one on one lunches to get to know key people better, and found them indispensable to develop rapport.

Events would often be held to coincide with the many visitors you receive: Ministers, members of Parliament, members of the Royal Family and distinguished people from many backgrounds. This is foreign policy at the top level, performative and symbolic but full of substance. I was involved with a State Visit by Her Majesty the Queen to Zimbabwe, and I worked on two visits by Prime Minister Margaret Thatcher, one to Poland and one to Zimbabwe, both remarkable, though in different ways. I was deeply struck by the ease of Margaret Thatcher's relationship with President Robert Mugabe and with the Mozambican President Machel, who joined them on the Zimbabwe visit. On the face of it they had nothing in common but in practice of course a great deal, not least as established powerful and successful leaders. This and other visits brought me into contact with senior local figures and helped to build relationships. This opportunity to meet so many remarkable people was one of the perks of the job.

In the day to day the diplomat occupies a variety of roles. If you are on your first posting you will have a narrow field to deal with, perhaps one subject, but as you get more senior then the portfolio will broaden, till at the top you are responsible for everything. Alongside the diplomat, there may be specialist attachés for subjects like agriculture or the environment, or representing the military services.

Managing and translating policy and politics are central to a diplomat's role. At the top level you may be advising your government on difficult policy decisions. For me, this ranged from how to attract support to your country's position on war with Iraq, to how to respond to a leak of reports from the ambassador in Washington that are embarrassing to the relationship with the United States, to how to respond when six political activists seek refuge from the South African police in your consulate in Durban. This last episode, that occurred in 1984, was particularly striking, and was one of the most difficult issues I dealt with, raising major questions of law as well as a huge row with the then-apartheid government of South Africa. I was in the FCO's Southern African Department at the time and so the issue was ours. I knew the South African diplomats at their London Embassy but, whether I liked them or not, I had to give them some very hard messages and accept the hard messages they brought me.

Understanding what is going on, and the politics of an issue, is therefore essential to the conduct of relations between your country and the host. In the case of disagreements there will be difficult messages to deliver. Yet it is vital that these are delivered. In Warsaw in the 1980s, I heard one of the Western ambassadors telling a Polish minister that personally he did not share the views of his government in condemning the violations of human rights in the suppression of opposition to the communist regime: not good practice. The politics of the role mean you have to stick to the script and tell your interlocutor what it says, even if you know and like the person you are talking to quite well, as you may. This is especially important now that public advocacy is a central part of an ambassador's role. Speeches, press interviews, appearances on TV and radio are now the daily stuff of life, and your job is to present the official point of view and persuade your audience to accept it.

At a consular level, the job is all about dealing with people. Locals may need visas and work permits to go to your country. Your own citizens may get into difficulty with the authorities, may fall ill and need evacuation, or they may simply lose their passports. This sometimes happens between leaving home and arriving at their destination. Every case needs attention, and sympathy as well as common sense and a thorough knowledge of the relevant laws and regulations. It can be harrowing. I had to inform a couple that their son had been killed in a motor accident. Consular work is critically important. After the terrorist attack in Bali in 2002, in which twenty-three Britons were killed (and many more Americans and others) the Embassy in Djakarta moved its whole consular operation to Bali to support the injured and the families of those killed. This will have demanded many qualities among the British team – compassion, of course, sympathy and human kindness, but also the ability to sum up the political situation and work out how to deal with a local government struggling to deal with this appalling incident.

Commercial work is a central part of any diplomat's job, especially as you become more senior. All embassies have a commercial section, and many British consulates, the embassy's outstations, are principally concerned with the protection and promotion of British business. British companies seek at advice on the local market, but they also look for support especially when seeking business with the local government. They want the access that the Embassy can provide, and the doors that the ambassador can open for them. The diplomat's skills for relationships can help businesses to meet the right people, and expand their markets. Diplomats can also mediate tensions between companies and their host countries. In Hungary, I encouraged British ministers to intervene with the Hungarian government when it sought to punish a British retailer for opening its doors on Hungarian National Day, something the government had prohibited any retailer from doing. This was tricky: the British company had not broken the law, merely gone against the government's wishes. It was coincidence that a senior British minister was in town, but we were able to turn it to our advantage, and, with some delicate phrasing, solve the problem.

All these sort of things happen in a department or an embassy comprising many people and having many assets at its disposal. There are administrative staff to look after the people and the material assets (houses, flats, cars and so on), but at a senior level overseas you will be carrying considerable management responsibility, and signing off an account that may be millions of pounds. You are directly responsible for those people working for you, and if you are the head of post in charge of the whole Embassy. This will include, of course, not only British diplomatic staff but also locally engaged staff, nationals of the country as well as some of the partners of your British team. All need careful and sympathetic handling.

To equip people for this role, the Service has spent a lot of time in the last forty years developing management skills among its senior members, having dropped the idea that such skills were innate and training was unnecessary. This has paid dividends. The challenge of management in a difficult post overseas, where perhaps living conditions are hard or the authorities are hostile, is quite different to that of managing people in a department in London. First of all, there is the question of accommodation – is it up to the standard of the home an officer would enjoy in Britain? Then there is the question of unhappy officers or a family in difficulty, suffering from the stress of separation form their children or some other issue. Managers are much more involved with the nitty gritty of people's lives overseas.

The Diplomatic Service

Learning how to be a diplomat, and the practices and behaviours it entails, usually involves learning on the job. When I started out, I was working under the direction of a more senior member of the Office, who was brilliantly clever and very talented. I tried to glean from him and from other colleagues what I should be doing, how I should set out my written work and how I should deal with the issues in my purview. It was vital to be able to turn to one of my older colleagues for advice.

For many of us our career starts with language lessons. For some this is easy, but for those of us who are not natural linguists it is hard work. I learnt Polish and then Hungarian, as well as trying to improve my French. This is lonely work, usually undertaken as you prepare for your posting. Once there you need to adjust to the new country, find your way about, learn the job and try to improve the language. Learning the job abroad involved more learning from colleagues, watching and listening to what others did to achieve their many and varied tasks. I also learnt from my contacts who would guide me on appropriate conduct and tips to truly understand the country where I was posted. When first in Warsaw in communist Poland, I was advised by a Polish journalist to spend 1 November at the main Warsaw cemetery. It was All Saints' Day, a special day for Catholic Poles. I had not previously appreciated the depth of Polish commitment to the Church but then I understood it. This was Communist Poland, ruled by a party of atheists who saw the Catholic Church as an ideological enemy. So, a good lesson.

The daily life of a diplomat has changed significantly. When I joined the Foreign and Commonwealth Office the main working room of a department was called the Third Room. It's no longer in use but in those days, a coal fire in winter and a bell which if pressed the right number of times would bring a man with a fresh supply of coal. In 1969 we started work at the Foreign Office's grand building in Whitehall at 10am, followed by departmental coffee at 11, then lunch, and tea at 4pm. I went home at 6. For all of us the hours have lengthened. In my last job in London I started at 7am and rarely left the office before 7.30pm. Partly this was because I was more senior, and carried responsibility for my department, but also I think the demands of the Office had intensified. This in turn was partly due to technological change and the ease and speed of communication.

The Service was always friendly but there has been a huge effort to make it less formal. Heads of mission are now often called by their first names and embassies are expected to be welcoming, not forbidding, places making life generally more relaxed. In the period after the war, until around the early 1970s, a new entrant was given a handbook on protocol (originally written by Marcus Cheke, Vice Marshal of the Diplomatic Corps in London), giving the fundamentals on how to behave, including tips on what to do with visiting cards and how to arrange seating at a dinner.

The terms and conditions of work have changed greatly and for the better. In late 1969 I received a phone call at my desk from the Foreign and Commonwealth Office Personnel Department to tell me that I was to be posted to the Embassy in Warsaw the next year. There was no question. It was an order, and I was conditioned to obey. Nowadays you apply for jobs, and face a competitive process of selection.

In particular, there have been initiatives to improve equality and diversity. When I began the Service was rather old school and many people were from private schools and Oxford and Cambridge. Although they had all the qualities required, and included many very able people, they reflected a pattern of recruitment from rather traditional backgrounds. That has, slowly, changed. At that time women members of the Service had to resign if they got married. The Equal Opportunities Act of 1972 rightly changed this, and now there are lots of senior female officers, sometimes accompanied by their partners rather than the other way round. LGBTQ officers no longer face objections on security grounds (although this can be an issue in countries where homosexuality is still illegal). Fortunately, the Service now reflects more accurately the society that it represents. We are a long way from the recruitment process that took an applicant to a country house for a weekend and studied his (he would have been male) behaviour, and conversation to make a decision without the need for a written or oral examination and interview.

Nonetheless, the Service has retained two very important qualities. The first is a sense of collegiality – you feel that you are really part of one organization, and with that a sense of belonging and loyalty. Because of the postings cycle, and the mix of overseas and home postings, you get to know a surprising number of your Service colleagues, and often run into people you know wherever you go. The second is a sense of service. As a diplomat you are there to serve your government, country and the Queen. In this we are closer to the armed forces than probably to other departments of the Civil Service.

The many lives of a diplomat

As a diplomat the question I most feared from my children was, 'What do you do at work?' In reality, there are two different roles and two different lives: one at home in London and the other abroad. A key challenge in the life of a diplomat is to separate the personal from the professional.

The London life is essentially that of the standard civil servant: the daily commute on public transport to the office, an office-based job, meetings with other officials and ministers in the Office and in other government departments, often long hours and a job very much focused ultimately on giving advice to Ministers, be it on longer-term policy or the latest crisis. Interestingly there are relatively few social engagements. The skills needed are more or less the same as in any government department. Perhaps the big difference is that many home departments are very Parliament-focused and have to put legislation through Parliament to effect policy. In contrast the Foreign Office has little need for legislation. But the work you are doing can still retain the drama and excitement.

It was in the Foreign and Commonwealth Office in London in 1978 that I found myself part of the five-nation team (working with the United States, Canada, France and Germany – the Contact Group) negotiating a plan for the independence of Namibia. At the time it was occupied by South Africa and I was the desk officer who wrote the papers (called submissions) to ministers recommending the course of action we should take with our partners on all the many issues that came up. We ended our work with an agreement, endorsed by the South Africans and the Namibian parties, for Namibian independence. It took another ten years to implement but, in the end, it worked, so I suppose that was a success story.

The domestic and the international are constantly intertwined. Back again in London in 1994, I was head of the Central European Department of the Foreign and Commonwealth Office. Among my responsibilities was policy towards Poland, a country I had served in twice and which was close to my heart. When the Polish government announced a big celebration to mark the 50th Anniversary of the Warsaw Uprising of 1944 against the Nazi occupiers, my first instinct was to recommend that the prime minister, John Major, should attend. The UK had gone to war over the invasion of Poland in 1939, the Poles had fought bravely alongside British forces and we had supplied the insurgents at some cost in the lives of RAF crew. To my surprise Mr Major agreed and very quickly I was in a small RAF plane flying to Warsaw and briefing the prime minister on the events of 1944, and the day ahead.

It was a steamy day in Warsaw and Mr Major was in an English woollen suit, ill-matched for the weather. We embarked on a heavy programme of meetings, including lunch with President Wałęsa, before the main event, which was an outdoor performance of an opera specially written for the Anniversary. It seemed interminable but with a mighty clap of thunder the heavens opened and it poured with rain. It was a sudden end to the day, but as we all ran for our transport and got back to the ambassador's residence, where a waiter was ready with drinks, there was a sense of relief that the day was over but also an understanding that, however difficult, we had taken an important step in building our relationship with the newly democratic Poland.

Your domestic, personal life is like that of most other people. Life at home is 'normal'. You are living in your own home, spending evenings and weekends with your family and friends, many of whom you will have known for many years. If you have children and a partner, their lives will go on as usual. They will not generally have to support you in your professional role or be affected by it, meaning a partner can pursue their career.

Life abroad is quite different. It may look exotic and glamorous, but you are living a strange type of life, not only in the Embassy but also at home. Overseas postings can be lush, but they can also be in very difficult places. Posts in very poor societies can be challenging because of the experiences of extreme poverty deprivation that can cause serious culture shock, in which a person is revulsed by all that he or she sees. It can take months to come to overcome. Equally, in places that are dangerous, where the rule of law is not strong or where the government is hostile, personal security can be at risk. On top of this, there can be challenges of climate or living conditions that can make it harder.

In your private life, such as it is when you are abroad, there are many challenges. It is after all a foreign country, and you may be there for the first time. You may arrive not knowing not only the place but nobody there, even in the Embassy you are joining. Firstly, you need to find somewhere to live. Sometimes the Embassy will simply allocate a house or flat but in my experience the options are unsatisfactory. This is a question of money for the Service and further budgetary pressures have reduced the options. You usually expect a home that suits your family circumstances, and is comparable to what you enjoy at home. However, you may not get this. On top of this, you need a car and to find your way around a strange city. There are shops to be found, and perhaps clubs to join.

Food it particular can be difficult. In two of my postings we had Embassy shops, stocked by orders from Denmark or Sweden (for Warsaw) and Singapore (for Bangladesh) which ensured that many staples of the British diet were available. Otherwise life would have been bleak, especially when you need creature comforts in a real shortage economy like Communist Poland. Bangladesh was a dry state, so alcohol had to be imported and beer and spirits were always on the order. From Bangladesh we travelled regularly to Calcutta (now Kolkata) for rest and recreation, where you could buy clothes and shoes, which were almost unobtainable in Bangladesh then, and go out for a meal.

In many poorer countries it is normal to have domestic staff. In Bangladesh I arrived to find already established in the house I was allocated a cook, a bearer, a gardener and a night guard. I did not choose these people and I was not sure I wanted them. They lived in their own quarters and looked after me very well. But I had not expected this sort of responsibility and was unprepared for it. Similarly, in Zimbabwe I inherited a cook, a maid, a gardener and a night guard. This is not only a responsibility, it is a management challenge raising all sorts of issues, including dealing with pilfering and a very difficult loss of role for a partner or indeed yourself when you no longer run your house. You have a sort of family that is not in fact yours. As a head of post in Budapest I had two cooks, a butler, maid, driver and gardener. They had nearly all been there for a long time and I was just another ambassador passing through the Residence (as the house ambassadors live in is known). It may seem a small thing, but it was very difficult to assert control over what happened in the house. You were and still are expected to know how to manage it all. One other aspect of all this is that traditionally the Service expected the partner of the head of post to run the Residence, effectively a small hotel and restaurant. It is only recently that a small salary has been available for a Residence housekeeper, a way in practice of paying the partner for carrying out this duty.

The two big issues for families are work for the partner and schooling for any children there may be. A partner may have given up a good well-paid job and their own life at home. It is a big sacrifice to tag along to a foreign posting, where the opportunity to work may be very limited. Sometimes there are jobs available in the Embassy, as a locally engaged officer in the visa or administration sections. Sometimes the partner can work in the local economy. Finding opportunities for partners has become more important as more couples both work.

Diplomats with children face the problem of schooling for very young children in post (often possible though the quality of available schooling is very variable) and then having to decide what to do for their secondary education. The choice is invidious. You can take your children around the world with you and they run the risks of whatever local or international schools they can attend. This may give them a wonderful experience but it means they will grow up not knowing much about Britain. Alternatively, you leave them behind in boarding schools in Britain. Allowances for this have shrunk, as school fees have risen. Moreover, the idea of boarding school is alien to many staff today. If you send them away to school you miss them growing up. In the 1960s the Service paid for only one trip a year for a child to join parents overseas, so the other two holidays had to be dealt with by finding relatives to look after the child. That has changed and there are now three trips a year. The postings cycle also brings problems, for instance, of securing school places in London when you return. Families with children with special needs faced particular difficulties. I always found this an uncomfortable aspect of Diplomatic Service life. Nowadays it is possible to stay in jobs at home through this period and so get over that problem but at a cost to career development.

Much of the burden of adjusting to all the challenges of the overseas life falls to the partner in a couple. The diplomat is often busy at the office, learning a new job and meeting a lot of new people. Whereas the partner will be trying to make the house work and deal with all the domestic issues, perhaps missing children who are away at school in Britain, probably missing the home she/he has left behind, and possibly feeling rather lonely and wondering how they will spend the days. Certainly, such experience varies enormously with each person. Fortunately, all posts have a social network for dealing with this and the solidity of the partners'/spouses' network is a vital backstop. It is important not to underestimate the challenge of starting life in a new post, and there is plenty of evidence that partners in particular find it harder in a foreign posting.

Indeed, loneliness and isolation are always a risk for those posted overseas, especially those who are single or whose partners and families are at home. It is exacerbated by restrictions in certain locations. During the communist period, for example, many staff were forbidden to have contact with the local population for security reasons. It remains true for places like China and North Korea. This can lead to a very isolated life and postings are often short as a result.

Fortunately, technology has mitigated some of these challenges. Diplomats are no longer dependent on the weekly unclassified bag for letters from family and friends. Email means you are never out of touch, and Skype means you can see and talk to loved ones easily and for free. Other developments like cheap flights have helped to stop isolation and a sense of being a long way from home. Mobile phones mean instantaneous contact between family and friends. It is hard to imagine that calling home from Warsaw in the 1980s used to involve dialling the UK number tens of times before finally the switchboard was able to connect you. Social media has expanded a diplomat's reach. Most embassies now have Facebook group pages, which help to share information and keep people in the loop over what is happening. There are websites that bring expatriates together, valuable tools to address the isolation and culture shock that can occur in any post.

Conclusion

Now that I have retired from diplomatic life I look back on it with nostalgia and a wealth of memories that still enrich my life: from accompanying Prime Minister Margaret Thatcher on a historic visit to Communist Poland, to landing on a cricket pitch in a light aircraft on a visit to the Bangladesh police academy. People often ask me what was my favourite posting, or most exciting time. I always say that I enjoyed it all, but in truth all of us in the Embassy in Warsaw in the late 1980s, witnessing the decline and fall of the communist world, think back on that as a wonderful, interesting and exciting time to be a British diplomat, with the Thatcher visit the crowning moment. Having spent a considerable part of my life abroad, sometimes in places that were difficult, I revel in the diplomat's unusual way of life. But perhaps the most extraordinary thing has been observing the ways in which the world I was working has changed beyond all our expectations.

In a career spanning almost thirty years, I watched the end of the Soviet Union and of its empire in Central Europe, the reunification of Germany after over forty years of division since the end of the Second World War, the growth of the West European alliance into the European Union, the rise of China as a major economic and political force, the globalization of the world economy and the emergence of climate change and terrorism as dominating global issues. Technology has quickened the pace and means of diplomacy, and democratized access. Events have forced cooperation and alliances where it was thought impossible, and non-state actors have challenged the conventional sovereignty of nations. Since 2016, Brexit yields new challenges and the 2020 global COVID-19 pandemic will have a long-lasting impact on international affairs. These changes have paralleled developments in the ways of working and how the diplomatic service is adapting to the modern world.

Having seen the evolution of Britain's role in Europe from inside the diplomatic service, its decision to leave the European Union will have profound implications for its place in the world, as well as in Europe. At a simple level, Britain will find itself excluded from the largest club of like-minded states in the world. British ambassadors may find themselves more isolated as they no longer enjoy the close political cooperation that has characterized the last thirty or more years. This departure will have ramifications for all the UK's international relations, as Britain can no longer speak as part of such a formidable group which includes France and Germany.

All this is happening as the money available to support British diplomacy has declined, and staff numbers have been cut apparently by over 1,000 at home and a further 1,000 overseas. Some functions have been handed to local staff, and language skills have been neglected. Many posts are now a fraction of the size they should be, with sometimes only two UK-based staff. At the policy level responsibility for leaving the European Union was given to the Department for Exiting the EU and to the Department for International Trade, whereas since 1973, when Britain joined the then European Economic Community, policy on all EC/EU matters had been coordinated by the Foreign and Commonwealth Office and Diplomatic Service staff generally had the key roles in the British Embassy at the EU in Brussels. It is a long way back from this situation, and it will need a bold and an able foreign secretary to rebuild a Diplomatic Service that is in full charge of all foreign policy and is properly staffed and funded to carry out its functions.

Successive British governments have benefitted from the Diplomatic Service's skills and expertise, its worldwide reputation and the extent of its presence. Some prime ministers, notably Margaret Thatcher, mistrusted the Service and felt it was too prone to go native and see the other side's point of view, though in my experience this was not correct. But even she had a Diplomatic Service officer as her key advisor on foreign affairs. As the country faces the consequences of the result of the 2016 referendum it more than ever needs the skills and knowledge of the Diplomatic Service.

Conclusion

Professor Jack Spence, Dr Claire Yorke and Dr Alastair Masser

The ten chapters contained in this volume provide a series of new perspectives of diplomacy. Together, they cover a broad thematic and geographical range, making expert use of both historical and contemporary examples to illustrate the changing theory and practice of diplomacy. Viewed collectively, they highlight a number of major themes, as well as posing some fundamental questions.

Diplomacy remains, fundamentally, about engagement. It requires an ability to not only identify but to understand the economic, societal, and political pressures that shape the foreign policies of other states. As Claire Yorke highlights, a more concerted effort to understand the intrinsically human element of such engagement – using empathy and emotional resonance to connect with others – offers us a new means of looking at the study of diplomacy, as well as an opportunity to improve its efficacy in practice.

The necessity of diplomatic engagement also requires individual nations to address their unique strengths and weaknesses, and to formulate a foreign policy that enables them to maximize their influence, whilst minimizing their vulnerabilities. For small states, as James Gow makes clear, this requires active engagement with others to achieve a critical mass of influence. Others have taken a more malign approach to their engagement, with Gerrit Kurtz shining a welcome spotlight on the use of counter-diplomacy to deliberately undermine trust and unity between nations.

For others, it requires them to identify how – and where – they can achieve greatest impact, whether as a leading proponent of soft power levers such as cultural diplomacy, as a business hub, or by acting as a trusted intermediary or interlocutor. As Flavia Gasbarri highlights, this presents particular challenges for nations and leaders seeking to establish themselves in the international arena. However, finding this 'gap in the market' has arguably added an entrepreneurial element to contemporary diplomacy.

The analysis contained within the chapters of this volume also indicates that diplomats are under increasing pressure to be more representative of, and responsive to, the societies they serve. The ubiquity of the internet and the smartphone has helped to make foreign policy – and its implications – more visible to a larger demographic. Consequently, public opinion is able to influence the domestic politics that underpin foreign policymaking to an unprecedented degree. This suggests that the audience for diplomacy is widening, with diplomats required to be more cognizant of the impact of their work upon their own population at home.

As Pablo de Orellana indicates, such influences are key in shaping the identities of actors within the scope of diplomatic practice, and in governing states' response to them. They also suggest an important distinction between notions of agency and power. Though the public today enjoys greater agency in international relations, this has to translate – consistently at least – into greater power. In short, governments remain the ultimate arbiters of foreign policy; citizens wishing to effect change still look to their political leaders to respond. However, it is far from clear whether governments have established how best to do so, to demonstrate they are suitably attentive to public concerns, whilst maintaining their own ability to determine foreign policy.

Public engagement in foreign policy manifests itself most often in opposition to, rather than support for, government actions. As such, it is typically limited to a single issue, and therefore overlooks the nuance required in nations' management of multiple priorities through its interaction with numerous states. Put simply, the public tend to oversimplify foreign policy, often reacting disproportionately to the seemingly black-and-white ethical or moral questions. This poses a quandary for diplomats themselves who, as Mervyn Frost suggests, are not able to use their own moral and ethical principles to guide their work. And, as Daniel Lomas highlights, it poses unique challenges for those features of foreign policymaking that do not lend themselves to public scrutiny, namely secret intelligence.

The insights contained within this volume indicate the rapid pace of change within the international order. The more prominent role of public opinion is symptomatic of the growing number and impact of non-state actors in the diplomatic process and, consequently, its increasing informality. Too much of today's practice of diplomacy has failed to reflect this change, and instead appears bound by methods, institutions and attitudes that appear increasingly anachronistic.

The pace of change of the international order, as well as its inherent unpredictability, has been laid bare by the COVID-19 pandemic. The rapid spread of coronavirus has illustrated how quickly the priorities and norms of nations states and the international community can be upended, and has thrown our interconnectedness into stark relief. The crisis has had – and will continue to have – profound effects on the societies and economies of nations around the world.

It will also have a profound impact on international relations, and the diplomacy that helps shape it. Multilateral diplomacy has been indispensable to coordinating the international response, with the requirements of social distancing necessitating a novel form of interaction – Zoom diplomacy. At the time of writing, the international cooperation that was the hallmark of the first months of the outbreak is slowly giving way to international recrimination. The pandemic promises to become a major fault line in US-China relations, with President Trump threatening to withhold funding from the WHO in response to its handling of the crisis, and alleged collusion with the Chinese authorities.

The multinational nature of such challenges suggests another theme evident in the chapters of this volume: the need for greater cooperation. As Barbara Zanchetta makes clear, summitry is an irreplaceable feature of such cooperation, playing a leading role in convening and coordinating national representatives. Yet the urgency and scale of the challenges under discussion often sees presidents and prime ministers – rather than diplomats – taking on the role of their country's most senior representative.

Viewed collectively, the chapters contained within this volume point towards an ever-expanding range of responsibilities for modern diplomats. Formulating the varied approaches required to the plethora of issues and audiences is a complex undertaking. Whilst this still requires the kinds of varied competencies outlined by Nigel Thorpe, it requires us to examine whether we are asking too much of our diplomats, expecting them, simultaneously, to be experts in consular affairs, advocates for trade, crisis negotiators, security specialists and expert media performers. This is even more important in a climate where the funding and prestige of diplomacy appear to be in decline.

Finally, the varied insights contained within this volume suggest that diplomacy must react to a shifting dynamic between notions of power and order, with profound – and as yet unclear – implications for how nations conceptualize and pursue their national interests. In much of the world, power is becoming less centralized, as a greater number of diplomatic actors seek influence within an increasingly disordered international system. This poses fundamental questions over the continued relevance of diplomacy, and to what extent it needs to evolve. Hard coercive power has its limitations, as Jean-Francois Belanger demonstrates, and it has ramifications for engagement between societies considered open, and those that are closed, like North Korea.

The scope of modern diplomacy is vast. It is, by its very nature, multidisciplinary, encompassing every element of the relationship between nation states, from cooperation over trade, to war and peace. Providing a meaningful analysis of its innumerable incarnations across every nation and region of the world is therefore impossible. The analysis contained in this volume, alongside its counterpart, is instead intended to provide new perspectives of diplomacy. As such, it has sought to be as inclusive as possible, embracing a wide variety of approaches, methodologies and specialisms.

By illustrating some of the many ways in which the theory and practice of diplomacy are evolving to meet the new demands and priorities of twenty-first-century statecraft, it hopes to encourage academics, practitioners and the public to reconsider the role of diplomacy in today's world, specifically to stimulate greater debate about how we can think about diplomacy differently, by re-examining how we define notions of national interest in an increasingly interconnected world and how we can accommodate the increasing number of people seeking a voice in foreign policy.

The new perspectives promise to contribute to a more constructive dialogue between those dedicated to the study and practice of diplomacy. Though practice theory approaches feature prominently in both volumes, this prominence is unintentional. It does, however, reflect a growing desire on the part of many within academia to make their research more directly applicable to addressing some of these challenges. By embracing the multidisciplinary nature of the subject, and developing ideas of praxis, we can benefit from both conceptual innovations and historical insights to strengthen diplomacy's theoretical foundations. These new perspectives are intended to encourage us to be more innovative in how we conceptualize the role of diplomacy, and bolder in identifying how it can be strengthened to continue its fundamental role in managing international relations. In turn, this can help nations navigate a rapidly changing international order.

Select bibliography

Abrahamsen, R., and Michael Williams, 'Security beyond the State: Global Security Assemblages in International Politics', *International Political Sociology* 3 (2009): 1–17.

Adelmann, M., 'Quiet Diplomacy: The Reasons behind Mbeki's Zimbabwe Policy', *Africa Spectrum* 39, no. 2 (2004): 249–76.

Adler, E., and V. Pouliot (Eds), *International Practices* (Cambridge: Cambridge University Press, 2011).

Adler-Nissen, R. and V. Pouliot, 'Power in Practice: Negotiating the International Intervention in Libya', *European Journal of International Relations* 20, no. 4 (2014): 889–911.

Baram, A., 'Deterrence Lessons from Iraq', *Foreign Affairs* 91, no. 4 (July/August 2012): 76–90.

Barnett, B. and R. Duvall, 'Power in International Politics', *International Organization* 59, no. 1 (2005): 39–75.

Barston, R., *Modern Diplomacy*, 4th edition (Oxon: Routledge, 2019).

Bellamy, Alex J., 'The Humanisation of Security? Towards an International Human Protection Regime', *European Journal of International Security* 1, no. 1 (2016): 112–33.

Bergman, R., *Rise and Kill First: The Secret History of Israel's Targeted Assassinations* (London: John Murray, 2019).

Berridge, G. R., *Diplomacy: Theory and Practice* (New York City: Springer, 2015).

Berridge, G. R., H. M. A. Keens-Soper, and T. G. Otte, *Diplomatic Theory from Machiavelli to Kissinger* (Basingstoke: UK Palgrave Macmillan, 2001).

Bjola, C., *Digital Diplomacy: Theory and Practice* (London: Routledge, 2015).

Blight, J. G. and J. M. Lang, *The Fog of War: Lessons from the Life of Robert S. Mcnamara* (Maryland, USA: Rowman & Littlefield Publishers, Inc, 2005).

Booth, K. and N. Wheeler, *The Security Dilemma: Fear, Cooperation, and Trust in World Politics* (New York City: Palgrave Macmillan, 2008).

Braithwaite, R., *Armageddon and Paranoia: The Nuclear Confrontation* (London: Profile Books, 2017).

Bull, H., *The Anarchical Society – A Study of Order in World Politics*, 4th edition (Basingstoke: Palgrave Macmillan, 2012).

Campbell, D., *Writing Security: United States Foreign Policy and the Politics of Identity*, 2nd revised edition 1998 (Manchester: Manchester University Press, 1992).

Von Clausewitz, C., *On War*, edited and translated by Michael Howard and Peter Paret (Oxford: Oxford University Press, 2008).

Cogan, C., 'Hunters not Gatherers: Intelligence in the Twenty-First Century', *Intelligence & National Security* 19, no. 2 (2004): 304–21.

Coker, C., *Globalisation and Insecurity in the Twenty-First Century: NATO and the Management of Risk* (Oxford: Oxford University Press, 2004).

Colley, T., *Always at War: British Public Narratives of War* (Ann Arbor: University of Michigan Press, 2019).

Connolly, W. E., 'Identity and Difference in Global Politics', in *International/Intertextual Relations: postmodern readings of world politics*, edited by James Der Derian, Michael J. Shapiro (Lexington, MA: Lexington Books, 1989), 323–43. https://discover.libraryhub.jisc.ac.uk/search?ti=International%2FIntertextual%20Relations&rn=1.

Constantinou, C., P. Kerr, and P. Sharp (Eds), *The SAGE Handbook of Diplomacy* (London: Sage, 2016).

Cooper, A. F., J. Heine, and R. Thakur (Eds), *Oxford Handbook of Modern Diplomacy* (Oxford: Oxford University Press, 2013).

Costigliola, F., '"Unceasing Pressure for Penetration": Gender, Pathology, and Emotion in George Kennan's Formation of the Cold War', *The Journal of American History* 83, no. 4 (1997): 1309–39.

Crowards, T., 'Defining the Category of Small States', *Journal of International Development* 14, no. 2 (2002): 143–79.

Daalder, I., 'Responding to Russia's Resurgence: Not Quiet on the Eastern Front', *Foreign Affairs* 96, no. 6 (November/December 2017): 29–38.

Darst, R., *Smokestack Diplomacy* (Cambridge: MIT Press, 2001).

Davis, P. K. and B. M. Jenkins, *Deterrence and Influence in Counterterrorism: A Component in the War on al Qaeda* (Santa Monica, CA: Rand Corporation, 2002).

De Waal, A., *The Real Politics of the Horn of Africa. Money, War and the Business of Power* (Cambridge: Polity Press. 2015).

Der Derian, J., *Antidiplomacy: Spies, Terror, Speed, and War* (Cambridge, MA: Blackwell, 1992).

Der Derian, J., 'Mediating Estrangement: A Theory for Diplomacy', *Review of International Studies* 13, no. 2 (1987): 91–110.

Der Derian, J., *On Diplomacy: A Genealogy of Western Estrangement* (Oxford: Oxford University Press, 1987).

Duncombe, C., *Representation, Recognition and Respect in World Politics: The Case of Iran–US Relations* (Manchester: Manchester University Press, 2019).

Duncombe, C., 'Twitter and the Challenges of Digital Diplomacy', *SAIS Review of International Affairs* 38, no. 2 (2018): 91–100.

Duncombe, C., 'Twitter and Transformative Diplomacy: Social Media and Iran-US Relations', *International Affairs* 93 (2017): 546.

Farrow, R., *War on Peace: The End of Diplomacy and the Decline of American Influence* (New York City: W. W. Norton, 2018).

Ferris, J., *Intelligence and Strategy: Selected Essays* (Oxon: Routledge, 2005).
Fletcher, T., *The Naked Diplomat: Understanding Power and Politics in the Digital Age* (London: HarperCollins UK, 2016).
Freedman, L., *Strategy: A History* (Oxford: Oxford University Press, 2013).
Fridman, O., *Russian 'Hybrid Warfare': Resurgence and Politicisation* (New York: Oxford University Press, 2018).
Frost, M., 'Putting the World to Rights: Britain's Ethical Foreign Policy', *Cambridge Review of International Affairs* 12, no. 2 (1999): 80–9.
Fukuyama, F., *The End of History and the Last Man* (New York: Free Press, 1992).
Gaddis, J. L., *The Cold War* (New York: Penguin, 2006).
Galeotti, M., 'Hybrid, Ambiguous, and Non-Linear? How New Is Russia's "New Way of War"', *Small Wars & Insurgencies* 27, no. 2 (2016): 282–301.
Gheciu, A., *NATO in the "New Europe": The Politics of International Socialization after the Cold War* (Stanford: Stanford University Press, 2005).
Gilboa, E., 'Searching for a Theory of Public Diplomacy', *Annals of the American Academy of Political and Social Science* 616 (2008): 393–415.
Gow, J. and Cathie Carmichael, *Slovenia and the Slovenes: A Small State in the New Europe*, 2nd edition (London: Hurst and Co., 2010).
Granelli, F., *Trust, Politics and Revolution: A European History* (London: I.B. Tauris, 2019).
Haas, R. N., 'Supporting US Foreign Policy in the Post-9/11 World', *Studies in Intelligence* 46, no. 3 (2002). https://www.cia.gov/library/center-for-the-study-of-intelligence/csi-publications/csi-studies/studies/vol46no3
Hall, T. H., *Emotional Diplomacy: Official Emotion On the International Stage* (Ithaca, NY: Cornell University Press, 2015).
Hamilton, K. and Richard Langhorne, *The Practice of Diplomacy: Its Evolution, Theory, and Administration* (London: Taylor & Francis, 2011).
Hansen, L., *Security as Practice: Discourse Analysis and the Bosnian War* (London: Routledge, 2006), 18–54.
Harding, L., *The Snowden Files* (London: Faber & Faber, 2014).
Harding, L., *Wikileaks: Inside Julian Assange's War on Secrecy* (London: Faber, 2013).
Head, N., 'A Politics of Empathy: Encounters with Empathy in Israel and Palestine', *Review of International Studies* 42, no. 1 (2016): 95–113.
Head, N., 'Transforming Conflict Trust, Empathy, and Dialogue', *International Journal of Peace Studies* 17, no. 2 (2012): 33–55.
Herman, M., 'Diplomacy and Intelligence', *Diplomacy & Statecraft* 9, no. 2 (1998).
Herman, M., 'Ethics and Intelligence after September 2001', *Intelligence & National Security* 19, no. 2 (2004): 342–358.
Herman, M., *Intelligence Services in the Information Age* (London: Frank Cass, 2005).
Hibbert, R., 'Intelligence and Policy', *Intelligence & National Security* 5, no. 1 (1990): 110–28.
Holmes, M. and K. Yarhi-Milo. 'The Psychological Logic of Peace Summits: How Empathy Shapes Outcomes of Diplomatic Negotiations', *International Studies Quarterly* 61, no. 1 (2016): 107–22.

Holsti, O. R., *Public Opinion and American Foreign Policy* (Ann Arbor: University of Michigan Press, 2004).

Howard, M., 'Reassurance and Deterrence: Western Defense in the 1980s', *Foreign Affairs* 61, no. 2 (1982): 309.

Jabri, V., *Discourses on Violence: Conflict Analysis Reconsidered* (Manchester: Manchester University Press, 1996).

Janis, Irving L., *Victims of Groupthink; A Psychological Study of Foreign-Policy Decisions and Fiascoes* (Boston: Houghton, 1972).

Jeffery, K., *MI6: The History of the Secret Intelligence Service, 1909–1949* (London: Bloomsbury, 2010).

Jervis, R., 'Cooperation Under the Security Dilemma', *World Politics* 30, no. 2 (January 1978): 167–214.

Jervis, R., 'Deterrence Theory Revisited', *World Politics* 31, no. 2 (January 1979): 289–324.

Jervis, R., *The Meaning of the Nuclear Revolution: Statecraft and the Prospect of Armageddon* (Ithaca, NY: Cornell University Press, 1989).

Johansen, Robert C., 'The Impact of US Policy toward the International Criminal Court on the Prevention of Genocide, War Crimes, and Crimes against Humanity', *Human Rights Quarterly* 2, no. 28 (2006): 301–31.

Jonsson, O., *The Russian Understanding of War: Blurring the Lines between War and Peace* (Washington, DC: Georgetown University Press, 2019).

Keens-Soper, M., 'Abraham De Wicquefort and Diplomatic Theory', *Diplomacy and Statecraft* 8, no. 2 (1997): 16–30.

Kennedy, G. C. and K. Neilson (Ed), *Incidents and International Relations: People, Power, and Personalities* (Westport: Praeger, 2002).

Kennedy, P., *The Realities Behind Diplomacy: The Background Influences on British External Policy, 1865–1980* (London: Fontana Press, 1989).

Kennedy, P., *The Rise and Fall of the Great Powers: Economic Change and Military Conflict from 1500 to 2000* (London: Unwin Hyman, 1988).

Keys, B., 'Henry Kissinger: The Emotional Statesman', *Diplomatic History* 35, no. 4 (2011): 587–609.

Keys, B. and Claire Yorke, 'Personal and Political Emotions in the Mind of the Diplomat', *Political Psychology* 40, no. 6 (2019): 1235–49.

Kissinger, H., *Diplomacy* (London: Simon and Schuster, 1994).

Kissinger, H., *World Order* (London: Penguin, 2014).

Koschut, S., 'Emotion (Security) Communities: The Significance of Emotion Norms in Inter-Allied Conflict Management', *Review of International Studies* 40, no. 3 (2014): 533–58.

Kurtz, G. and P. Rotmann, 'The Evolution of Norms of Protection: Major Powers Debate the Responsibility to Protect', *Global Society* 1, no. 30 (2016): 3–20.

Landsberg, C., 'African Solutions for African Problems: Quiet Diplomacy and South Africa's Diplomatic Strategy Towards Zimbabwe', *Journal for Contemporary History* 41, no. 1 (2016): 126–48.

Langhorne, R., 'The Diplomacy of Non-State Actors', *Diplomacy and Statecraft* 16 (2006): 331–9.
Lechner, S. and Mervyn Frost, *Practice Theory and International Relations*, Cambridge Studies in International Relations (Cambridge: Cambridge University Press, 2018).
Lomas, D. and Christopher Murphy, *Intelligence & Espionage: Secrets and Spies* (Oxon: Routledge, 2019), 94.
Markwica, R., *Emotional Choices: How the Logic of Affect Shapes Coercive Diplomacy* (Oxford: Oxford University Press, 2018).
Martin, C. and L. Jagla, *Integrating Diplomacy and Social Media* (Washington, DC: The Aspen Institute, 2013).
Martin, P., 'Yoga Diplomacy: Narendra Modi's Soft Power Strategy', *Foreign Affairs* 25 (2015): 25.
McDermott G., *The New Diplomacy and Its Apparatus* (London: Plume Press, 1973).
Melissen, J. (Ed), *Innovation in Diplomatic Practice* (Basingstoke: Springer, 2016).
Melissen, J. (Ed), *The New Public Diplomacy: Soft Power in International Relations* (Basingstoke: Palgrave, 2005).
Mercer, J., 'Emotion and Strategy in the Korean War', *International Organization* 67, no. 2 (2013): 221–52.
Mercer, J., *Reputation and International Politics* (Ithaca, NY: Cornell University Press, 1996).
Mitzen, J., "Ontological Security in World Politics: State Identity and the Security Dilemma," *European Journal of International Relations* 12, no. 3 (2006): 341–70.
Mohamed, A. N., *The Diplomacy of Micro-States*, Discussion Papers in International Diplomacy, no. 78 (The Hague: The Netherlands Institute of International Relations, Clingendael, 2002).
Morgenthau, H. J., *Politics among Nations: The Struggle for Power and Peace* (New York: Knopf, 1966).
Mueller, R. S., *Report On The Investigation Into Russian Interference In The 2016 Presidential Election* (Washington, DC: US Department of Justice, 2019).
Murray, C., *Dirty Diplomacy* (New York: Scribner, 2007).
Murray, W., R. Hart Sinnreich and J. Lacey (Eds), *The Shaping of Grand Strategy: Policy, Diplomacy, and War* (Cambridge: Cambridge University Press, 2011).
Nicolson, H., *Diplomacy* (London; Oxford; New York: Oxford University Press, 1969).
Nicolson, H., 'Diplomacy Then and Now', *Foreign Affairs* 40 (1961): 39.
Nye Jr., J., *Soft Power: The Means to Success in World Politics* (New York: Public Affairs, 2005).
Nye, J. S., *The Paradox of American Power* (Oxford: Oxford University Press, 2002).
O'Shaughnessy, N., *Politics and Propaganda: Weapons of Mass Seduction* (Manchester: Manchester University Press, 2000).
Pahlavi, P., "Evaluating Public Diplomacy Programs," *Hague Journal of Diplomacy* 3 (2007): 255–81.
Pamment, J., *New Public Diplomacy in the 21st Century: A Comparative Study of Policy and Practice* (London: Routledge, 2012).

Pedwell, C., *Affective Relations: The Transnational Politics of Empathy* (Basingstoke: Palgrave Macmillan, 2014).
Pouliot, V., *International Pecking Orders: The Politics and Practice of Multilateral Diplomacy* (New York: Cambridge University Press, 2016).
Puri, S., *The Great Imperial Hangover* (London: Atlantic, 2020).
Putnam, R. D., *Bowling Alone: The Collapse and Revival of American Community* (London: Simon & Schuster, 2000).
Putnam, R. D., 'Diplomacy and Domestic Politics: The Logic of Two-Level Games', *International Organization* 42, no. 3 (1988): 427–60.
Rachman, G., *Zero Sum World* (London: Atlantic, 2010).
Regan, R. J., *Just War: Principles and Cases* (Washington, DC: The Catholic University of America Press, 1996).
Rice, C., *No Higher Honor: A Memoir of My Years in Washington* (New York: Crown, 2011).
Rifkin, J., *The Age of Access: The New Culture of Hypercapitalism* (Penguin Random House, 2001).
Risse-Kappen, T., 'Public Opinion, Domestic Structure, and Foreign Policy in Liberal Democracies', *World Politics* 43, no. 4 (1991): 479–512.
Ross, A. G., *Mixed Emotions: Beyond Fear and Hatred in International Conflict* (Chicago: The University of Chicago Press, 2014).
Rubin, M., 'The Temptation of Intelligence Politicisation to Support Diplomacy', *International Journal of Intelligence and CounterIntelligence* 29, no. 1 (2016): 1–25.
Sagan, S. D., 'Why Do States Build Nuclear Weapons? Three Models in Search of a Bomb', *International Security* 21, no. 3 (1997): 54–86.
Sandre, A., *Digital Diplomacy: Conversations on Innovation in Foreign Policy* (Lanham, MD: Rowman & Littlefield, 2015).
Satow, E. M., *Satow's Guide to Diplomatic Practice* (London: Longman, 1979).
Schake, K., *Safe Passage: The Transition from British to American Hegemony* (Cambridge, MA: Harvard University Press, 2017).
Schelling, T. C., *Arms and Influence* (New Haven, CT: Yale University Press, 2008).
Schelling, T. C., *The Strategy of Conflict* (Cambridge: Harvard University Press, 1960).
Schmidt, E., *Foreign Intervention in Africa: From the Cold War to the War on Terror* (Cambridge: Cambridge University Press, 2013).
Scott, L., 'Secret Intelligence, Covert Action and Clandestine Diplomacy', *Intelligence & National Security* 2, no. 19 (2004): 322–41.
Seib, P. M., *Real-Time Diplomacy: Politics in the Social Media Era* (Malden, MA: Polity Press, 2012).
Sevin, E., and D. Ingenhoff, 'Public Diplomacy on Social Media: Analyzing Networks and Content', *International Journal of Communication* 12 (2018): 1–23.
Siko, J., *Inside South Africa's Foreign Policy: Diplomacy in Africa from Smuts to Mbeki* (London: I.B. Tauris, 2014).
Slaughter, A. M., 'America's Edge', *Foreign Affairs* 88, no. 1 (2009): 94–113.

Sobelman, D., 'Learning to Deter: Deterrence Failure and Success in the Israel-Hezbollah Conflict, 2006–16', *International Security* 41, no. 3 (January 2017): 151–96.

Sofer, S., 'The Diplomat as a Stranger' *Diplomacy and Statecraft* 8, no. 3 (1997): 179–86.

Soroka, S. N., 'Media, Public Opinion, and Foreign Policy', *Harvard International Journal of Press/Politics* 8, no. 1 (2003): 27–48.

Srinivasan, K., James Mayall, and Sanjay Pulipaka, *Values in Foreign Policy* (London: Rowman and Littlefield, 2019).

Steiner, Z., *The Foreign Office and Foreign Policy, 1898–1914* (Cambridge: Cambridge University Press, 1969)

Surowec, P. and Ilan Manor, *Public Diplomacy and the Politics of Uncertainty* (Switzerland: Palgrave, 2020).

Susskind, L. E., *Environmental Diplomacy: Negotiating More Effective Global Agreements* (Oxford: Oxford University Press, 1994).

Talbott, S., 'Globalization and Diplomacy: A Practitioner's Perspective', *Foreign Policy* 108 (1997): 69–83.

Tolba, M. K. and I. Rummel-Bulska, *Global Environmental Diplomacy: Negotiating Environmental Agreements for the World, 1973–1992* (Cambridge: MIT Press, 1998).

Trager, R. F. and Dessislava P. Zagorcheva, 'Deterring Terrorism: It Can Be Done', *International Security* 30, no. 3 (Winter/2006 2005): 87–123.

Trenin, D., *Should We Fear Russia?* (Cambridge: Polity Press, 2016).

United Nations, 'Vienna Convention on Diplomatic Relations 1961', Done at Vienna on 18 April 1961. Entered into force on 24 April 1964. United Nations, Treaty Series, Vol. 500.

Watson, A. *Diplomacy: The Dialogue between States* (London: Eyre Methuen, 1982).

Watts, J. F. and Fred L. Israel (Ed), *Presidential Documents: The Speeches, Proclamations, and Policies That Have Shaped the Nation from Washington to Clinton* (New York: Routledge, 2000).

Weldon, L., *When Protest Makes Policy: How Social Movements Represent Disadvantaged Groups* (Ann Arbour: University of Michigan Press, 2011).

Wendt, A., *Social Theory of International Politics* (Cambridge: Cambridge University Press, 1999).

Wenger, A. (Ed), *Deterring Terrorism: Theory and Practice* (Stanford: Stanford University Press, 2012).

Wheeler, N. J., 'Investigating Diplomatic Transformations', *International Affairs* 89, no. 2 (2013): 477–96.

White, R. K., 'Misperception and the Vietnam War', *Journal of Social Issues* 22, no. 3 (1966):1–164.

Williams, P., *War and Conflict in Africa*, 2nd edition (Cambridge: Polity, 2016).

Wilner, A. S., *Deterring Rational Fanatics* (Philadelphia: University of Pennsylvania Press, 2015).

Wilner, A. S., 'Deterring the Undeterrable: Coercion, Denial, and Delegitimization in Counterterrorism', *Journal of Strategic Studies* 34, no. 1 (February 2011): 3–37.

Wong, S. S., 'Emotions and the Communication of Intentions in Face-to-Face Diplomacy', *European Journal of International Relations* 22, no. 1 (2016): 144–67.

Wong, S. S., 'Stoics and Hotheads: Leaders' Temperament, Anger, and the Expression of Resolve in Face-to-Face Diplomacy', *Journal of Global Security Studies* 4, no. 2 (2019): 190–208.

Xia, Y., *Negotiating with the Enemy: Us-China Talks during the Cold War, 1949–1972* (Bloomington: Indiana University Press, 2006).

Zagare F. C. and D. Marc Kilgour, *Perfect Deterrence* (New York: Cambridge University Press, 2000).

Index

adversaries 3, 7, 11, 39, 42, 44, 46, 103–6, 110, 117, 125, 128, 130, 134
Afghanistan 4, 42
Africa Cup of Nations 188
African National Congress 185
African Union (AU) 17
Agrokor 171
Al-Assad, Bashar 38, 41
Al-Qaeda 61, 80, 89–90, 93–4, 210
alliances 5, 6, 9, 11, 67, 77–9, 110, 161, 165, 166, 178, 222
America First 5
anarchy 22, 26, 27
Ancient Greece 124
Angola 185, 187, 189–92, 197
    Movimento Popular de Libertacao de Angola (MPLA) 187, 191
    Uniao Nacional para a Independencia Total de Angola (UNITA) 187, 191
Anti-Ballistic Missile (ABM) system 113–14, 116
Apartheid 6, 16, 27, 145, 185–7, 192, 196–9
Arab Spring 61, 66, 87
arms control 104, 106, 109, 111, 113, 115–17
Arusha process 152
audiences 124, 132, 143–4, 149, 214
Austria 166, 169–70
Axis powers 57

balance of power 110
balance of terror 114, 117
Balkans, the 161, 162, 166, 167, 170, 179
Baltic states, the 38, 161, 162, 166–8, 174, 175, 177, 179
Bangladesh 208, 211, 212, 219
Begin, Menachem 104
Benghazi 87, 91, 94
Blair, Tony 66, 92, 94, 104
Blumenthal, Sidney 90, 94
Bosnia and Herzegovina 171, 175

Brezhnev, Leonid 104, 106, 110, 115, 116
Brexit 65, 167, 172, 176, 177, 222
BRICS 185
Bureau of Intelligence and Research (INR) 62
Bush, George W. 43, 104, 152

Cameron, David 84
Canada 5, 63, 64, 208, 218
Carter, Jimmy 62, 104, 116
Central Intelligence Agency (CIA) 59–60, 62, 64–5, 69–70, 111
chemical weapons 38, 41–3, 91
China, People's Republic of 11, 38, 42–3, 63–5, 104–13, 115–19, 128, 131, 134, 138–9, 142, 152, 166, 211, 222, 227
Churchill, Winston 103–4, 123
civil society 22–4, 28–30, 33, 93, 107, 151
civil war 38, 82–3, 87, 89–90, 91, 93, 95, 151, 186, 187
climate change 4, 23, 135, 210, 222
Clinton, Bill 37, 45
Clinton, Hillary 81, 84, 87, 90–2, 94, 125
coercion 10, 37–53
coexistence 113, 117
Cold War 1, 12, 38, 39, 44, 57, 67, 69, 103–6, 113–15, 117–18, 146, 166, 185, 189, 199, 207–8
Commonwealth 67, 163, 164, 165, 188, 193, 207
communications 2, 4, 9, 10, 11, 25, 59, 60, 63, 65, 67, 68, 71, 79, 92, 105, 108, 116, 123, 124, 127, 130–2, 135, 141, 211, 216
communism 24, 61, 82, 106, 110, 115, 134, 162, 166, 168, 170, 179, 207–11, 214, 216
compellence 39
conflict 3, 5, 6, 9, 15, 37, 39, 41, 43, 44, 47, 56, 61, 79, 80, 84, 87, 89–93,

95, 105, 106, 143, 146, 147, 149,
    167, 173, 175, 185, 192, 193, 195,
    199
conflict resolution 58, 185–8, 196, 197,
    199
Congo, Democratic Republic of 185, 186,
    188, 191, 192, 193, 195, 199
  Alliance des Forces Democratiques
    pour la Liberation du Congo-Zaire
    (AFDL) 188, 189
Convention on Diplomatic Relations
    (1961) 1, 62
cooperation 4, 5, 15, 66, 92, 109, 113, 136,
    145, 146, 150, 162, 166, 169, 170,
    187, 195, 207, 222, 227, 228
covert action 56, 62, 63, 69–71
COVID-19 4, 33, 135, 222, 227
Crimea 144, 156, 173
Croatia 168–72, 175
Cuba 64
Cuban Missile Crisis 111
cyber 42, 65, 175

Darroch, Sir Kim 68
Dearlove, Sir Richard 65–6
democracy 87, 91, 146, 153, 186, 196, 198,
    199, 207
denuclearization 45
Department of Defense, US 61, 62
détente 11, 66, 104–6, 110, 111, 117,
    198
deterrence 39, 42, 44, 115
development 17, 91, 93, 163
diplomacy
  art of 6, 124
  backchannel 66, 111, 116
  counter-diplomacy 11, 141–59, 225
  decline of 1
  future of 2
  multilateral 106
  Ping Pong 108
  quiet 193, 197, 198
  secret 8, 25, 108
  shuttle 194
diplomatic
  cables 67, 68, 81, 82, 83, 129
  communication 78, 95, 124
  competences 38, 80, 133, 211–12, 227
  cultural 225

disposition 127, 133
expulsions 64
life 207–23
practices 15, 77, 81, 104, 105, 116,
    124–5, 130, 132–3, 142, 154, 207,
    211, 215, 226
recognition 116
service 207, 215
signalling 131
texts 79, 81, 125, 134
transformations 105, 125
diversity 24, 27–9, 33, 217
Djibouti 166
Dobrynin, Anatoly 111, 116, 120
Dos Santos, Jose Eduardo 187
drones 41, 42, 48, 50, 70

Eastern Bloc 57
embassies 16, 26, 63, 68, 214, 215, 220
emotions 7, 11, 46, 95, 123–140, 178
empathy 7, 11, 116, 123–140, 225
empire 27, 169, 172, 222
Enlai, Zhou 108–9, 116, 128
environment 3–5, 15, 17, 23, 213
espionage 55, 56, 65, 68
Estonia 165, 167, 174–9
ethics 7, 10, 15–35, 226
Ethiopia 152, 185
Europe 5, 11, 56, 66, 106, 113, 146, 161,
    165–9, 170–9, 207–10
European Union (EU) 9, 12, 30–2, 65, 84,
    146, 149, 162, 164, 166–9, 170–9,
    207–10, 222, 223
Europol 65–6
extraordinary rendition 70

Facebook 132, 211, 221
Falklands War 61
Finland 166, 167
First World War 57, 170
force, use of 3, 38–44, 47, 186
Ford, Gerald 116
Foreign and Commonwealth Office (FCO)
    59, 61, 66, 209
foreign fighters 89, 90, 92
foreign policy 3, 5, 8, 11, 12, 17, 31, 38,
    41, 42, 48, 56, 58, 59, 61, 62, 64, 67,
    71, 107–10, 112, 129, 135, 136, 143,
    144, 146, 166, 175, 178, 186,

187, 189, 192, 198, 211, 213, 218,
    223, 225, 226, 228
Former Yugoslavia 146, 166, 170
France 5, 8, 68, 169, 176, 218, 222
freedom 22–4, 27–30, 32, 33, 83, 87, 93

Gaddafi, Muammar 45, 66, 77–80, 83–4,
    87–93
Gaddafi, Saif al-Islam 91
game theory 37
GCHQ 59, 68–9
General Agreement on Tariffs and Trade
    (GATT) 209
Genocide 84, 87, 88, 90–1, 189, 191
Georgia 175
German Reunification 222
Germany 4, 32, 57, 69, 145, 151, 218, 222
    Federal Republic of 113
global governance 79
global market 22, 28
Gorbachev, Mikhail 104, 117, 129, 209
GRU (Russia) 70, 173

hegemony 110, 185, 187
Huawei 68
human rights 16–18, 29, 31–3, 84, 87, 93,
    141, 143, 145–7, 152–4, 186, 188,
    214
humanitarian intervention 17
Hungary 5, 32, 207, 208, 210, 212, 215
Hussein, Saddam 38, 39, 43, 46
hybrid warfare 70, 144

identity 10, 11, 23, 77–101, 125, 127–8,
    130, 178, 226
immigration 5
information war 6, 144
intelligence 10, 55–76, 90–1, 128, 226
    Human (HUMINT) 58, 62
    Imagery (IMINT) 58
    OSINT 59
    Signal (SIGINT) 58, 61, 63, 65–6, 68
Inter-Congolese dialogue 193–4
intercontinental ballistic missiles (ICBMs)
    111–12, 114
International Criminal Court 17
international law 15, 41, 70, 146, 175
international order 1–4, 15, 141–2, 145,
    152, 154, 226, 227, 228

interpersonal relations 12, 126–31, 148
international society 21, 24, 25, 27, 141
Iran 7, 38, 40, 43, 46, 68, 117, 128, 131,
    132, 142, 149, 151, 210
Iranian Hostage Crisis 7
Iranian Revolution 61, 210
Iraq 4, 10, 38–9, 42, 43, 46, 58, 62, 89, 90
Iraq War 16, 104, 212, 213
Islamic extremists 90–1
Italy 56, 91, 169

Joint Comprehensive Plan of Action
    (JCPOA) 46
Joint Intelligence Committee (JIC) 60–1
Jong Il, Kim 61
Jung-Un, Kim 45, 148
justice 15, 17, 18, 146, 147, 153, 166

Kabila, Laurent-Desire 188–97
Kagame, Paul 191, 202
Kai-shek, Chiang 106, 108
Kennan, George 80, 127, 137
Kennedy, John F. 62, 104, 129
Kerry, John 128
KGB 63
Khashoggi, Jamal 26, 70
Khruschev, Nikita 104, 129–30
Kissinger, Henry 9, 11, 95, 106–16, 127,
    131
knowledge 77–80, 133, 211
    bureaucratic 79, 81, 95
    cultural 123
    production 78, 93–6
Kuwait 39

language 77, 79, 84, 87, 115, 130, 131, 134
languages, foreign 211, 216, 222
Latvia 167, 174–6
leadership 7, 46, 63, 104, 107, 109, 117,
    129, 146, 147, 197, 199, 208
Lesotho 192
Libya 3, 45, 66, 77, 78, 80–95, 133, 188
Libyan nuclear program 45
Lithuania 167, 174, 176
Lusaka agreement 193–4

Machiavelli, Niccolo 78, 95
Major, John 218
Mandela, Nelson 11, 185–94, 197–9

Mao, Chairman 107-9, 116-19, 134
May, Theresa 65
Mbeki, Thabo 187, 189, 190, 191, 193-7
McCarthyism 134
McGuiness, Martin 128
media 8, 25, 91, 211, 227
mediation 12, 151, 185-8, 190-3, 197, 199
Medvedev, Dmitry 64
Merkel, Angela 69
Middle East War 117
migration crisis 167, 172, 176, 177
military 2, 3, 37, 40-5, 48, 58, 59, 63-70, 87, 91, 92, 107, 113, 134, 144, 147-9, 152, 161, 163, 166, 167, 169, 172-7, 186, 188-92, 194, 196, 198, 209, 212, 213
Mobutu, Joseph 188-91, 196, 197
Montenegro 172-4
Mossadegh, Mohammed 7
Mozambique 185
Mugabe, Robert 192, 193, 197, 198, 203, 213
Multiple Independently targeted Re-entry Vehicles (MIRVs) 112-14, 120
multipolarity 10, 42
Mutual Assured Destruction (MAD) 113-14, 117
Myanmar 30, 31

Namibia 192, 218
National Cyber Security Center 68
National Security Agency (NSA) 55, 59, 60, 68
National Security Council (UK) 68
National Transitional Council (NTC) 89-91
nationalism 5, 141, 146
negotiations 11, 25, 46, 47, 80, 90, 91, 103-17, 124, 128, 131, 132, 141, 144, 145, 151, 152, 185, 187, 190, 191, 193, 195, 196, 198, 208, 209
Netherlands 164, 165, 178
New Zealand 4, 5, 188
Nicolson, Harold 1, 18
Nigeria 187, 188, 197, 198
Nixon, Richard 11, 106-10, 112, 114-16
non-state actors 3-5, 8-9, 40, 57, 68, 69, 135, 154, 222, 226

norms 1, 5, 7, 11, 55, 70, 80, 95, 135, 141, 143-7, 149, 152-4
North Atlantic Treaty Organization (NATO) 9, 11, 38, 84, 162, 164, 166, 167-70, 172-9, 207, 210
North Korea 10, 31, 37-40, 45-7, 61, 92, 106, 141-2, 148, 221, 228
Northern Ireland Peace Process 128
Northern Ireland Troubles 66
nuclear disarmament 92, 141
Nuclear Non-Proliferation Treaty (NPT) 151
nuclear weapons 3, 38, 40-3, 46, 47, 65, 111, 113-15

Obama, Barack 38, 41, 42, 46, 50, 64, 69, 83-4, 87, 89-91, 93, 95, 98, 132, 168
Organization of American States (OAS) 15
Organization of African Unity 15, 186, 188, 194
Organization for Security and Co-operation in Europe (OSCE) 173, 175, 176
Operation Desert Storm (1991) 39

Paisley, Iain 128, 138
Pakistan 46-7, 64, 108, 116
Paraguay 63, 164
Poland 208-11, 216, 218, 219
politics 9, 11, 12, 25, 26, 30, 40, 88, 95, 124, 125, 127, 135, 141, 161, 170, 172, 207, 213, 214, 226
Pompeo, Mike 45, 68
Portugal 187
poststructuralism 10, 77-79
Power, Samantha 92
Practice Theory 10, 19-33, 38, 78-80, 95, 142, 228
Primakov, Yevgeny 175
proxy groups 3
public opinion 27, 41, 88, 226
Putin, Vladimir 41, 76, 156, 168, 175

radicalization 4-5
rapport 124, 128, 131, 132, 136, 213
Reagan, Ronald 104, 117, 129, 198
realpolitik 18, 127
rebels 83, 87-95, 154, 188, 192-6
refugees 5, 17, 25, 30, 31, 189, 191

Responsibility to Protect (R2P) 31–2
Richardson, Bill 189, 191
Romania 210
Rumsfeld, Donald 61
Russia 3, 6, 31, 38, 43, 63–5, 70, 123, 127, 144, 149, 162, 166–8, 170–2, 179, 187
Rwanda 146, 188–94
Rwandan genocide 189

Sadat, Anwar 104
sanctions 40, 44, 45, 47, 84, 92, 151, 188, 193, 197, 198
Sarkozy, Nicolas 84, 89, 91
Saudi Arabia 26, 31, 35, 70, 89
Savimbi, Jonas 187
Schelling, Thomas 37, 40, 48, 49
Second World War 57, 170
Security Council 43, 80, 84–6, 146, 147, 150, 151, 153, 207
11 September 2001 3, 61, 69
Serbia 172–5
serious organized crime 66
Shanghai Communiqué 109–10
Skripal, Sergei 64, 70
Slaughter, Anne-Marie 90, 91, 95, 234
Slovakia 210
Slovenia 164, 168–72, 178
small states 4, 6, 11, 161–83, 225
Snowden, Edward 55, 59, 67–9, 71, 231
social media 8, 132, 135, 221
social movements 8
soft power 64, 199, 225
Solidarity movement 208, 210, 213
South Africa 6, 11, 16, 27, 30, 33, 145, 151, 185–205, 208, 213–14, 218
South African Development Community (SADC) 186, 188, 192–9
South America 146
South Korea 40, 45, 49, 61, 109
South Sudan 142, 148–51
sovereignty 15–18, 21–33, 81, 124, 143, 144, 164, 165, 169, 175, 177, 178, 222
Soviet Union 11, 61, 63, 103–21, 123, 127–8, 154, 166, 175, 176, 207–10, 222
Sri Lanka 142, 147
Stalin, Joseph 123

statecraft 41, 48, 56, 59, 228
State Department, US 59, 60, 62–3, 68, 81–2, 89–90, 91, 94, 116, 127, 133–4
Strategic Arms Limitation Treaty (SALT) I and II
Sudan 148, 152
summits 2, 7, 11, 19, 31, 45, 59, 103–21, 227
   Beijing 105
   G7/8
   G20 59
   Hanoi 45
   Moscow 105, 117
   Singapore 45

Taiwan 106–8
technology 4, 6, 8, 10, 23, 29, 39, 47, 48, 59, 65, 67, 68, 71, 80, 111, 135, 207, 211, 216, 221, 222, 226, 227
terrorism 3, 4, 5, 41, 65, 66, 69, 70, 83, 88, 93, 167, 210, 214, 222
   counter-terrorism 55, 89, 92–3
terrorists 41, 70, 135
Thatcher, Margaret 209, 210, 213, 222, 223
Thucydides 161
Thunberg, Greta 4, 135
torture 16, 22, 70
trade 8, 15, 25, 56, 60, 108 214, 223, 227
Treaty of Vienna 163
Trump, Donald 7, 31, 42, 45–6, 67–8, 149, 153, 168, 176, 177, 227
trust 8, 11, 12, 63–4, 68, 69, 71, 105, 109, 110, 115–17, 128–9, 131, 144, 153, 154, 225
Twitter 67, 132, 139, 211

Uighurs 152
Ukraine 3, 64, 144, 149, 167, 173, 177
United Kingdom 3, 9, 27, 32, 57, 58, 61, 65, 67, 69, 167–9, 174, 207, 211, 222
United Nations 15, 17, 31, 39, 81, 145, 152, 153, 186, 193
UN, General Assembly 31, 173
UN, Human Rights Council 146–7, 153
United States 3, 4, 5, 9, 27, 30, 31, 37–47, 57, 62–5, 67–9, 87–8, 92, 97, 104–18, 141, 146, 148, 150–3,

156, 158, 159, 162, 164, 166–70, 174, 176, 177, 187, 198, 212, 213, 218, 227
United States Information Agency (USIA) 133
Uruguay 164
U.S. Opening to China (1972) 11, 104–18, 128
Uzbekistan 16

Verhofstadt, Guy 65
Vietnam 6, 107–8, 112, 131, 235
violent extremism 4
vulnerability 161, 164–166, 172–5, 177–9, 225

Wałęsa, Lech 209, 210, 218
war 3, 6, 15, 25, 27, 37–9, 41–5, 48, 191–3, 195, 207

war crimes 31, 84, 87
war on terror 4, 69, 78, 83, 88, 89
Warsaw Pact 208
weapons of mass destruction 38, 43, 72, 91
Wikileaks 7, 10, 68, 71, 98
Wilson, Woodrow 8
women 18, 217
World Health Organization (WHO) 4, 9, 227
World Trade Organization 209

Zaire 188–91
Zarif, Mohamad Javad 128
Zimbabwe 188, 192, 193, 197, 198, 213, 220